ELEMENTARY NORTH INDIAN VOCAL

Fifth Edition, Revised and Expanded

by

David Courtney
and
Chandrakantha Courtney

Sur Sangeet Services
Houston
1995

price $34.95

First Edition published in 1992. Fifth Edition 1995
Printed in United States of America
Eighth Impression, August 1997

The authors can be reached at:
David Courtney or Chandrakantha Courtney
(telephone) (713) 665 4665
(email) tabalji@aol.com
(fax) (713) 665 0186
(Chandrakantha's Home Page) http://home.aol.com/chandrakan
(David's Home Page) http://home.aol.com/tabalji

Distributed by Sur Sangeet Services
Box 270685
Houston, TX 77277

Library of Congress Catalog Number: 95-068751

Softbound
ISBN 0-9634447-4-3

Elementary North Indian Vocal

CONTENTS

v

PREFACE TO THE FIFTH EDITION

This book has undergone quite a transformation from the first edition. Three years ago it was half its present size (and cost considerably less). There has also been a change in focus; it now presumes that the student is starting from the very beginning.

This is an introductory book on North Indian classical vocal music. The entire field of Indian music is so broad, it is highly unlikely that a single book could ever completely describe it. We have tried to concentrate on the material required by a new student. Beginning compositions and exercises form the mainstay of this work. However, we have also tried to include reference matter that may be of use to a musician of any stage. An extensive glossary of Hindi terms is one example. All of this is intended to present a concise yet relatively complete picture of North Indian classical vocal music.

There is a shortage of material on Indian music. This dearth of material has always been a major impediment to students. Although this modest little edition will certainly not fill the void, we hope that it may be of some help.

As with any book there are a number of people who have made it possible. I would especially like to thank Shailaja Garde for her editorial input and help with Hindi translations. Manika Sapru, Uma Aggarwal, Dr. Rucha Sheth, Dr. Mohini Sindhawani and Rathna Kumar have also been very helpful with the translations. I would also like to thank Lal Thukral, Dr. Victor Parr, and Dr. Ashutosh Patwardhan, and Jo Anne Courtney for their editorial suggestions.

D. Courtney, Feb. 28, 1995

CHAPTER 1.

INTRODUCTION

The North Indian system of classical music is called *Hindustani sangeet.* It is the classical system of northern India, Pakistan, Bangladesh and even much of Afghanistan.

We can begin our discussion with the concept of *Sangeet* (संगीत). *Sangeet* is considered synonymous with classical music; however it is actually a threefold artform of vocal music, instrumental music, and dance. Since classical dance is also a component, it is not strictly synonymous to the Western term "music". In this work we will concentrate only upon the musical side and say very little about dance. We find two approaches to viewing the origins of *sangeet*; one mythical and the other historical. The myths show clear cultural relationships which are not easily seen in a simple historical / anthropological approach.

MYTHOLOGICAL ORIGINS - An example of the significant role that *sangeet* has played in Indian culture may be seen in the story concerning its origin. Perhaps the clearest mythological *raison de etre* may be seen in Bharata's *Natya-Shastra* (Rangacharya 1966):

> Once, a long time ago, during the transitional period between two Ages it so happened that people took to uncivilised ways, were ruled by lust and greed, behaved in angry and jealous ways with each other and not only gods but demons, evil spirits, yakshas and such like others swarmed over the earth. Seeing this plight, Indra and other gods approached god Brahma and requested him to give the people a toy (Kridaniyaka), but one which could not only be seen but heard and this should turn out a diversion (so that people gave up their bad ways)

Although it was decided to give the celestial art of *sangeet* to mankind, a suitable human had to be found who was capable of receiving this gift. *Sangeet* had always been in the realm of the demigods (*gandharva* गंधर्व). A super-human of superior spiritual ability was required to convey this celestial artform to the world of man. It fell

Figure 1.1.

upon the great sage Narada (नारद) to be the first mortal recipient of this divine art. Through Narada, we are indebted for the presence of classical music.

The introduction of this artform to the mortal world was only the first step. Traditional pedagogy had to accommodate it. Classical music is considered more than mere entertainment; it is a moral and spiritual redeemer. Therefore, the divine qualities inherent in the artform imply certain prerequisites; key among them are *guru* (गुरु), *vinaya* (विनय) and *sadhana* (साधना) (Shankar 1968): this translates to teacher, humility, and discipline.

The *guru*, or teacher is the most important prerequisite in traditional musical pedagogy. Music is said to be a *guru-mukha-vidhya* (i.e., knowledge which must come from a teacher). This is considered the highest form of knowledge. Traditional pedagogy is based upon the transfer of knowledge from the teacher (*guru*) to the disciple (*shishya* शिष्य) in an unbroken tradition (*parampara* परम्परा) (Courtney 1980). The tradition of *guru-shishya-parampara* (गुरु शिष्य परम्परा) extends back countless millennia.

The second prerequisite is *vinaya* (humility). This also reflects the divine origins of the artform. Classical music is said to be a worship that involves both the listener and the artist alike. Any negative emotions such as arrogance (*abhiman* अभिमान) become an impediment. This is an impediment from both the divine aspect as well as a matter of simple pedagogy (e.g., "If you think you already know everything, then what is there to learn?")

The final prerequisite for a student of classical music is *sadhana* (discipline and practice). *Sadhana* is necessary at two levels. At one level, the divine origins of the artform require that the student "be prepared" to be a recipient of this knowledge. However, from a simple pedagogic standpoint, the music is so incredibly difficult that if the student does not devote countless hours of practice spread over many years, the student certainly will not be able to master the music. This may clarify many points of pedagogy, but what about the artform itself? Any art must deal with the topic of aesthetics. The Indian tradition has much to say on this point as well.

The ancient scriptures describe nine fundamental emotions from which all complex emotions may be produced. Just as all hues may be produced by mixing the three primary colors, so too, all emotions are said to be derived from these principal emotions (Shankar 1968). They are called *navaras* (नवरस) and are shown in table 1.1.

These emotions form the aesthetic foundation for *sangeet*. We must remember that we are talking about music. This requires an acoustic vehicle to convey these emotions.

This main acoustic vehicle is known as *rag* (राग). *Rag* may be thought of as the melodic foundation upon which classical Indian music is based. During the last few centuries it was customary to anthropomorphize the *rag* in the form of *Gandharva*s (demigods) and *Apsaras* (अप्सरा) (celestial nymphs)[1] .

The divine quality of music is perhaps best illustrated in *nad siddha* (नाद सिद्ध). This is the ability to perform miracles by singing or playing certain *rags*. The most famous miracle working musician was Tansen (तानसेन)(Garg 1984). It is often said that he was able to create fire by singing *rag Dipak* (दीपक), or create rain by singing *rag Megh Malhar* (मेघ मल्हार).

We have seen how this artform is considered divine. This divine quality influences concepts such as aesthetics and pedagogy. The reverence that Indians have for this system may only be seen in a traditional approach. However, this does not bar us from taking a more objective approach; one based upon a historical standpoint.

Table 1.1 The Nine Moods	
Shringar ------------	Love
Hasya --------------	Comic
Karuna --------------	Sadness
Raudra --------------	Furious
Veera ---------------	Heroic
Bhayanaka ----------	Terrible / Frightful
Vibhatsa ------------	Disgusting
Adbhuta ------------	Wonderment
Shanta --------------	Peace

[1] This characterization has given rise to a style of painting known as *ragmala* (रागमाला). However, this anthropomorphism with its application to painting, is of little importance to the student of music.

HISTORICAL ORIGINS - There are many milestones in the evolution of Indian music. These

milestones show clearly the development of musical thought from early history to the present day.

The early prehistory of Indian music may be explained by the Indo-European theory. According to this theory, there was a culture, or group of cultures who were so successful that they spread throughout Europe and parts of Asia. Although no one knows where they came from, present thought tends to place their origins somewhere in Eurasia, either north of the Black sea or north of the Caspian (Mallory 1989). The classical music of India is said to have its roots in this culture.

The connection between Indo-European expansion and Indian music may be seen in mythology. Mythology refers to music being brought to the people of India from a place of celestial beings. This mythical land (*Gandharva Desh* गंधर्व देश) is usually equated with heaven. However, some are of the opinion that this mythical land could actually be Kandahar in what is the modern Afghanistan. Therefore, the myths of music being given to the world by the celestial beings (*gandharva*) may actually represent a cultural connection with this ancient Indo-Aryan homeland.

Further evidence may be seen in musical structure. In the first few centuries B.C., Indian music was based upon seven modes (scales). It is probably no coincidence that Greek music was also based upon seven modes. Furthermore, the Indian scales follow the same process of modulation (*murchana* मूर्च्छना) that was found in ancient Greek music.

The link to Sanskrit is another strong indication of Indo-Aryan roots. Many of the earliest texts were written in Sanskrit. It is also generally believed that classical music is derived from the *Samaveda* (सामवेद). However it should be stressed that this belief is hard to justify because intermediate forms have never been found.

In the final analysis, the roots of classical music being Indo-Aryan are a reflection of modern paradigms concerning ancient Indian history. Although supporting evidence may be slim, conflicting evidence is conspicuous by its absence. Until we are faced with significant conflicting evidence we should accept the Indo-Aryan theory.

The nature of music in prehistoric India may be obscure but the picture begins to become clear in the first few centuries B.C.. Bharata's *Natya-Shastra* (नाट्यशास्त्र) (circa 200 B.C.), provides a detailed account of stagecraft in that period. Here we find mention of seven *shuddha jati* (शुद्ध जाति) (pure modes) and eleven mixed *jatis* (modal forms not produced by simple modulation). There is also a very detailed discussion of the musical instruments.

The *Brihaddeshi* (बृहद्देशी) written by Matanga (circa 700 A.D.) is another major milestone in the development of Indian music. It is in this work that we first find the word "*rag*" mentioned. However, there is some doubt whether the concept was the same as it is today.

The "*Sangeet Ratnakar*"(सङ्गीत रत्नाकर) by Sharangdev (शार्ङ्गदेव) is another treatise on Indian music. This work, written around the thirteenth century, gives extensive commentaries about numerous musical styles that existed at that time.

Perhaps one of the most significant milestones in the development of Indian music was the life of Amir Khusru (अमीर खुसरो) (Bhatkhande 1934). Although the extent of his contribution to Indian music is more legendary than factual, he nevertheless symbolizes a crucial turning point in the development of Indian music. Amir Khusru is an icon representing a growing Persian influence on the music. This influence was felt to a greater extent in the North than in the South. The consequence of this differing degree of influence ultimately resulted in the bifurcation of Indian music into two distinct systems; the *Hindusthani sangeet* (हिंदुस्तानी संगीत) of the North and the *Carnatic sangeet* (कर्नाटक संगीत) of the South.

The musical career of Tansen is another landmark in the development of Indian Music (Mital 1960). He is significant because he symbolizes the maturing of the north Indian system as a distinct entity from south Indian music (fig. 1.2).

The early part of the 20th century brings the most recent revolution in north Indian music. This is provide by two people: V. N. Bhatkhande (भातखन्डे) and V. D. Paluskar (पलुस्कर). These two men revolutionized the concept of Indian music. Paluskar is responsible for the introduction of the first music colleges while Bhatkhande is responsible for the introduction of an organized system which reflects current performance practice.

In the preceding section we have given a fair description of the Indian concept of *Sangeet*. This threefold artform of vocal music, instrumental music and dance, provides the foundation for the classical arts in India. As in any art, the ultimate goal is the emotional quality. The primary musical vehicle for the conveyance of this emotion is *rag*.

PRESENT MUSICAL SYSTEMS - Today there are two
systems of Indian music (fig. 1.3). One system is found in Northern India, Pakistan, and Bangladesh. This system is called *Hindusthani sangeet*. There is another system found in southern India. This system is called *Carnatic Sangeet*. These two systems are both based upon similar concepts of *rag* and *tal* (rhythm). They both are said to be derived from the *Vedic* tradition. However, they differ in terms of theory, nomenclature and performance.

The *Hindusthani* (Northern) system may be thought of as a mixture of traditional Hindu musical concepts and Persian performance practice. The advent of Islamic rule over northern India caused the musicians to seek patronage in the courts of the new rulers. These rulers, often of foreign extraction, had strong cultural and religious sentiments focused outside of

Figure 1.2. Tansen (from The Hindu, Sunday March 2, 1941)

India. Yet they lived in, and administered kingdoms which retained their traditional Hindu culture. Several centuries of this arrangement caused the Hindu music to absorb a Persian character.

The *Carnatic* (Southern) system was relatively immune to the cultural impact of the Islamic invasion. South Indian musicians still enjoyed the patronage of the temples and Hindu rulers. Therefore the south Indian system evolved along different lines from its northern counterpart. In some ways the south Indian system is closer to the older forms.

It is helpful for us to summarize the important points of this chapter. We have seen that there are differences between the Northern system of music and the Southern. The Northern system evolved under cultural pressure from Persia and acquired a different character from the Southern system. There are numerous aspects of theory and practice. We have seen in this chapter that the music of India is part of one of the oldest musical traditions in the world. As such, it is inextricably linked to the ancient stagecraft. Therfore the Indian word for music *(sangeet)* does not restrict itself to melodic forms, but

HINDUSTANI

CARNATIC

Figure 1.3. Geographical Breakdown of the Hindustani and Carnatic Musical Systems.

also encompasses the classical dance. The three aspects of *sangeet* will be discussed in greater detail in the coming chapters.

WORKS CITED

Bhatkhande, Vishnu Narayan
1934   *A Short History of the Music of Upper India.* Bombay, India: (reprinted in 1974 by Indian Musicological Society, Baroda).

Courtney, D.R
1980   *Introduction to Tabla.* Hyderabad, India: Anand Power Press.

Garg, Lakshminarayan
1984   *Hamare Sangeet-Ratna.* Hathras, India: Sangeet Press.

Mallory, J. P.
1989   *In Search of the Indo-Europeans; Language Archaeology and Myth.* London: Thames and Hudson Ltd.

Mital, Prabhudayal
1960   *Sangeet Samrat: Tansen: Jivani aur Rachanaen.* Mathura, India: Sahitya Samsthan.

Rangacharya, Adya
1966   *Introduction to Bharata's Natya-Sastra.* Bombay, India: Popular Prakashan.

Shankar, Ravi
1968   *Ravi Shankar: My Music, My Life.* New Delhi, India: Vikas Publishing House Pvt. Ltd.

CHAPTER 2.

MELODIC FUNDAMENTALS

There are certain melodic fundamentals which must be mastered before one can learn to sing. There are definite structures and set of rules. Understanding these rules is important if one is form the proper conceptual framework in which to perform ones art.

S WAR -The *swar* (स्वर) is a convenient place to begin. *Swar* is nothing more than the seven notes of the Indian musical scale. At a fundamental level they are similar to the *solfa* of Western music. These are shown in table 2.1.

Two of these *swar* are noteworthy in that they are immutably fixed. These two notes are *shadj* (षड्ज) (*Sa*) and *pancham* (पंचम) (*Pa*) and are referred to as *achala swar* (अचल स्वर). These two *swar* form the tonal foundation for all the Indian classical music.

The other notes are not immutably fixed for they have alternate forms. The notes; *rishabh* (ऋषभ) (*Re*), *gandhara* (गंधार) (*Ga*), *dhaivat* (धैवत) (*Dha*), and *nishad* (निषाद) (*Ni*) may be either natural (*shuddha* शुद्ध) or flattened (*komal* कोमल). *Madhyam* (मध्यम) (*Ma*) is unique in that its alternate form is augmented or sharp. This note is called *tivra ma* (तीव्रा म). Therefore, we find that we are actually dealing with 12 *swar*. This extended concept is shown in table 2.2. These are roughly comparable to the keys on a harmonium, or piano (chromatic scale).

This brings us to the topic of musical notation. One may have noticed that the natural notes (*shuddha swar*) do not have any marks while the alternate notes do. The *komal* notes (i.e., *Re, Ga, Dha, Ni*) are denoted by a line underneath. The *tivra ma* (augmented fourth) is denoted by a vertical line over it. This is a convenient, intuitive approach to the notation.

We may summarize the the topic of *swar* quite simply. *Swar* is the basic concept of a "note". These notes are similar to the diatonic scale of Western music. The notation of Indian music is simply the writing down of theses notes with appropriate marks to denote the timing.

Table 2.1. Indian Scale (Sargam)	
Shadj -------------	Sa
Rishabh -------------	Re
Gandhara -----------	Ga
Madhyam -----------	Ma
Pancham ------------	Pa
Dhaivat -------------	Dha
Nishad -------------	Ni

Table 2.2 Extended Scale	
Shadj --------------------	Sa
Komal Rishabh ----------	R̲e̲
Shuddha Rishabh ------	Re
Komal Gandhara -------	G̲a̲
Shuddha Gandhara ---	Ga
Shuddha Madhyam ---	Ma
Tivra Madhyam ---------	Má
Pancham -----------------	Pa
Komal Dhaivat ----------	D̲h̲a̲
Shuddha Dhaivat -------	Dha
Komal Nishad -----------	N̲i̲
Shuddha Nishad --------	Ni

THAT - The concept of *that* is essentially the same as the Western concept of mode. It has already been pointed out that several of the *swar* have alternate forms. The permutations of these various forms give rise to numerous scales with vastly differing intervals.

A simple mathematical approach tells us that there are 32 seven-note combinations of the *swar*. However, only ten are conventionally accepted as *thats* (Jairazbhoy 1971).

The ten *thats* are :

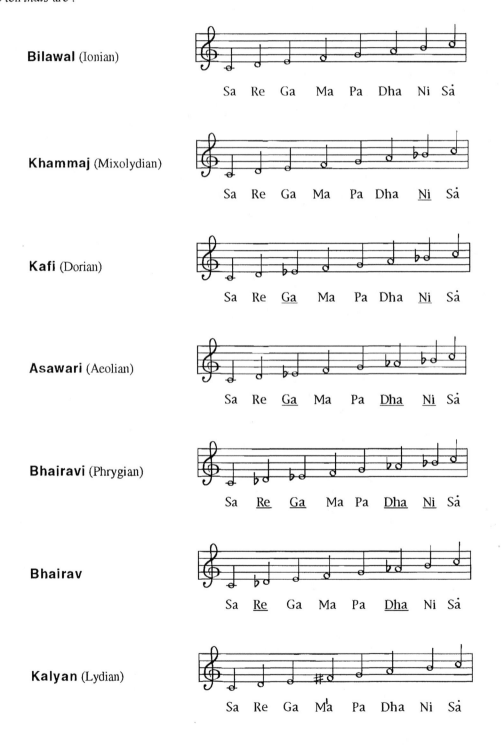

Bilawal (Ionian)

Sa Re Ga Ma Pa Dha Ni Sa

Khammaj (Mixolydian)

Sa Re Ga Ma Pa Dha <u>Ni</u> Sa

Kafi (Dorian)

Sa Re <u>Ga</u> Ma Pa Dha <u>Ni</u> Sa

Asawari (Aeolian)

Sa Re <u>Ga</u> Ma Pa <u>Dha</u> <u>Ni</u> Sa

Bhairavi (Phrygian)

Sa <u>Re</u> <u>Ga</u> Ma Pa <u>Dha</u> <u>Ni</u> Sa

Bhairav

Sa <u>Re</u> Ga Ma Pa <u>Dha</u> Ni Sa

Kalyan (Lydian)

Sa Re Ga Ma' Pa Dha Ni Sa

Marwa
Sa Re Ga M'a Pa Dha Ni Sá

Purvi
Sa Re Ga M'a Pa Dha Ni Sá

Todi
Sa Re Ga M'a Pa Dha Ni Sá

There are problems whenever one is talking about the number of *thats*. Generally only ten are acknowledged; twenty are in common usage; while 32 are possible given present concepts of scale construction. This has created a certain amount of confusion in north Indian pedagogy.

The concept of *that* is summarized easily. Five of the seven notes have alternate forms; therefore, a simple process of mathematical permutation shows that 32 seven-note scales are possible. Of these, only 20 are normally found in the north Indian system, and only ten are acknowledged for pedagogic purposes.

SAPTAK - The *saptak* (सप्तक) may be directly translated to mean octave; as such it has two common definitions. The most fundamental definition is of the Indian gamut (i.e., the seven *swar*)(Shankar 1968). This is shown in expressions such as *shuddha swar saptak* (natural scale).

However, a more common definition is the register (table 2.3). The middle register is referred to as *madhya saptak*; the upper register is referred to as *tar saptak*; and the lower register is referred to as *mandra saptak*. Additionally, two octaves above the middle is called *ati-tar saptak*; three octaves is called *ati-ati-tar saptak*, etc. In a similar manner two octaves below is called *ati-mandra saptak*; three octaves below is called *ati-ati-mandra saptak*, etc.

The register is indicated by a new notational element shown in our discussion of *that*. The dot over a *swar* indicates that it is *tar saptak*. Two dots over the *swar* indicate that it is *ati-tar saptak*. Conversely, a dot below indicates that it is *mandra saptak*. Two dots below indicate that the *swar* is *ati-mandra saptak*.

The *saptak* may be easily summarized as being the register or octave of Indian music. Only three are traditionally acknowledged (i.e., *tar*, *madhya*, and *mandra*) but others may easily be denoted by appending the prefix

Table 2.3. The Registers (Saptak)
Ati-ati-tar-saptak . Three octaves above middle
Ati-tar-saptak . Two octaves above middle
Tar-saptak . Upper octave
Madhya-saptak . Middle octave
Mandra-saptak . Lower octave
Ati-mandra-saptak . Two octaves below middle
Ati-ati-mandra-saptak . Three octaves below middle

"ati" to an existing designation. The center *(madhya)* is determined according to what is convenient to the instrumentalist or vocalist.

RAG

- The *rag* (राग) is the most important concept that any student of music should understand. Unfortunately, it is not easy to describe what a *rag* is in a few words. It is easier to say what it is not. It is not a tune, melody, scale, mode, or any concept for which an English word exists. It is instead a combination of different characteristics. It is these characteristics which define the *rag*.

One of the sources of confusion is that the *rag* may be defined at different levels. There are cases where a *that* has only a single *rag* in it. In such cases the *that* (modality) is sufficient to define the *rag*. However, most *thats* have several *rags* in them; therefore, we must look to increasingly subtle levels to make the distinctions.

The *jati* (जाति) is one such level. *Jati* is the number of notes in the *rag*; for not every one uses all seven notes. Normally, a *rag* will consist of either five, six, or a full seven notes. A five-note *rag* is said to be an *audhav jati* (औड्व जाति); a six note *rag* is said to be *shadav jati* (षाड्व जाति); and one of seven notes is said to be *sampurna jati* (सम्पूर्ण जाति). Furthermore, *rags* may have different *jatis* for the ascending and the descending structures. For instance, a *rag* which has only five notes in the ascending, but all seven notes in the descending would be called *audhav-sampurna*.

We now have two levels that may be used to define the *rag*. We have the *jati* and the *that*. These two characteristics are sufficient to define a few *rags*. Yet, this is not yet sufficient to define all *rags*. We need a further level of distinction.

Arohana (आरोहन) and *avarohana* (अवरोहन) are another level of definition. The *arohana*, also called *aroh* (आरोह), is the pattern in which a *rag* ascends the scale. The *avarohana*, also called *avaroh* (अवरोह), describes the way that the *rag* descends the scale.

Both the *arohana* and *avarohana* may use certain characteristic twists and turns. Such prescribed twists are referred to as *vakra* (वक्र). Furthermore, notes may have different levels of significance. Notes may be strong or weak.

The fact that the notes may have a different level of significance is very important. The note which is strongly emphasized is referred to as the *vadi* (वादी). Another note which is strong but only slightly less so is the *samavadi* (संवादी). A note which is neither emphasized nor deemphasized is called *anuvadi* (अनुवादी). Notes which are deemphasized are referred to as being *durbal* (दुर्बल) while notes which are excluded are called *vivadi* (विवादी).

The concept of *vadi* and *samavadi* are particularly problematic for the music student. Although certain notes clearly show importance, the "official" *vadi* and *samavadi* are sometimes quite different. In many cases this reflects the fact that the theory was laid down quite a few years ago while the performance of the *rags* has continued to evolve. In other cases it reflects Bhatkhande's efforts to develop a cohesive theory about the structure of rags.[1]

Implicit in the *arohana/ avarohana* is the *pakad* (पकड़). This is a defining phrase or a characteristic pattern for a *rag*. Not every *rag* has a clear *pakad*, but a large number of *rags* require one to distinguish them from related *rags*. *Pakad* is sometimes called *swarup* (स्वरूप).

Therefore, these are the characteristics which make the *rag*. Collectively, the *vadi, that, jati, pakad*, etc., define a *rag*.

There are a few other characteristics which should be mentioned. Although these do not have the same level of importance they still should be kept in mind.

The *samay* (समय) or time is one such quality. Tradition ascribes certain *rags* to particular times of the day, seasons, or holidays. It is said that appropriate performance may bring harmony, while playing at different

---

[1] *Vadi* and *samavadi* play a crucial role in Bhatkhande's system of time theory of *rags*. In many cases he declared that certain notes were *vadi/samvadi*, not because of their usage, but rather to come up with a system which would describe the timings by an internal structure.

times may bring disharmony. Stories are even told of musicians who were able to create rain by singing a monsoon *rag*.

There is not a universal agreement as to the correctness of *samay*. There are some musicians who argue that a *rag* must be performed at the time of day that it is assigned; conversely, other musicians argue that one may play a *rag* at any time if one wishes to evoke the mood of that time. For instance, if one simply wished to evoke the mood of a monsoon day, one could perform *Megh Malhar;* even in the middle of summer. The concept of *samay* is complicated by the fact that there are a number of *rags* that have different times ascribed by different musical traditions.

This question is further complicated by an absence of any scientific process to determine *samay*. The great musicologist Bhatkhande attempted to develop a description of *samay* which could be explained in terms of the structure. Unfortunately, the exceptions to his system were so many that his system must be considered a failure. If one is disposed to follow the system of *samay*, one can only accept that it is merely a question of tradition. Attempts to justify the concept by looking at the internal structure of the *rag* have failed.

The concept is further weakened by the influx of *rags* from South India. Many years ago *Carnatic* musicians and musicologists abandoned the concept of *samay*. It seems that it did not fit into their rational, scientific system. The result is that when *Carnatic rags* enter the *Hindusthani* system, they come stripped of any conventionally accepted timings.

The concept of "families" of *rags* is another characteristic worthy of note. It was briefly mentioned that *rags* were ascribed to certain demigods. A natural consequence of such anthropomorphism is that there be a familial relationship between them. Therefore, in the past few centuries there arose a complicated system of *rags* (male *rags*), *raginis* (रागिणी) (female *rags*), *putra rags* (पुत्र राग) (sons of *rags*), etc. (Kripalvanand 1972). This was the basis for a system of classification before the advent of modern musicology. Although this may have been a great inspiration to the painters of the old *ragmala* tradition, it proved to be worthless as a means of taxonomy. The obvious problem was that there was no way to accommodate the new *rags* that were coming into existence.

Ornamentation is essential to the proper performance of the *rag*. When one hears Indian music, it is the ornaments which first make an impression. However this is often a confusing subject. The concept implies a technique which is used for artistic reason yet not necessarily of theoretical importance. This is usually the case, however there are many instances where such ornamentation is a defining characteristic of the *rag*.

Here are some of the more common ornaments. *Meend* (मींड) is the the most common; it is basically a slide or *glissando*. *Andolan* (आन्दोलन) is another common ornament; this may be described as a slow vibrato. *Krantan* (क्रन्तन) is a purely instrumental ornament; this may be described as a hammering action of the left hand. *Krantan* is often used on the *sarod* or *sitar*. Notes may also be sharpened or flattened. *Rags* such as *Todi* (तोड़ी) or *Darbari Kanada* (दरबारी कानड़ा) use lower forms of some notes as part of their definition. In many other cases these are mere ornaments and have no theoretical significance.

We have tried to cover in some detail the nature of *rag*. Any music student should understand these principles. Concepts such as *that* (the mode), *vadi* (important note), *samavadi* (consonant of the *vadi*), etc. must be mastered if the student is to have a firm background.

WORKS CITED

Jairazbhoy, N. A.
1971   *The Rags of North Indian Music*. Middletown, CT: Wesleyan University Press.

Kripalvanand, Swami
1972   "Purush Rag, Stri Rag Aur Putra Rag", *Rag-Ragini Ank*. Hataras: Sangeet Karyalaya; pp. 7-51.

Shankar, Ravi
1968   *Ravi Shankar, My Music, My Life*. New Delhi: Vicas Publishing House.

CHAPTER 3.

FUNDAMENTALS OF TAL

It has been argued that rhythm is fundamental to the creation of any musical system. Certainly from a historic standpoint rhythm existed many centuries before the word *rag* was ever used. Given this historical preeminence, it is not surprising that rhythm occupies an important position in the Indian system of music.

BASIC TERMS - There are a number of terms used in the Indian science of rhythm. The first of which is *tal* (ताल). *Tal* literally means "clap" (Kapoor - no date). Today, the *tabla* has replace the clap in the performance, but the term still reflects the origin. The basic concepts of tal are: *tali* (ताली) or *bhari* (भरी), *khali* (खाली), *vibhag* (विभाग) or (*ang* अंग), *matra*(मात्रा), *bol* (बोल), *theka* (ठेका), *laya* (लय) and *avartan* (आवर्तन). We will now discuss these terms in greater detail.

Tali (*Bhari*) - This is the pattern of clapping. Each *tal* is characterized by a particular pattern and number of claps.

Khali - In addition to the claps, there are also a number of "waves". These have a characteristic relationship to the claps.

Vibhag (Ang) - Each clap or wave specifies a particular section or measure. These measures may be of any number of beats, yet most commonly 2, 3, 4, or 5 beats are used.

Matra - This is the beat. It may be subdivided if required.

Bol - This is the mnemonic system where each stroke of the drum has a syllable attached to it. These syllables are known as *bol*. It is common to consider the bol to be synonymous to the stroke itself.

Theka - This is a conventionally established pattern of *bols* and *vibhag (tali, khali)* which define the *tal*. This is very important, yet we will postpone our discussion until later.

Laya - This is the tempo. The tempo may be either slow(*vilambit* विलंबित), medium (*madhya* मध्य), or fast (*drut* द्रुत). Additionally ultra-slow may be referred to as *ati-vilambit* or ultra-fast may be referred to as *ati-drut*.

Avartan - This is the basic cycle. It has been stated that the *tal* revolves around an established number of beats. This number of beats represents one cycle. Therefore, one *avartan* (cycle) of *tintal* will be 16 beats; one avartan of *ektal* will have 12 beats, etc.

Sam - The first beat of the cycle is referred to as *sam*. It is important because it marks a point of convergence between the vocalist, instrumentalist and percussionist.

These are the most common terms used in the Indian science of rhythm. They are delt with in much greater detail in other sources (Courtney 1994). Let us now look more closely at the accompaniment forms.

THEKA - The basic concepts behind *tal* are much easier to comprehend than to implement. It is very difficult for beginner to sing with the *tabla*. It is usually difficult because the student has not bothered to memorize the *thekas* that the tablist plays. The memorization of basic *thekas* is absolutely crucial to the musical development of the vocal student.

Here is a list of common thekas:

Tintal - This is the most common *tal* in North Indian classical music. It is a 16 beat *tal* composed of 4 measures *(vibhag)* of four beats *(matra)* each. It has the clapping arraignment of clap, clap, wave clap.

$$\overset{X}{\text{Dha Dhin Dhin Dha}} \Big|\overset{2}{\text{Dha Dhin Dhin Dha}} \Big|\overset{0}{\text{Dha Tin Tin Na}} \Big|\overset{3}{\text{Na Dhin Dhin Dha}} \Big|$$

Jhaptal - This *tal* is declining in popularity. Today it is used primarily in *Rabindra sangeet*, and for a few older style *kheyals*. It is a 10 beat *tal* composed of four *vibhag*. The number of *matras* per *vibhag* is two, three, two, and three *matras* respectively. It has the clapping arrangement of; clap, clap, wave, clap.

$$\overset{X}{\text{Dhin Na}} \Big|\overset{2}{\text{Dhin Dhin Na}} \Big|\overset{0}{\text{Tin Na}} \Big|\overset{3}{\text{Dhin Dhin Na}} \Big|$$

Rupaktal - *Rupak tal* is unique among the *tals* in that the *sam* is *khali*. Therefore, the firsts clap has no major significance. It is also interesting to note that it is asymmetric; for the last few centuries it has been usual for *tals* to be an even number of beats with a strong sense of symmetry. *Rupak tal* has seven *matras* arranged into three *vibhag*. The number of *matras* is three, two, two. It has the clapping arrangement of wave, clap, clap. This *tal* is quite common in a broad variety of styles, including *gazal*, classical instrumental, classical vocal, and even occasionally film songs.

$$\overset{0}{\text{Tin Tin Na}} \Big|\overset{1}{\text{Dhin Na}} \Big|\overset{2}{\text{Dhin Na}} \Big|$$

Ektal - *Ektal* is very common in a style of vocal known as *kheyal*. This *tal* is 12 *matras* divided into six *vibhag* of two *matras* each. It has the clapping arrangement of clap, wave, clap, wave, clap, clap. Although the medium tempo *theka* is shown here, it is usually found in either very fast or very slow tempo.

$$\overset{X}{\text{Dhin Dhin}} \Big|\overset{0}{\text{Dha Ge Ti Ri Ki Ta}} \Big|\overset{2}{\text{Tun Na}} \Big|\overset{0}{\text{Kat Ta}} \Big|$$
$$\overset{3}{\text{Dha Ge Ti Ri Ki Ta}} \Big|\overset{4}{\text{Dhin Na}} \Big|$$

Dadra - This *tal* is very common in the semiclassical styles. It is used extensively in *gazal*, *bhajan*, *Rabindra sangeet*, and film songs. It is six *matras* divided into two *vibhags*. Each *vibhag* is of three *matras*. It has the clapping arrangement of: clap, wave.

$$\overset{X}{\text{Dha Dhin Na}} \Big|\overset{0}{\text{Dha Tin Na}} \Big|$$

Kaherava (standard) - This is a very common *tal* of light, and semiclassical music. It is eight *matras* divided into two *vibhags* of four *matras* each. It has the clapping arrangement of clap, wave.

$$\overset{X}{\text{Dha Ge Na Ti}} \Big|\overset{0}{\text{Na Ka Dhin Na}} \Big|$$

Kaherava (Bhajan ka Theka) - This is a variety of *kaherava* which is used extensively in *bhajans*. It is nominally considered to be an eight-beat *tal*. However, it is often easier to conceive of it as a fast 16-beat *tal*.

X | Dhin - | Na Dhin | - Dhin | Na Ga | 0 | Tin - | Na Tin | - Tin | Na Ga |

<u>Choutal</u> - This is a very ancient *tal* which was much used in the *dhrupad* style of singing. It is composed of 12 *matra*s divided into four *vibhag*s, of four, four, two, and two *matra*s each. It has claps for all of the *vibhag*s. There are some interpretations which divide *choutal* into six *vibhag*s in a manner similar to *ektal*, however this interpretation is probably of recent origins.

X | Dha Dha Din Ta | 2 Ti Ta | Dha Din Ta | 3 Ti Ta | Ka Ta | 4 Ga Di | Ge Na |

We have covered here the basic rhythmic material that a beginner should know. These were the basic concepts *(bhari, khali, vibhag,* etc.). Furthermore, we have presented a list of common *theka* that the student should know.

WORKS CITED

Courtney, David R.
1994   *Fundamentals of Tabla.* Houston, TX: Sur Sangeet Services.

Kapoor, R.K.
no date   *Kamal's Advanced Illustrated Oxford Dictionary of Hindi- English.* Delhi, India: Verma Book Depot.

CHAPTER 4.

INSTRUMENTAL MUSIC AND DANCE

One cannot learn vocal music without an understanding of the related disciplines of instrumental music and dance. It takes all three components to make up the field of *sangeet*. Let us begin with a study of instrumental music.

INSTRUMENTAL MUSIC - Instrumental music has the closest conceptual similarity to vocal music. In Bharat's time it was part of the overall tradition of stagecraft (Rangacharya 1966), but today it is a fully developed artform in its own right. There is a traditional system for the classification of instruments. This system is based upon; non-membranous percussion (ghan घन), membranous percussion (*avanaddh* अवनद्ध), wind blown (*sushir* सुषिर), plucked string (*tat* तत्), bowed string (*vitat* (वितत).[1] Here are the classes and representative instruments.

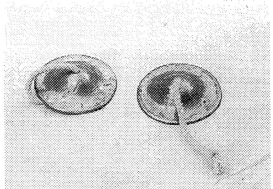

Figure 4.1. Jal Tarang

NON-MEMBRANOUS PERCUSSIVE (GHAN) - This is one of the oldest classes of instruments in India. This class is based upon percussive instruments which do not have membranes, specifically those which have solid resonators. These may be either melodic instruments or instruments to keep *tal*.

Kasht tarang (काष्टतरंग) - *Kasht tarang* is a type of xylophone. It is characterized by the use of wooden resonating bars.

Jal tarang (जलतरंग) (fig. 4.1) - *Jal tarang* is a set of china bowls that are filled with water. Each bowl is struck with a light wooden mallet to cause it to ring.

Manjira (मञ्जीरा) (fig. 4.2) - *Manjira* is a set of small cymbals. It is a ubiquitous component of dance music and bhajans.

Figure 4.2. Manjira

Ghatam (घटम) - *Ghatam* is nothing more than a large clay pot. It is very commonly played in south Indian classical performances. There are two actions of resonance. The primary one is the ringing of the pot caused by striking. A very low resonance is also produced by the cavity. This pitch is raised or lowered by opening or closing the hole with the stomach.

---

[1] The *Ain-i-Akbari* gives a slightly different version. According to its author, Abul-Fazl Allami (circa 16th century) the classes are *Tata* (stringed instruments), *Vitata* (instruments with skin stretched over them), *Ghana* (percussive instruments based upon solid bodies), *Sushira* (wind instruments).

Murchang (मुरचंग) - *Murchang* is a Jew's harp. It is commonly played in south Indian performances.

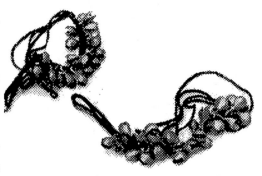

Cabas (कबास) - *Cabas* is an instrument imported into India. It is usually constructed by weaving beads upon a coconut shell. It produces a rasping sound which is appropriate for light music.

Ghungharu (घुंघरू) (fig. 4.3) - *Ghungharu* are the "tinklebells" or "jingle bells" which are used to adorn the feet of dancers. When tied to the feet it is played by the act of dancing. It may also be played by hand. This instrument evolved from the tinkling of the *payal* (पायल), which are traditional anklets worn by women in India.

Figure 4.3.   Ghungharu

Kartal (कर्ताल) (fig. 4.4) - *Kartal* are a pair of wooden blocks or frames with small metal jingles mounted in them. They are simply beaten together to provide a rhythmic support to *bhajans*, *kirtan*, folk and other light music.

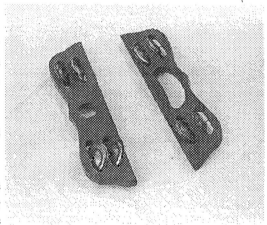

BLOWN AIR (SUSHIR) - This class of instruments is characterized by the use of air to excite the various resonators.

Bansuri (बंसुरी) / Venu (वेणु) (fig. 4.5) - *Bansuri* and *venu* are common Indian flutes. They are typically made of bamboo or reed. There are two varieties; transverse and fipple. The transverse variety is nothing more than a length of bamboo with holes cut into it. This is the preferred flute for classical music because the embouchure gives added flexibility and control. The fipple variety is found in the folk and filmi styles but seldom used for serious music. This is usually considered to be just a toy because the absence of any embouchure limits the flexibility of the instrument. The flute may be called many things in India: *bansi* (बंसी), *bansuri*, *murali* (मुरली), *venu* and many more. Although names may vary across India, there are two main types; *bansuri* and *venu*.

Figure 4.4.   Kartal

The *bansuri* is found in the North. It typically has six holes, however there has been a tendency in recent years to use seven holes for added flexibility. It was previously associated only with folk music, but today it is found in classical, *filmi*, and numerous other genre.

Venu is a south Indian flute. It typically has eight holes. The venu is very popular in all south Indian styles.

The flute has special significance in India because of its association with lord Krishna. Numerous common names reflect these epitaphs; Venugopal, Bansilal, Murali, Muralidhar, etc.

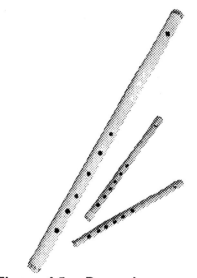

Figure 4.5.   Bansuri

Shehnai (शहनाई) (fig 4.6) - *Shehnai* may be thought of as a north Indian oboe. Although it is referred to as a double reeded instrument it is actually a quadruple reed instrument. This is because it has two upper reeds and two lower reeds. The instrument has a wooden body with a brass bell. The reed is attached to a brass tube which is wrapped in string. The *shehnai* has eight holes but it is common to find some of the holes partially or completely occluded with wax.

The sound of the *shehnai* is considered particularly auspicious. For this reason it is found in temples and is an indispensable component of any north Indian wedding. In the past, *shehnai* was part of the *naubat* (नौबत) or traditional ensembles of nine instruments found at royal courts.

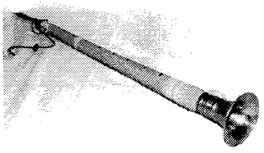

Pungi (पुंगी) or (Bin)(बीन) - *Pungi* is a snake charmer's instrument. The word "*pungi*" is a generic term for many reeded noisemakers. The term *bin* is really a misnomer. The word *bin* is a typical East Indian corruption of *vina*. The term *vina* implies a stringed instrument so it could not be applied to a reeded instrument.

Figure 4.6. Shehnai

Harmonium (हारमोनियम)(fig. 4.7) - The harmonium is not a native Indian instrument. It is a European instrument which was imported in the last few centuries. It is a reed organ with hand pumped bellows. Although it is a relatively recent introduction, it has spread throughout the subcontinent. Today, it is used in virtually every musical genre except the south Indian classical.

Although this is a European invention, it has evolved into a truly bicultural instrument. The keyboard is European, but it has a number of drone reeds which are particularly Indian. European models came in both hand pumped and foot pumped models. The foot pumped models disappeared in India many years ago. This is because the foot pedals required one to sit in a chair; something which is unusual for an Indian musician. Also the only advantage of the foot model was that it freed both hands so that both melody and chords could be played. Indian music has no chords, so this was no advantage. Although the hand pumped models required one hand to pump they were more comfortable when played on the floor.

Figure 4.7. Harmonium

Shankh (शङ्ख) - *Shankh* is a conch shell. This instrument has a strong association with the Hindu religion. It is said that when it is blown it announces the victory of good over evil. This instrument has limited musical applications.

Nadaswaram (नादस्वरम) - *Nadaswaram* is a South Indian version of the *shehnai*. It is substantially larger than the *shehnai* and has a simple double reed rather than the more complex quadruple reed. It is considered a very auspicious instrument and is found at temples and at weddings.

PLUCKED STRINGED INSTRUMENTS (TAT) - This class of instruments is characterized
by plucked strings. In ancient times virtually all instruments of this class were referred to as *vina*.

Sitar सितार (fig. 4.8) - *Sitar* is perhaps the most well known of the Indian instruments. Artists such as Ravi Shankar have popularized this instrument around the world. Sitar is a long necked instrument with an interesting construction. It has a varying number of strings but 17 is usual. It has three to four playing strings and three to four drone strings. These strings are plucked with a wire finger plectrum called *mizrab*. There are also a series of sympathetic strings lying under the frets. Although these strings are almost never played, they vibrate in sympathy whenever the corresponding note is sounded. The frets are metal rods which have been bent into crescents. The main resonator is usually made of a gourd and there is sometimes an additional resonator attached to the neck.

Rabab रबाब (fig. 4.9) - *Rabab* is a very ancient instrument found primarily in Kashmir. It is a hollowed-out body of wood with a membrane stretched over the opening. Combinations of gut (or nylon) and metal strings pass over a bridge which rests on the taught membrane. The *rabab* is mentioned quite frequently in old texts. This may indicate that the *rabab* was once quite popular in India. However, some are of the opinion that this is actually a different *rabab* from what we think of today.

Figure 4.8. Sitar

Sarod सरोद (fig. 4.10) - *Sarod* is an instrument which is derived from the *rabab*. It is not an ancient instrument, probably no more than 150 to 200 years. It is essentially a bass *rabab*. It has a metal fingerboard with no frets. The bridge rests on a taut membrane which covers the resonator. The *sarod* has numerous strings, some of which are drone, some are played, and some are sympathetic. It is played with a pick made of coconut shell.

Saraswati Vina सरस्वती वीणा(fig. 4.11) - *Saraswati vina* is the instrument associated with Saraswati, the goddess of learning and the arts. It is made of wood and has frets which consist of brass bars set into wax. Unlike north Indian instruments, the *saraswati vina* has no sympathetic strings. It has only playing strings and drone strings (*thalam*). It is played with wire plectra on the fingers. This instrument is common in south India.

Figure 4.9. Rabab

Figure 4.10. Sarod　　　　　　**Figure 4.11. Saraswati Vina**

Surbahar सुरबहार - *Surbahar* is essentially a bass *sitar*. It is substantially larger and is tuned anywhere from four steps to an octave lower than a regular *sitar*. Its technique is similar enough to *sitar* so that musicians have no trouble going from one instrument to another. The *surbahar* has an advantage over *sitar* in that it has a longer sustain and an ability to *meend* (*glissando*) up to an octave in a single fret. Therefore it is possible to play complex melodies without using more than a single fret. This instrument is very well suited to long slow *alaps*. The instrument's main weakness is that its long sustains cause a fast *jhala* to become indistinct and muddy. It is for this reason that some artists prefer to play the *alap* with *surbahar* but shift to *sitar* for *gat* and *jhala*.

Figure 4.12.   Rudra Vina

Gotuvadhyam गोटूवाद्यम - *Gotuvadhyam* is exactly like *saraswati vina* except it has no frets. It is played with a slide in a manner somewhat like a Hawaiian guitar. This instrument is common in Southern India.

Rudra Vina रुद्र वीणा (Bin) बीन (fig. 4.12) - *Rudra vina* appears to be the oldest style of vina. Such evidence is readily seen in elements of its construction, and from its depiction on the walls of ancient temples. This instrument is basically a bamboo stick with two gourds attached. It has frets which are set into wax. This instrument is quite rare nowadays.

Vichitra Vina (विचित्र वीणा) - *Vichitra vina* instrument is like the *rudra vina* except it has no frets. It is played with a slide like a Hawaiian guitar.

Ektar (एकतार) - *Ektar* is a simple folk instrument. It may be the oldest stringed instrument in the Indian subcontinent. In its simplest form it is nothing more than a gourd which has been penetrated by a stick of bamboo. Another piece of bamboo forms the tuning peg. The bridge is nothing more than a coin, piece of coconut, plastic or similar object. *Ektars* such as this are common in the south. In the north, their construction is a little more complicated. A membrane is stretched over the gourd and the bridge is placed over the taut membrane.

Figure 4.13.   Tanpura

Tanpura (तानपूरा)(fig. 4.13) - This is a drone instrument. It resembles a *sitar* except it has no frets. It is composed of a resonator made of a gourd and a long neck. The usual number of strings is four, but one occasionally finds five or even six string models. This instrument is also called *tambura* in the south.

Dotar (दोतार) - This is a two stringed version of the ektar. However, in Bengal there is an unrelated instrument also called *dotar* which is very similar to the Afghani *rabab*.

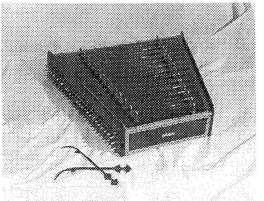

Figure 4.14.   Santur

page 21

Santur (संतूर)(fig. 4.14) - This is an instrument indigenous to Kashmir but nowadays played throughout the North. It is a hammered dulcimer which is struck with light wooden mallets. The number of strings may be as few as 24 or more than 100.

Typical sizes tend to be around 80. It has a vibrant tone and has become very popular in the last 20 years.

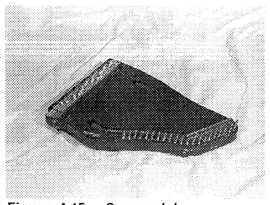

Surmandal (सुरमंडल)(fig. 4.15) - *Surmandal* is basically a small harp. It is generally used for the accompaniment of vocalists. Although it is considered a minor instrument, as a class the harps are very old.

Figure 4.15. Surmandal

BOWED-STRINGED INSTRUMENTS (VITAT) - This
is a class of stringed instruments which are bowed. This class appears to be quite old, yet these instruments did not occupy a place in classical music until the last few centuries (Bor 1987). Even today only the Western violin is free of a stigma which has become attached to this class.

Sarangi (सारंगी)(fig. 4.16) - *Sarangi* is a common representative of *vitat*. It has three to four main playing strings and approximately sixty sympathetic strings. The instrument has no frets or fingerboard. The strings float in the air. Pitch is determined by sliding the fingernail against the string rather than pressing it against a fingerboard (like violin). This instrument is extremely difficult to play, as a consequence its popularity is on the decline. This instrument has traditionally been associated with the *kathak* dance and the vocal styles of *thumri*, *dadra* and *kheyal*.

Saringda - *Saringda* is a folk version of the *sarangi*. It is found in Rajasthan and northwest India.

Figure 4.16. Sarangi

Violin - Although not native to the subcontinent, the violin has become so popular that it must be mentioned in this book. There appears to be no difference in construction between the Indian violin and its Western counterpart, however the technique is quite different. The most refined technique is to be found in south India. Instead of holding the instrument under the chin, the musician props it between the shoulder and the foot. This gives a stability which cannot be matched by either north Indian nor occidental technique. North Indian technique, though not as refined, is still impressive.

Esraj (एसराज) - *Esraj* is a combination between *saringda* and *sitar*. The base of the instrument is like *saringda* while the neck and strings are like *sitar*. It gives a sound very much like *sarangi* without being as difficult to play.

Dilruba (दिलरूबा) (fig. 4.17) - *Dilruba* is extremely close to the *esraj*. It so close that most people are unable to tell them apart. The difference is to be found in the shape of the resonator and the manner in which the sympathetic strings attach. Still they are so similar that a *dilruba* player has no trouble playing an *esraj* and vice versa.

Figure 4.17. Dilruba

MEMBRANOUS PERCUSSIVE

(AVANADDH) - This is a class of instruments which have struck membranes. These typically comprise the drums.

Figure 4.18.   Tabla

Tabla (तबला)(fig. 4.18) - This is a pair of drums. It consists of of a small right hand drum called *danya* and a larger metal one called *banya*.

The *tabla* has an interesting construction. The *danya* (right hand drum) is almost always made of wood. The diameter at the membrane may run from just under five inches to over six inches. The *banya* (left hand drum) may be made of iron, aluminum, copper, steel, or clay; yet brass with a nickel or chrome plate is the most common material. Undoubtedly the most striking characteristic of the *tabla* is the large black spot on each of the playing surfaces. These black spots are a mixture of gum, soot, and iron filings. Their function is to create the bell-like timbre that is characteristic of the instrument.

Pakhawaj (पखावज)(fig. 4.19) - *Pakhawaj* is an ancient barrel shaped drum with two playing heads. It was once common throughout north India but in the last few generations *tabla* has usurped its position of importance. It has a right head which is identical to *tabla* except somewhat larger. The left head is similar to the *tabla* banya except that there is a temporary application of flour and water instead of the black permanent spot. It is laced with rawhide and has tuning blocks placed between the straps and shell. This instrument was very much tied to dhrupad, consequently as *dhrupad* has declined the *pakhawaj* has has also fallen out of use. Today this instrument is rare.

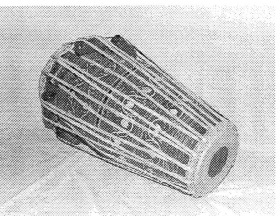

Figure 4.19.   Pakhawaj

Mridangam (मृदंगम)(fig 4.20) - This is a south Indian version of the *pakhawaj*. It bears a strong superficial resemblance to *pakhawaj* but there are major differences in construction and technique. The tone of the instrument is quite different (Courtney 1993). This is due in part to the heavier annular membrane around the right side and a number of pieces of straw which are placed radially between the annular membrane and the main membrane. The left side also uses a mixture of flour and water to provide a proper tone. The sustain of this side is substantially less due to a large-double annular membrane rather than a small single layer as found on the *pakhawaj*.

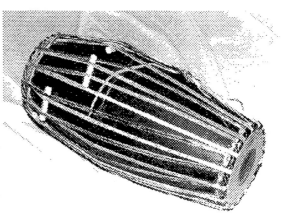

Figure 4.20.   Mridangam

Tabla Tarang (तबला तरंग) - *Tabla tarang* consists of a number of *tabla danya* tuned to different notes of the scale. Complete melodies are played by striking the appropriate *danyas*.

Dholak (ढोलक) - *Dholak* is a very popular folk drum of northern India. It is barrel shaped with a simple membrane on the right hand side. The left hand is also a single membrane with a special application on the inner surface. This application is a mixture of tar, clay and sand (*dholak masala* ढोलक मसाला) which lowers the pitch and provides a well defined tone. It is said that this instrument used to occupy a position of considerable prestige (Stewart 1974). Today it is merely relegated to film and folk music.

Figure 4.21. Nagada

Khol (खोल) - This instrument is also called mridang. It is a folk drum of northeast India. It has a body made of clay, a very small head on the right side (approximately 4 inches), and a larger head on the left side (approximately 10 inches). A fiberglass version of the *khol* has become popular in the West among the members of ISKON.

Nagada (नगाड़ा)(fig. 4.21)- These are the kettle drums of the old *naubat* (traditional ensemble of nine instruments). It is played with sticks. Today this instrument is usually used to accompany *shehnai*.

Dholki (ढोल्कि) or (Nal)(नाल) - *Dholki*, also called *nal* is an drum with a barrel shaped shell. The left side resembles the *banya* (large metal drum of the *tabla*) except that it uses *dholak masala* (oil based application) on the inner surface instead of a *syahi* (permanent black spot). The right head is unique in its construction. Goat skin is stitched onto an iron ring. In the center of this skin is a *syahi*, similar to *tabla* except much thinner. The traditional *nals* were laced with rope and had sticks to function as turnbuckles. Today, metal turnbuckles have replaced the rope lacing in most models.

The *nal* is very popular in the *tamasha* तमाशा (street performance) of Maharashtra. It has been absorbed into the Hindi film industry and today the *nal* is very popular for this style.

Duff (डफ) - *Duff* is a tambourine. It is commonly used in folk music but is rarely heard in other styles. It is also called *dapphu*, *daffali*, or a number of other names.

Kanjira (कंजीरा) - The *kanjira* is also a tambourine. It is made by stretching lizard skin over a wooden frame. The frame is about seven inches in diameter with one metal jingle mounted in it. The *kanjira* is very popular in South Indian classical performances.

Tavil (ताविल) - This is an instrument found only in the extreme south. It has a shell of nearly spherical proportions which is open on both sides. There are two skins wrapped around two large hemp hoops. The left side is played with a stick. The right side is played with the hands with metal thimbles placed over the fingers to give a sharp sound. This instrument is commonly played in south Indian temples and weddings.

We have given a brief overview of the Indian instruments. It was mentioned that the instruments fall into five categories: *tat* (plucked stringed), *vitat* (bowed stringed), *sushir* (wind blown), *avanaddh* (membranous percussion) and *ghan* (non membranous percussion). Within these five classes there are a large number of individual instruments. Although we have talked in great detail about the instruments we have mentioned nothing about the instrumental style of music.

INSTRUMENTAL STYLES - There is a general tendency for the instrumental styles to follow quite closely the vocal styles. Yet, the degree to which an instrument follows is primarily linked to the dynamics of the instrument.

Dynamics is the nature of the loudness of an instrument. This is not intended to mean loudness in the usual interpretation, but rather the amplitudinal characteristics of the instrument. The *sitar* and flute offer a good illustration. A flute is continuously excited, therefore there is a steady sound as long as the breath is applied. Since it is possible to sustain a sound for a long time, it is possible to perform all kinds of delicate *meends (glissando)*. Contrast this to a sitar with its rapid decay. The sound is essentially inaudible within about two seconds. Many types of ornamentation cannot be executed due to the quick decay.

This creates an artistic pressure for these instruments to develop their own styles. These styles enhanced the strong points while avoiding the weaknesses. Over the years they have become formalized into four major instrumental styles known as: *alap, jor, gat* and *jhala*.

Alap (आलाप)- The *alap* of instrumentalists is virtually identical to the *alap* of the vocalists. It is a slow, rhythmless exposition of the *rag*. It is usually the beginning movement. There may be a slight difference in interpretation due to the limitations of many instruments.

Jor (जोड़) - *Jor* is an instrumental rendition of a vocal style called *nomtom*. It is characterized by the use of a slow to medium rhythm. There is not a fully developed cycle so it is never accompanied by *tabla*. Although the *nomtom* has fallen out of use among the vocalists it is still a ubiquitous component of instrument concerts. The dynamics of most stringed instruments lends themselves well to this style.

Gat (गत) - Gat is a structure very much like like the main theme, or *sthai* of the vocal tradition. It has a fully developed cycle and is invariably accompanied by the *tabla*. There are two basic approaches; *masitkhani* (मसीतखानी) and *razakhani* (रज़ाखानी). The *masitkhani gat* is the basic slow gat. The *razakhani* is the fast gat. In recent years, the distinction between the two styles has become blurred.

Jhala (झाला) - *Jhala* is undoubtedly the most characteristic of the instrumental styles. Indian instruments are noted by a few special purpose drone strings called *chikari* (चिकारी). These strings are never fretted but are struck whenever the tonic needs to be emphasized. The *jhala* is a fast paced alternation of main melody string and *chikari*. This lends itself to interesting permutations of both *rag* and *tal* simultaneously. This exciting style has become an obligatory conclusion to any *sitar* or *sarod* recital.

The last chapter has dealt extensively with many aspects of the instrumental traditions. If we return to our definition of *sangeet* we find that dance also occupies an important position. Let us look at the Indian dance traditions.

DANCE - There are numerous dance forms in India. The acknowledged classical dances are: *Bharatnatyam* (भरतनाट्यम), *Kathakali* (कथकलि), *Kuchipudi* (कूचिपूडि)(fig.4.22), *Manipuri* (मणिपुरि), *Orissi* (उड़ीसी), and *Kathak* (कथक). Each of these styles has a strong regional connection and none can claim to be representative of the entire Indian subcontinent. Of the above styles, the *Orrisi* and *Kathak* are clearly linked with the north Indian system of music.

CONCLUSION - We have endeavored to give a good background for the instrumental styles. We have only briefly touched upon the dance tradition. This background has allowed us to place Indian vocal in perspective. We see that vocal music does not

Figure 4.22. Kuchipudi Dancer

exist in isolation but as part of a larger musical tradition; one based upon the disciplines of vocal music, instrumental music and dance. Each of these three disciplines has differentiated into a myriad of particular styles. Additionally a bewildering array of musical instruments have evolved.

WORKS CITED

Allami, Abu l-Fazl
Circa 1590 *Ain-i Akbari*. (Translated by H. Blockmann). Delhi 1989: Reprinted by New Taj Office

Bhatkhande, Vishnu Narayan
1934   *A Short History of the Music of Upper India*. Bombay, India: (Reprinted in 1974 by Indian Musicological Society, Baroda).

Courtney, D.R
1980   *Introduction to Tabla*. Hyderabad, India: Anand Power Press.
1993   "Mrdangam et Tabla: un Contraste". *Percussions: Cahier Bimensiel d'Études et d'Informations sur les Arts de la Percussion*. Chailly-en-Biere, France; Vol 28, March/April 1993; pp 11-14.

Bor, Joep
1987   "The Voice of Sarangi: An Illustrated History of Bowing in India". *Quarterly Journal for the National Centre for the Performing Arts*. Bombay: NCPA. Vol XV and XVI Nos. 3, 4, & 1; Sept, Dec, & March 87.

Garg, Lakshminarayan
1984   *Hamare Sangeet-Ratna*. Hathras, India: Sangeet Press.

Rangacharya, Adya
1966   *Introduction to Bharata's Natya-Sastra*. Bombay, India: Popular Prakashan.

Shankar, Ravi
1968   *Ravi Shankar: My Music, My Life*. New Delhi, India: Vikas Publishing House Pvt. Ltd.

Stewart, R. M.
1974   *The Tabla in Perspective*. Ann Arbor: University Microfilms International. (Ph.D. Dissertation).

CHAPTER 5.

VOCAL STYLES

The vocal tradition is especially strong in Indian music. It is considered the highest of the three aspects of *sangeet* (vocal, instrumental, dance). There are many different styles and approaches.

PARTS OF THE SONG

Alap (आलाप) - The *alap* is an approach which is common to most of the above examples. It is a totally rhythmless style based upon a free elaboration upon the *rag*. It is usually the introductory section to any of the previously mentioned musical styles. The *alap* may vary in length from a few seconds to over an hour.

Nomtom (नोमटोम) - This is an intermediate introductory style. It contains a simple rhythm but no developed rhythmic cycle. This is found in *dhrupad* and related styles but today is virtually extinct.

Fixed Compositions - The fixed composition has a special role in *Hindusthani sangeet*. Such compositions may be as simple as a standard elaboration or refined as a traditional piece. In general the fixed compositions fall into two classes: pedagogic material, and themes.

Swarmalika (स्वरमालिका) - This is a style of singing where the vocalist sings the *sargam* (सरगम) of the song. The note-for-note relationship between the lyrics and the melody is very powerful in delineating the *swar*.

Most fixed compositions are not complete pieces but themes used in a larger improvised performance. Such composed themes form a melodic base to which the improvisation frequently returns. Even a very heavily improvised style like *kheyal* (ख्याल) is built around a couple of fixed themes. These themes may be several hundred years old and have been passed down for many generations.

Sthai (स्थाई) - The *sthai* may be thought of as a primary theme. It is fairly fixed and forms the basis for most north Indian vocal performances. This theme is typically short; generally one to three cycles in length and may be recognized by its prominence. It is usually performed in the *madhya saptak* (middle register).

Antara (अंतरा) - This is the secondary theme of a vocal performance. It is easily recognized because it is introduced well after the *sthai*. It is also easy to recognize because it tends to be performed in the *tar saptak* (upper register). Although a classical piece has only a single *antara*, the semi-classical and light pieces may have numerous versions.

Sanchari (संचारी) - This is the tertiary theme of a vocal performance. This is usually found in the old *dhrupad* styles and is seldom heard today.

Abhog (आभोग) - This is the quaternary theme of a vocal performance. Like the *sanchari* it is characteristic of the older forms like dhrupad and is seldom heard today.

STYLES OF SINGING - There are many styles of singing, some old and some new. Here are some major styles.

Lakshan Git (लक्षण गीत) - This is probably the most typical fixed composition used for vocal instruction. This is a style of singing where the lyrics of the song actually describe the features of the *rag*. If the *lakshangit* is memorized, one will never forget the *rag*. Throughout ones life, whenever the *rag* is heard the words keep coming back.

Dhrupad (धुपद) - This is perhaps the oldest style of classical singing in north Indian music today. The heyday of this style was in the time of Tansen. It is a very heavy masculine style performed to the accompaniment of the *pakhawaj* (an ancient *mridang*). It is known for its austere quality and strict adherence to the *tal*. The moods of *dhrupad* may vary, but themes revolving around the victories of great kings and mythological stories are common. Devotional themes are also very common.

     The dhrupad usually adheres to a four part structure of *sthai, antara, sanchari, abhog*. It is usually set to *chautal* (चौताल) of 12 beats, *tivra* (तिव्रा) of 7 beats, or *sulfak* (सूलफाक) of 10 beats. Its formal structure makes it a very difficult style to master. Unfortunately, this rigidity has also made it very difficult for the average person to appreciate. Today this style is almost extinct.

Dhammar (धम्मार) - This has many similarities to *dhrupad*. Its major difference is that it is slightly more romantic. Themes of *dhammar* typically revolve around Krishna and the *Holi* festival. In fact the *dhammar* is often called *"hori"* (holi). It is typically performed in *dhammar tal* of 14 beats. *Dhammar*, like its cousin the *dhrupad*, is rarely heard today.

Kheyal (खयाल) -This has a special place in Indian music. The near extinction of the *dhrupad* and *dhammar* styles has made it the *de facto* standard for classical music. It is probably the most improvised of the Indian styles.

     There are two major movements of *kheyal*. There is an extremely slow section which is called *vilambit*, or *bada kheyal*: and a fast section called *drut* or *chotta* (छोटा) *kheyal*. The *vilambit* section is extremely slow and usually played in *ektal* of 12 beats. The fast section is usually played in *drut tintal* or *drut ektal*.

Tarana (तराना) This is a style which has its origins in the Mogul period. This style is based upon the use of meaningless syllables in a very fast rendition. There is an interesting legend concerning its origin:

     The story refers to a music competition in the court of Allaudin Khilji. It had come to two finalists; a Hindu by the name of Gopal Nayak, and a Muslim named Amir Khusru. Gopal Nayak was well aware that he was up against a formidable opponent. He therefore sang a very fast song in Sanskrit, knowing quite well that Amir Khusru did not know the language. Amir Khusru then sang the same song, note for note, but substituting Persian words for the Sanskrit. The resulting performance was thrilling even though it was unintelligible. In this way Amir Khusru won the competition and invented *tarana*.

     This legend is entertaining but highly unlikely. It is likely that the transformation from intelligible Persian lyrics to the present unintelligible syllables took a long time.

Thumri (ठुमरी) - This is a common style of light classical music. The text is romantic and devotional in nature, and usually revolves around a girl's love for Krishna (Devangan1984). The language is a dialect of Hindi called *Brij bhasha* . This style is characterized by a greater flexibility with the *rag*. The compositions are usually set to *kaherava* (कहरवा) of 8 beats, *addha tal* (अद्धा ताल) of 16 beats, or *dipchandi* (दीपचंदी) of 14 beats. It arose in popularity during the 19th century. Lighter *rags* such as *Mand* or *Khammaj* are usually used.

Dadra (दादरा) - This is a light classical style which is very similar to *thumri*. The most important difference is that the lyrics tend to be in Urdu, and the themes are purely romantic in character. The *tals* used are *dadra* of 6 beats, *kaherava* of 8 beats, or any other light tal. This too is based upon lighter *rags*.

Bhajan (भजन) - This has been popular for many centuries. Unfortunately, it is difficult to describe musically because the *bhajan* is defined by a sense of devotion (*bhakti* भक्ती) rather than any musical characteristics. *Bhajans* cover a broad spectrum of musical styles from the simple musical chant (*dhun* धुन) to highly developed versions comparable to *thumri*.

The poetic content of the *bhajan* also covers a broad spectrum. The more traditional ones by great saint-musicians such as Mira (मीरा), Surdas (सुरदास), or Kabir (कबीर) are considered of the highest literary quality. Many modern ones, although more easily understood by the masses, usually have a literary value no greater than a typical film song (a popular form of music generated for the masses). The lowest poetic form is the *dhun*, which is actually nothing more than a musical version of a chant.

The structure of *bhajan* is very conventional. It contains a single *sthai* and numerous *antara*. The last antara has special significance because it contains the *nom de plume* of the author.

Kawali (कव्वाली) - This is an Islamic devotional song. It is a lively, light style which has a popular appeal for both Muslims and Hindus alike. The *kawali* may or may not be based upon a *rag*, and it is usually set to *kaherava* (8 beats), *dadra* (6 beats) or any of the lighter *tals*.

Tappa (टप्पा) - This is a light classical style which is declining in popularity. It is basically a classical style of music from the Punjab.

Shabad (शबद) - This is a style similar to *bhajan*. However, these songs are from the *Guru Granth Sahib*, the holy book of the Sikhs, while the *bhajan* is found among the Hindus.

Kirtan (कीर्तन) or Dhun - These styles are related to *bhajan*. The major difference is that *bhajan* is usually performed by a soloist, while *kirtan* and *dhun* usually involve the audience. The musical quality is consequently much simpler to accommodate the uncertain musical abilities of the participants.

Gazal (ग़ज़ल) - Nowadays this is considered a style of singing. In a strict sense this is not true; it is a style of poetic recitation (Mukri 1990). Because of its poetic origins there is a very heavy emphasis upon the literary quality of the lyrics. Invariably such lyrics revolve around philosophic and romantic themes. Since this is a mere musical adaptation of Urdu poetry, concepts such as *sthai* and *antara* have no significance. The flow is determined by the structure of the poem. The language is a very formal Urdu and the *tals* tend to be *kaherava* (8 beats), *rupak* (7 beats), or *dadra* (6 beats). The melodies may be based upon lighter *rags* or they may be based upon folk themes.

Geet (गीत) - This may or may not be considered a distinct style. The word "*geet*" actually means "song". However, there is a tendency to use the term for many of the lighter styles which do not fit the rigid classification of the more classical forms. The *geet* may or may not be based upon a *rag*, and it is usually set to the lighter *tals*.

Folk styles - Each particular region has its own styles of song. These may have little to do with styles found in other regions. The text, style, and structure vary considerably.

Film Styles - This is the music from the Indian film industry. It is a commercial genre comparable to the Western "Top 40". Although it is of questionable artistic value, the industry and the extent of popular appeal make this style impossible to dismiss. Since it is a haphazard syncretism, it is impossible to define musically. Classical and traditional elements may be found, yet it is more likely to be dominated by Western jazz, rap, disco or whatever styles may be in vogue. The constant flux makes any definitive musical discussion impossible.

This was a brief introduction to the classical and semi-classical vocal styles found in Northern Indian music.

WORKS CITED

Devangan, Tulsiram
1984   *Thumri-Gayaki*. Hathras: Sangeet Karyalaya.

Mukri, Naseem
1990   *Junoon*. Bombay: Intel Communications.

CHAPTER 6.

LANGUAGE

It is impossible to give a complete description of the north Indian languages in a music book. However, some degree of familiarity is necessary. In this chapter we will touch upon the development of North Indian languages and dialects and provide the briefest glimpse into the grammar and writing of the same.

NORTH INDIAN LANGUAGES - The languages of northern India share a remarkable kinship to each other. The similarity between them is most striking when compared to the South Indian Languages. The common south Indian Languages are Tamil, Telugu, Malyalam, and Kanada, and are said to belong to a family of Languages called Elamo-Dravidian. Conversely the languages of the North, such as Hindi-Urdu (Hindustani), Gujarati, Punjabi, Bengali, Marathi, or Asami, belong to the Indo-European family. These two families differ drastically in terms of grammar and vocabulary.

The Indo-European theory states that all the languages in this family were derived from a single language which is referred to as Proto-Indo-European. The Proto-Indo-Europeans were a group of tribes, leading a pastoral existence, who began to spread in the first few centuries B.C. They traveled and differentiated until their descendants now occupy most of Europe and much of Asia (Mallory 1989). Therefore these languages show a marked kinship with European languages such as English, French or German.

It is convenient that the musical division within India follow the linguistic divisions. The regions of the South which speak the Dravidian languages are also the areas which follow the Carnatic system of Music. Conversely the Northern states which speak Indo-European languages follow the Hindustani system of music. Since this is a book on North Indian music the south Indian languages play no part.

We can begin our discussion the with Sanskrit. This language was once considered to be nearly identical to Proto-Indo-European. However, contemporary linguistic thought places it at a considerably greater distance than once believed. Regardless of its position in the Indo-European family tree, there is no doubt about its importance to Indian culture.

Sanskrit is only minimally used in contemporary musical performances. The most common application is the *shloka*. *Shloka* is a prayer which is generally sung at the beginning of a performance.

Sanskrit has gone through several stages to arrive at its present position. Initially it was a vernacular language. It later became a literary language. After it had become a literary language, it was frozen into its present form. The extreme formalization was convenient for *Vedic* studies but it immediately proclaimed the death of Sanskrit as a viable *lingua franca* (Barz 1977). A language which is frozen in this manner quickly becomes unable to deal with day-to-day affairs. From that period numerous vernacular forms would come and go.

The period of Islamic expansion into the Indian subcontinent is especially important for the development of Hindustani (Hindi-Urdu). The influence of Persian, Turkish, and Arabic upon the Sanskrit derived vernacular created dialects which for the first time could be considered as Hindustani. Over the years many dialects of Hindi-Urdu (Hindustani) would come and go.

Some of these dialects assumed a special significance in the period between the 15th and 17th centuries. It was in this period that the Hindu *bhakti* movement was sweeping northern India. This movement was a grassroots revolution against the pressures of Islam on one hand and the brahmanic monopoly of Hinduism on the other. The essence of the *bhakti* philosophy was that anyone, of any race, caste, or social strata could obtain the grace of God. This created a strong movement away from Sanskrit towards the vernacular for religious purposes. One vernacular, called Brijbhasha is especially important for musicians. Brijbhasha is a dialect of Hindi which was used in Mathur (Barz 1977).

Brijbhasha is one of the most widely used dialects for musical lyrics. It is used extensively in *bhajans, kheyal,* and *thumri.* Brijbhasha is generally used whenever there are themes revolving around Krishna. Since Krishna is central to much of North Indian music, there is ample scope for the use of this dialect.

The rise of Urdu is historically linked to the formalization of Brijbhasha. Brijbhasha became so formalized that it could no longer function as an effective *lingua franca.* Urdu had not yet become a literary language, so it had not yet become burden with rigid rules and restrictions. Urdu's flexibility coupled, with its wide acceptance made it the prime choice for administrative purposes in the 19th century.

Urdu reached its artistic zenith in the 19th century. There is an extensive amount of poetry from which much of North Indian music derives its lyrics. The poetry of Ghalib is perhaps the most famous. Urdu is extensively used in *gazal* and *dadra* and it is sometimes found in *kheyal.*

History has a habit of repeating itself. Just as Sanskrit, Pali, and Brijbhasha started as a vernacular, evolved into a literary language, and then became frozen into a solid mass of grammatical rules and restrictions, so too did Urdu. In the last century, as it was gaining acceptance as a literary language it was becoming formalized. Today literary Urdu is flowery and poetic but impractical for day-to-day applications.

We find that a contemporary vernacular, sometimes referred to as Film-Hindi, is extensively used in a number of musical genre. For many years this vernacular was confined to the film music: however in recent years it has started to be used in other forms such as *bhajan* and *gazal*. Although such usage is not hailed as a great artistic achievement, it is certainly consistent with the natural linguistic ebb and flow.

The relationship between Hindi and Urdu deserves some discussion. Outside of academic circles Hindi and Urdu are generally considered to be separate languages. The distinction is based upon a number of criteria. One distinction is that Hindi uses the Sanskrit alphabet while Urdu uses an Arabic script. Another difference is that the majority of Hindi speakers are Hindu while the majority of Urdu speakers are Muslim. Unfortunately, these are not linguistically valid criteria. It would be more correct to say that Hindi, Urdu, Brijbhasha, Pahadi, etc. are all dialects of one language which most linguists refer to as Hindustani.

We have seen in this section that the north Indian languages all belong to the Indo-European group of languages. Of these languages, the dialects of Urdu, Brijbhasha, and Standard Hindi, are especially important to the vocalist.

HINDI SCRIPT
- The Hindi Script, also known as *Devnagri,* is a model of elegance. It is phonetic and easy. The rules are consistent and clear. It is not surprising that the majority of north Indian languages have adopted this script or one of its derivatives (e.g., Guru Mukhi, Bengali)(Greaves 1983). In table 6.1 we see that the alphabet is clearly divided into vowels and consonants. One interesting characteristic is that the only time the vowels are written in this form is when they occur in isolation (Van Olphen 1992). Usually the vowels are designated by a series of modifying marks place around the consonant. It would therefore be easier to think of the syllable as being the basic functional unit of the writing (Srinivasachari 1983). The most striking characteristic of *Devnagri* is the extremely clear phonetic nature of the script. The concept of "spelling" just doesn't even exist because words are written like they are pronounced. *Devnagri* is written from left to right, just like English. Words are clearly separated, and in modern forms one may find the full compliment of commas and other marks of punctuation. This finishes our brief description of the *Devnagri* script. Now it is appropriate for us to take a quick look at the Urdu script.

URDU SCRIPT
- Urdu uses a modified Arabic script. It would be more correct to say that it uses the Persian script because there are some letters which are common in the Persian and Indian dialects but are absent in the original Arabic. The Urdu alphabet is shown in table 6.2 (Ganathe 1981). Each letter has four forms: isolate, initial, medial, and final. This reflects its position in a word section. If the letter is by itself one uses the isolate form (table 6.2). If it comes at the beginning the initial form is used. If it comes in the middle or end the medial and terminal forms are used.

There are a few things which make Urdu difficult. The most fundamental difficulty lies in the fact that the vowels are ambiguous. There is a tendency to even leave them off entirely. This creates a situation similar to English, where one must be familiar with the correct spellings. Another problem lies in the calligraphy. Although Urdu calligraphy is exceptionally beautiful, there are such liberties taken with the placement of the various sections that it is sometimes difficult to decipher.

Table 6.1.
Dev Nagri Alphabet

Vowels

अ	आ	इ	ई	उ	ऊ	ऋ
a	ā	i	ī	u	ū	ṛ

ए	ऐ	ओ	औ	अं	अः
e	ai	o	au	am	ah

Consonants

क	ख	ग	घ	ड.
k	kh	g	gh	ṅ

च	छ	ज	झ	ञ
ch	chh	j	jh	ñ

ट	ठ	ड	ढ	ण
ṭ	ṭh	ḍ	ḍh	ṇ

त	थ	द	ध	न
t	th	d	dh	n

प	फ	ब	भ	म
p	ph	b	bh	m

य	र	ल	व	श
y	r	l	v	sh

ष	स	ह	क्ष	त्र	ज्ञ
ṣ	s	h	ksh	tr	jñ

Table 6.2.
Urdu (Modified Arabic) Alphabet

ا Alif	ب Be	پ Pe	ت Te
ط Ta	ث Se	ٹ Je	چ Che
ح He	خ Khe	ج Jeem	ڈ Da
ذ Zaal	ر Re	ڑ Ra	د Daal
ژ Zhe	س Seen	ش Sheen	ز Ze
ض Zuaad	ص Suaad	ظ Zoe	ع Ain
غ Ghain	ط Toe	ق Quaaf	ک Kaaf
گ Gaaf	ف Fe	م Meem	ن Noon
و Waao	ل Laam	ہ He	ی Ye
ے			

BASIC GRAMMAR - There are both similarities and differences between Hindustani and English. The grammar of Hindustani is remarkably similar to English and other Indo-European languages, yet the vocabulary is very different. It uses nouns, verbs, adjectives, etc. in process that is remarkably similar to English. The example in table 6.3. will illustrate this very easily.

This example illustrates quite clearly the structure of a typical sentence. There are a number other points which should be considered.

Gender is an area of great importance. Generally there are three approaches to gender: masculine feminine, common. Animate objects are generally referred to according to their sex: however, even inanimate objects have a gender. For instance a hammer (*hathodi*) is considered feminine and will be grammatically treated as such. The common gender is rare and represents situations where both genders are present, for instance the word for parents (*mata-pita*).

The number is another area of importance. The use of the plural form verses the singular form is usually quite clear. However there is one interesting exception.

TABLE 6.3

Translation	"The book is on the table"			
Parts of speech	subject	object	preposition (postposition)	verb
Hindi	किताब	मेज़	पर	है
Transliteration	kitab	mez	par	hai
Word-for-Word	book	table	on	is

The use of the plural form is generally considered a mark of respect. This is roughly analogous to a doctor's bedside manner when he says "How are *we* feeling today?".

The use of the term "you" is of special significance. Unlike English, there are three forms of the word "you". In India, one cannot even talk to a person without placing them in some social context with respect to yourself. For instance, when one is dealing with an elder, or social superior one will use the term *aap* (आप). If one is with friends, one will generally use the term *tum* (तुम). However, if one is dealing with children, servants or social inferiors one may use the term *tu* (तू). There are literary complications to this rule which are of tremendous importance to the vocalist. It is customary for God to be addressed in the familiar form *Tu*. This linguistic anomaly has been the subject of tremendous discussion.

OTHER NORTH INDIAN LANGUAGES - We have here-to-fore confined our discussion to the various dialects of Hindustani. We must not forget that there are other languages in the North as well.

Punjabi is a language of the area of northwest India and Pakistan. Punjabi is used in classical, semiclassical, and folk music. In the classical and semiclassical realm, the *tappa*, and *shabad* have attained a tremendous degree of sophistication. The folk music is also noteworthy for its strong popular appeal. Much of the Hindi film music has been influenced by the Punjabi folk music.

Bengali is another language which has great importance to north Indian musicians. This is a language which is used in north-east India and Bangladesh. It is especially important in the styles of music known as *Nazrul geet* and *Rabindra sangeet*.

There are other north Indian languages whose musical contributions are almost entirely in the folk styles. The most common ones are Orriya from the eastern state of Orrisa, Gujarati of the northwestern state of Gujarat. Assami from the northeastern state of Assam, Kashmiri from the northern state of Kashmir and Marathi from the western state of Maharashtra.

SUMMARY - Hindustani vocal music is inextricably linked to the languages of northern India. Unfortunately, the study of these languages is such a deep matter that it is not possible to give more than the briefest glimpse. In spite of these limitations there are a number of points that we have been able to make.

Unlike the south Indian languages, the Northern languages are part of the Indo-European family. This implies a certain similarity to each other as well as European languages such as English, German or French. One of the similarities is in certain grammatical concepts such as nouns, verbs, adjectives, preposition (postpositions), etc.

There are other areas that are hard for an English speaking person to comprehend. One area is the concept of gender: it is hard for many people to conceive of inanimate objects as having a gender, however that is how objects are treated. Another difficult concept is having to construct sentences differently depending upon whether a person is ones social superior, equal or inferior.

As if these differences were not enough, there is also the problem of script. There are a number of scripts used in north India, but from the standpoint of classical music, the two most important ones are Urdu (Arabic) and the *Devnagri* (Sanskrit).

If these few points are kept in mind then our discussion of vocal music becomes much easier.

WORKS CITED

Barz, R.K.
1977   *An Introduction to Hindi and Urdu.* Canberra, Australia: Australian National University Press.

Ganathe, N.S.R.
1981   *Learn Urdu in 30 Days.* Madras: Balaji Publications.

Greaves, Edwin
1983   *Hindi Grammar.* New Delhi: Asian Educational Services.

Mallory, J. P.
1989   *In Search of the Indo-Europeans; Language Archaeology and Myth.* London: Thames and Hudson Ltd.

Srinivasachary, K.
1983   *Learn Sanskrit in 30 Days.* Madras: Balaji Publications.

Van Olphen, H.H.
1992   *Hindi Pravesikaa- Beginners Hindi: Writing and Conversation.* Austin: University of Texas.

CHAPTER 7.

BILAWAL THAT

Bilawal that is considered the most fundamental musical mode in North Indian music. This *that* consists of only natural notes; therefore, it is referred to as the *shuddha swar saptak*. This *that* corresponds to the Western major scale, and to the south Indian *Dhirashankarabharanam mela*. Additionally, it is believed by many to be the *Nashadi jati* of the original *shuddha jati* mentioned in the *Natya-Shastra*. It would therefore be of great antiquity.

It is obvious that one does not suddenly start singing *Bilawal*. One must begin with exercises to acquaint oneself with the basic principles. One of the most fundamental is the relationship between the *swar*. Here are a few exercises in *Bilawal that* to aid in the development of these concepts:

Exercise 1.
Aroh   sa re ga ma pa dha ni sȧ
Avaroh   sȧ ni dha pa ma ga re sa

Exercise 2.
Aroh   sa re ga ma, re ga ma pa, ga ma pa dha, ma pa dha ni, pa dha ni sȧ
Avaroh   sȧ ni dha pa, ni dha pa ma, dha pa ma ga, pa ma ga re, ma ga re sa

Exercise 3.
Aroh   sa re ga, re ga ma, ga ma pa, ma pa dha, pa dha ni, dha ni sȧ
Avaroh   sȧ ni dha, ni dha pa, dha pa ma, pa ma ga, ma ga re, ga re sa

Exercise 4.
Aroh   sa re ga ma ga re, sa re ga ma pa dha ni sȧ
Avaroh   sȧ ni dha pa dha ni, sȧ ni dha pa ma ga re sa

Exercise 5.
Aroh   sa ga, re ma, ga pa, ma dha, pa ni, dha sȧ
Avaroh   sȧ dha, ni pa, dha ma, pa ga, ma re, ga sa

Exercise 6.
Aroh   sa re, sa re, sa re ga ma pa dha ni sȧ
Avaroh   sȧ ni, sȧ ni, sȧ ni dha pa ma ga re sa

Exercise 7.
Aroh   sa, sa re sa, sa re ga re sa, sa re ga ma ga re sa, sa re ga ma pa ma ga re sa, sa re ga ma
         pa dha pa ma ga re sa, sa re ga ma pa dha ni dha pa ma ga re sa, sa re ga ma pa dha ni sȧ
         ni dha pa ma ga re sa
Avaroh   sȧ, sȧ ni sȧ, sȧ ni dha ni sȧ, sȧ ni dha pa dha ni sȧ, sȧ ni dha pa ma pa dha ni sȧ, sȧ ni
         dha pa ma ga ma pa dha ni sȧ, sȧ ni dha pa ma ga re ga ma pa dha ni sȧ, sȧ ni dha pa ma
         ga re sa re ga ma pa dha ni sȧ

Exercise 8.

Aroh sa - sa re ga re sa -, re - re ga ma ga re -, ga - ga ma pa ma ga -, ma - ma pa dha pa ma -,
pa - pa dha ni dha pa -, dha - dha ni sȧ - sȧ -,

Avaroh sȧ - sȧ ni dha ni sȧ -, ni - ni dha pa dha ni -, dha - dha pa ma pa dha -, pa - pa ma ga ma
pa -, ma - ma ga re ga ma -, ga - ga re sa - sa -,

RAG BILAWAL

Rag Bilawal is the most basic *rags* in *Bilawal that.* Indeed the name of the *that* is derived from this *rag.* However, it has declined in popularity over the years. It is sometimes referred to as *Shuddha Bilawal* to distinguish it from the much more popular *Alhiya Bilawal.*

Bilawal is considered by most to be *sampurna-sampurna.* However, some are of the opinion that it should be considered *shadav-sampurna* due to the weakness of ga in the *arohana.* It is a morning *rag* with dha as the *vadi* and re as the *samavadi.* Its characteristics are :

Arohana	sa re ga ma pa dha ni sȧ
Avarohana	sȧ ni dha pa ma ga re sa
Jati	sampurna-sampurna
Vadi	dha
Samavadi	re
Time	morning
That	Bilawal

Rag Bilawal, Swarmalika - Tintal (Bhatkhande 1985a)

Sthai

ga pa dha ni	sȧ - sȧ -	sȧ rė sȧ ni	dha pa ma ga
3	X	2	0
ga ma pa ga	ma ga re sa	dha ni sȧ ni	dha pa ma ga
3	X	2	0

Antara

pa pa dha ni	sȧ - sȧ -	sȧ rė gȧ mȧ	gȧ rė sȧ -
3	X	2	0
gȧ rė sȧ rė	sȧ ni dha pa	dha ni sȧ ni	dha pa ma ga
3	X	2	0

Rag Bilawal - Tintal (Bhatkhande 1985a:34)

तें हरि नाम न सुमिरन कीनो	ten hari nam na sumiran kino
एक हूँ दिन रैन	ek hoon din rain
-	-
सुमिरन भजन करो केशव को	sumiran bhajan karo keshav ko
अभय दान ताहे दिन	abhay dan tahe din

i have not remembered the holy name of god for even a day or night
remember and chant the name of lord keshav
god grant me fearlessness
so that i may attain salvation

Sthai

ga pa ni ni	sȧ - sȧ sȧ	sȧ sȧrė sa ni	dha pa maga mare
ten - ha ri	na - m na	su mi ra n	ki - no -
3	X	2	0

ga ma pa maga	ma re sa -	sȧsȧ gȧrė sȧni dhani	sȧni dhapa maga mare
e - k hoon	di - n -	re - - -	- - - n
3	X	2	0

Antara

pa pa sȧ sȧ	sȧ rė sȧ sȧ	sȧ rė gȧ rė	sȧ sȧ dha nipa
su mi ra n	bha ja na ka	ro - ke -	sha v ko -
3	X	2	0

ga ma pa ga	ma re sa sa	sȧsȧ gȧrė sȧni dhani	sȧni dhapa maga mare
a bha ya da	- na ta he	di - - -	- - - n
3	X	2	0

ga pa - dhani
ten - - hari
3

Rag Bilawal - Tintal (Kulshreshtha 1983:17-18)

बेगि दरस दो, कृष्ण मुरारी ।   begi daras do, krishna morari

गोवर्धन गिरिधारी ।   govardhan giridhari

मोरमुकुट-छवि, बंशी-धुन पर   moramukut-chavi, banshi-dhun par

मोहत ब्रज के सब नर-नारी ।   mohat braj ke sab nar-nari

quickly give me a vision of you, my krishna, great lifter of mount govardhan,
with the beautiful peacock adorned crown, and player of the flute,
the one who enchants all of the people of brij

Sthai

sa - dha pa	ma ga ma re	ga ma pa ga	ma re sa -
be - gi da	ra sa do -	kri - shna mu	ra - ri -
0	3	X	2

ga - ma re	ga pa ni ni	sȧ - rė sȧ	ni dha pa -
go - va r	dha na gi ri	dha - - -	ri - - -
0	3	X	2

Antara

pa - pa pa	sȧ sȧ sȧ sȧ	sȧ - sȧ -	sȧ rė sȧ sȧ
mo - ra mu	ku ta cha vi	vam - shi -	dhu na pa r
0	3	X	2

sȧ - gȧ mȧ	gȧ rė sȧ ni	dha ni sȧ ni	dha pa ma ga
mo - ha t	bra j ke -	sa ba na ra	naa - ri -
0	3	X	2

Sthai Tans

#1	sa re ga pa	dha ni sȧ re	sȧ ni dha pa	ma ga re sa
	0	3	X	2

#2	sȧ rė gȧ rė	sȧ ni dha ni	sȧ ni dha pa	ma ga re sa
	0	3	X	2

Antara Tans

#1	ga pa dha ni	sȧ rė sȧ ni	dha pa ga pa	dha ni sȧ -
	0	3	X	2

#2	sȧ ni dha pa	ma ga re sa	ga pa dha ni	sȧ - sȧ -
	0	3	X	2

RAG BIHAG

This *rag* is very popular. Some common songs are *"Boliye Surili Boliyan"*, *"Hamare Dil Se Na Jana Dhokhna Na Khana"*, and *Tere Sur Aur Mere Geet"*. It is a late night *rag* (9 pm - midnight) of *audhav-sampurna jati*. Its strong characteristic is the use of both *madhyams*. Opinion differs as to which ma should be given prominence. The orthodox approach is to give importance to the *shuddha ma*. However, more modern interpretations tend to give importance to the *tivra ma*. It is this emphasis on *tivra ma* which causes some musicians to assign this *rag* to *Kalyan that*.

Bihag has a moderately complex structure. This is due to the large number of *rags* which use both *madhyams*. One must pay particular attention to the *pakard* or else one may impinge upon *Hamir, Yaman Kalyan, Kedar* or any of a number of related *rags*. The *swarup* is pa ma ga ma ga. The *vadi* is ga and the *samavadi* is ni. The re and dha are not used in the *arohana*, but all are used in the *avarohana*. Its characteristics are:

Arohana	ni sa - ga ma- pa ni sa
Avarohan	sa ni - dha pa - ma ga ma ga - re sa
Jati	audhav-sampurna
Vadi	ga
Samavadi	ni
Time	late night
That	Bilawal
Pakad	Pa ma ga ma ga ⸝ re sa ⸝

Rag Bihag, Swarmalika - Tintal (Bhatkhande 1985b:183)

Sthai

ga - sa -	- ga - ma	pa ni - pa	- ga - ma
X	2	0	3
ga - sa -	ni - pa -	ni sa - ma	ga - sa -
X	2	0	3
ni sa ga ma	pa ni - pa	ma ga - ma	ga - sa -
X	2	0	3

Antara

pa ma ga ma	pa ni - sa	- pa ni -	sa - - ma
X	2	0	3
ga - sa -	ni sa ga ma	pa ga - ma	ga - sa -
X	2	0	3
ni ni pa sa	- ni - pa	- ga - ma	ga - sa -
X	2	0	3

Rag Bihag, Lakshangit - Tintal (Bhatkhande 1985b:185)

शुद्ध सुरन को मेल करे, गुनि गावत राग बिहाग   shuddha suran ko mela kare, guni gavat rag bihag

औढव संपुर्ण कर मानत, उपजत नित अनुराग   audav sampurna kar manat, upajat nit anurag

वादी गंधार करे सुर सहचर ताको देत निखाद   vadi gandhar kare sur sahachar, tako det nikhad

रात समय नित दूजे पहर मे, गावत सब बड भाग   rat samay nit duje pahar me, gavat sab bad bhag

bihag incorporates all natural notes
it is audhav-sampurna in its structure
gandhara is the vadi swar
while nishad is the samavadi
the most proper time to perform bihag is the second part of the night

page 41

Sthai

ga ma ga ma	pa pa ni -	sȧ - sȧ sȧ	ni ni pa pa
shu - ddha su	ra n ko -	me - la ka	re - gu ni
0	3	X	2
pa - ga ma	pa - ga ma	ga - - -	sa - - sa
ga - va ta	ra - ga bi	ha - - -	- - - ga
0	3	X	2
nị - pạ pạ	nị - sa -	pa pa ga ma	ga - sa sa
au - da v	sum - pu -	ra na ka r	ma - na t
0	3	X	2
ni ni mȧ pa	ga ma pa ma	ga - - -	sa - - sa
u pa ja t	ni t a nu	ra - - -	- - - g
0	3	X	2

Antara

ga ma ga ma	pa - ni ni	sȧ - sȧ sȧ	sȧ rȧ sȧ sȧ
va - di gan	dha - r ka	re - su r	sa ha cha r
0	3	X	2
sȧ - sȧ -	ni - pa pa	pa - sȧ -	ni - pa pa
ta - ko -	de - t ni	kha - - -	- - - d
0	3	X	2
ga ma ga ma	pa - ni ni	nisȧ gȧ ni sȧ	ni ni pa -
ra - t sa	men - ni t	du - je pa	ha r men -
0	3	X	2
pa - ga ma	pa pa ga ma	ga - - -	sa - - sa
ga - va t	sa b ba d	bha - - -	- - - ga
0	3	X	2

Rag Misra Bihag, Bhajan - Dadra (Traditional lyrics - music by C. Courtney)

प्रेममुदित मनसे कहो राम राम राम	premamudit manse kaho ram ram ram
श्री राम राम राम, शी राम राम राम	shri ram ram ram, shri ram ram ram
-	-
पाप कटै, दुख मिटै लेत राम-नाम	pap katai, dukh mitai let ram nam
भव-समुद्र सुखद नाव एक राम-नाम	bhava samudra sukhad nav ek ram nam
-	-
परम सांति-सुख-निधान नित्य राम-नाम	param santi sukh nidhan nitya ram nam
निराधारको अधार एक राम-नाम	niradharako adhar ek ram-nam
-	-
परम गोप्य, परम इष्ट मंत्र राम-नाम	param gopya, param isht mantra ram-nam
संत-हृदय सदा बसत एक राम-नाम	sant hriday sada basat ek ram-nam
-	-
महादेव सतत जपत दिव्य राम-नाम	mahadev satat japat divya ram-nam
कासि मरत मुक्त करत कहत राम-नाम	kasi marat mukt karat kahat ram-nam
-	-
माता-पिता, बंधु-सखा, सबहि राम-नाम	mata-pita, bandhu-sakha, sabhi ram-nam
भक्त-जनन-जीवन-धन एक राम-नाम	bhakt-janan-jivan-dhan ek ram-nam

chant the name of ram with devotion
his name helps us remove our falsehoods and cross the ocean of life
by chanting his name the devotee becomes the recipient of of his grace.
the name of ram protects the helpless
the name of ram is the secret to attaining the lord.
the sage is always absorbed in chanting the name of ram
mahadev (shiva) meditated upon the uniqueness of the name ram
those who die in kasi achieve salvation by chanting his name
we need to see the presence of ram in our mother, father, and friends
lord ram is seen as a precious treasure by his devotees

Sthai

sa - sa	ga ga ma	pa pa pa	ni ni -
pre - ma	mu di t	ma n se	ka ho -
X	0	X	0

sȧ - ni	dha ni dha	pa - -	- mȧ pa
ra - m	ra - m	ra - m	- sri -
X	0	X	0

‿dhani, sȧ ni	dha ni dha	pa - pa	mȧ pa -
ra - m	ra - m	ra - m	sri - -
X	0	X	0

pa - mȧ	ga - ma	ga - pa	ga re sa
ra - m	ra - m	ra - m	- - -
X	0	X	0

Antara

pa - pa	mȧ pa -	mȧ pa mȧ	pa pa -
pa - p	ka te -	du - kha	mi tai -
X	0	X	0

‿mȧpa ‿nidha, pa	ga - ma	ga - -	- - -
le - t	ra - m	na - m	- - -
X	0	X	0

ga ga ma	pa ni ni	sȧ - sȧ	ni - pa
bha v sa	mu - dra	su kha d	na - v
X	0	X	0

‿mȧpa ‿nidha, pa	ga - mȧ	ga - pa	ga re sa
e - k	ra - m	na - -	- - m
X	0	X	0

2nd Antara

pa pa pa	ni dha ni	sȧ sȧ sȧ	sȧ - sȧ
pa ra m	shan - ti	su kh ni	dha - n
X	0	X	0

ni - dha	ni - rė	sȧ - -	ni - ‿dhapa
nit - ya	ra - m	na - m	- - -
X	0	X	0

ni sȧ ni	dha ni dha	pa - mȧ	pa - pa
ni ra -	dha - ra	ko - a	dha - ra
X	0	X	0

ga - re	ga - mȧ	ga - pa	ga re sa
e - k	ra - m	na - ma	- - -
X	0	X	0

(3rd and 5th antara has same melody as the first)

(4th antara has same melody as 2nd)

WORKS CITED

Bhatkhande, Vishnu Narayan
1985a   *Hindustani Sangeet Paddhati, Kramik Pustak Malika, Vol 1.* Hathras, India: Sangeet Karyalaya.

1985b   *Hindustani Sangeet Paddhati, Kramik Pustak Malika, Vol 3.* Hathras, India: Sangeet Karyalaya.

Kulshreshtha, J.S.
1983   *Sangeet Kishor.* Hathras, India: Sangeet Karyalaya.

CHAPTER 8.

KALYAN THAT

Kalyan that is characterized by the *tivra madhyam* (augmented 4th). It corresponds to the *Mechakalyani mela* of south Indian music. This *that* is reputed to have been *Gandharijati* (i.e., one of the seven *shuddhajatis* mentioned in the *Natya-shastra*). Therefore, it is considered one of the oldest musical modes, predating *rag* by at least a millennium. Here are some exercises in *Kalyan that.*

Exercise 1.
Aroh   sa re ga má pa dha ni sá
Avaroh   sá ni dha pa má ga re sa

Exercise 2.
Aroh   sa re ga má, re ga má pa, ga má pa dha, má pa dha ni, pa dha ni sá
Avaroh   sá ni dha pa, ni dha pa má, dha pa má ga, pa má ga re, má ga re sa

Exercise 3.
Aroh   sa re ga, re ga má, ga má pa, má pa dha, pa dha ni, dha ni sá
Avaroh   sá ni dha, ni dha pa, dha pa má, pa má ga, má ga re, ga re sa

Exercise 4.
Aroh   sa re ga má ga re, sa re ga má pa dha ni sá
Avaroh   sá ni dha pa dha ni, sá ni dha pa má ga re sa

Exercise 5.
Aroh   sa ga, re má, ga pa, má dha, pa ni, dha sá
Avaroh   sá dha, ni pa, dha má, pa ga, má re, ga sa

Exercise 6.
Aroh   sa re, sa re, sa re ga má pa dha ni sá
Avaroh   sá ni, sá ni, sá ni dha pa má ga re sa

Exercise 7.
Aroh   sa, sa re sa, sa re ga re sa, sa re ga má ga re sa, sa re ga má pa má ga re sa, sa re ga má pa dha pa má ga re sa, sa re ga má pa dha ni dha pa má ga re sa, sa re ga má pa dha ni sá ni dha pa má ga re sa
Avaroh   sá, sá ni sá, sá ni dha ni sá, sá ni dha pa dha ni sá, sá ni dha pa má pa dha ni sá, sá ni dha pa má ga má pa dha ni sá, sá ni dha pa má ga re ga má pa dha ni sá, sá ni dha pa má ga re sa re ga má pa dha ni sá

Exercise 8.

Aroh sa - sa re ga re sa -, re - re ga má ga re -, ga - ga má pa má ga -, má - má pa dha pa má -, pa - pa dha ni dha pa -, dha - dha ni sá - sá -,

Avaroh sá - sá ni dha ni sá -, ni - ni dha pa dha ni -, dha - dha pa má pa dha -, pa - pa má ga má pa -, má - má ga re ga má -, ga - ga re sa - sa -

RAG KALYAN

This *rag* is known by several names; *Kalyan, Iman, Eman, or Yaman*. Strangely enough *Yaman Kalyan* is a different *rag*. This is very popular and some commonly known exmples of songs in this *rag* are *"Ansu Bhari Hai Jai Jivan Ki Rahen", Ja Re Badara Bairi Ja Re Ja Re",* or *"Jiya Le Gayo Re Mora Sanvariya".* *Yaman* is a *sampurna rag* which is performed at the first part of the night. The *vadi* is ga and the *samavadi* is ni. Typically sa and pa are weak in the *arohana*. However, such omission is not obligatory. Its structure is:

Arohan	ni re ga má pa dha ni sá
Avarohan	sá ni dha pa má ga re - ni - re - sa
Jati	sampurna-sampurna
Vadi	ga
Samavadi	ni
Time	first part of night
That	Kalyan

Rag Kalyan, Swaramalika, Tintal. (Bhatkhande 1985a:28-29)

Sthai

ni dha - pa	má pa ga má	pa - - -	pa má ga re
0	3	X	2
sa re ga re	ga má pa dha	pa má ga re	ga re sa -
0	3	X	2
ni re ga má	pa dha ni sá	re sá ni dha	pa má ga má
0	3	X	2

Antara

ga ga pa dha	pa sá - sá	ni re gá re	sá ni dha pa
0	3	X	2
gá re sá ni	dha pa ni dha	pa má ga re	ga re sa -
0	3	X	2
ni re ga má	pa dha ni sá	re sá ni dha	pa má ga má
0	3	X	2

Rag Yaman, Kheyal - Tintal (Bhatkhande 1985a:29-30)

सदा शिव भज मना निस दिन	sada shiva bhaj mana nis din
रिधी सिधी दायक बीनत सहायक	ridhi sidhi dayak binat sahayak
नाहक भटकत फिरत अनवरत	nahak bhatkat firat anavarat

शंकर भोला पार्वती रमण   shankar bhola parvati raman

सित तन पन्नग भूषण अनुपम   sit tan pannag bhushan anupam

काहे न सुमिरन भटकत तू फिरत   kahe na sumiran bhatkat tu phirat

let me always chant the name of shiva
the source of the universe
without your help i am a lost soul wandering in this world
oh simple shankar (shiva), consort of parvati
whose head is adorned with the snake
i must chant his name continuously
instead of wandering aimlessly in this world

Sthai

ni dha - pa	ma pa ga ma	pa - - -	pa ma ga re
sa da - shi	va bha ja ma	na - - -	ni sa di na
0	3	X	2

sa re ga re	ga ma pa dha	pa ma ga re	ga re sa sa
ri dhi si dhi	da - ya ka	bi na ta sa	ha - ya ka
0	3	X	2

ni re ga ma	pa dha ni sa	re sa ni dha	pa ma ga ma
na - ha ka	bha ta ka ta	phi ra ta a	na va ra ta
0	3	X	2

Antara

pa ga pa dhapa	sa - sa -	sa re ga re	sa ni dha pa
sha an ka ra	bho - la -	pa - ra va	ti ra ma na
0	3	X	2

ga re sa ni	dha pa ni dha	pa ma ga re	ga re sa sa
si ta ta na	pan - na ga	bhu - sha na	a nu pa ma
0	3	X	2

sa re ga ma	pa dha ni sa	re sa ni dha	pa ma ga ma
ka - he na	su mi ra n	bha ta ka ta	tu phi ra ta
0	3	X	2

Rag Kalyan, Kheyal - Tintal (Bhatkhande 1985a:30)

गुरु बिन कैसे गुण गावे   guru bin kaise gun gave

गुरु ना माने तो गुण नही आवे   guru na mane to gun nahi ave

गुणियन मे बेगुणी कहावे   guniyan me beguni kahave

माने तो रिझावे सबको   mane to rijhave sabko

चरण गहे सा दीखन के जब   charan gahe sa dikhana ke jab

आवे अचपल ताल सुर   ave achpal tal sur

how can one sing the glory of god without the guidance of the guru
if you fail to follow your guru
you will fail to become virtuous
and the wise will consider you to be a fool
if you follow the guru's guidance
you will become a model for those seen as constant in following his path

<u>Sthai</u>

pa pa ni dha	ma̍ dha pa -	ma̍ ga ma̍ -	pa - - -
gu ru bi na	kai - se -	gu na ga -	ve - - -
0	3	X	2

pa ni dha pa	- ma̍ ga -	ga re ga pa	re - sa -
gu ru na ma	- ne to -	gu na na hi	a - ve -
0	3	X	2

ni̤ ni̤ re re	ga - ma̍ -	ma̍ dha ni dha	ma̍ dha pa -
gu ni ya na	me - be -	gu ni - ka	ha - ve -
0	3	X	2

<u>Antara</u>

pa - ma̍ -	ga - - re	ga pa ni dha	ni rė sȧ -
ma̍ - ne -	to - - ri	jha - ve -	sa ba ko -
0	3	X	2

ni rė gȧ rė	ni rė sȧ -	ni dha sȧ sȧ	ni dha pa pa
cha ra na ga	he - sa -	de - kha na	ke - ja ba
0	3	X	2

pa ga pa -	re re sa sa	sare gama̍ padha nisȧ	
a - ve -	a cha pa la	ta - - -	
0	3	X	

nidha pama̍ gare ni̤sa
- la su ra
2

Rag Yaman-Dhrupad, Choutal (Bhatkhende 1989:60)

तू ही भज भज रे मन   tu hi baj baj re man

कृष्ण वासुदेव पद्मनाभ परमपुरुष   krishna vasudev padmanabh parampurush

परमेश्वर नारायण   parmeshwar narayan

—   —

जोग जाग जप तप कर   jog jag tap jap tap kar

वामदेव नारदमुनी वशिष्ठ सनकादिक   vamadev naradamuni vashisht sanakadik

सकल सुर गावत ध्यावत   sakal sur gavat dhyavat

अष्ट जाम करत रहत पारायन   asht jam kart rahat parayan

oh my mind, praise and pray to god
lord krishna, son of vasudev
who emerged from lord vishnu with much sacrifice, devotion and discipline
all the sages sang your glory
throughout the day they chanted and meditated upon your greatness

Sthai

ga - re -	sa sa sa ga	re ga	ma pa
tu - hi -	bha ja bha ja	re -	- -
X	2	3	4

ni pa - ma	- ga ga ma	⟍gare⟍ ga	re sa
ma na - kri	- shna va -	su de	- va
X	2	3	4

sa re ga re	- sa sa re	ga re	⟍sare⟍ sa
pa - dma na	- bha pa ra	ma pu	ru sha
X	2	3	4

sa re ga ma	pa pa pa re	ga re	⟍sare⟍ sa
pa re me -	shwa ra na -	ra -	ya na
X	2	3	4

Antara

	* * ma ga	ma pa	dha pa
	* * jo -	ga ja	- ga
	2	3	4

ni dha sa ni	re sa ni -	ni ni	dha dha
ja pa ta pa	ka ra va -	ma de	- va
X	2	3	4

sa - ni ni	pa pa pa pa	ni dha	ma dha
na - ra da	mu ni va shi	- sta	sa na
X	2	3	4

pa ma ga ma	pa pa pa ma	ga re	sa re
ka - - di	ka sa ka la	su ra	ga -
X	2	3	4

sa sa sa re	sa sa ma ga	ma pa	- pa
va ta dhya -	va ta a -	shta ja	- ma
X	2	3	4

ni sa ni ni	ma pa pa re	ga re	⟍sare⟍ sa
ka ra ta ra	ha ta pa -	ra -	ya na
X	2	3	4

Rag Yaman, Bhajan - Tintal (lyrics by Surdas, - music by Lal Bahadur Singh 1977:153)

जित देखो तित श्याम मई है ।	jit dekho tit shyam mai hai
श्याम कुंज-बन, यमुना श्यामा,	shyam kunj-ban, yamuna shama
श्याम गगन घन-घटा छई है ।	shyam gagan ghan-ghata chai hai
	—
सब रंगन में श्याम भलो है,	sab rangan men shyam bhalo hai
लोग कहत यह बात नई है ।	log kahat yaha bat nai hai
मद बौराने लोगन की है,	mad baurane logan ki hai
श्याम पुतरिया बदल गई है ॥	shyam putriya badal gai hai
	—
नीलकंठ को कंठ श्याम है,	nilakanth ko kanth shyam hai
मृगमद श्याम काम विजयी है ।	mragamad shyam kam vijayi hai
चंद्र सुर को हृदय श्याम है,	chandra sur ko hraday shyam hai
जलधि जगत सब श्याम मई है ॥	jaladhi jagat sab shyam mai hai
	—
श्रुति के अक्षर श्याम देखिए,	shruti ke akshar shyam dekhiye
दीप-सिखा पर श्याम मई है ।	dip-sikha par shyam mai hai
नर देवन की मोहर श्याम,	nar devan ki mohar shyam
अलख ब्रह्म-छबि श्याम भई है ॥	alakh brahma-chhabi shyam bhai hai

everywhere we see the reflection of krishna's darkness
we see him in the forest, and the river jamuna, and in the darkness of the thunderclouds
black is the best colour although most people disagree
however this is misconception which has perpetuated through the generations
shiva's neck is also dark
the musk which subdues the passions is also dark
the center of the sun and moon is dark
even the depths of the ocean are dark like krishna
the words of eternal knowledge are written in black
the tip of the lamp is black
the darkness of krishna symbolic of divinity
the unseeable image of the ultimate creator is dark

<u>Sthai</u>

ga re ga re	ni re sa sa	ga - ga re	ga ma pa -
jit ta de -	kho - ti ta	shya - m ma	i - hai -
0	3	X	2

sa - sa sa	- sa sa sa	ni dha ni dha	ma dha pa -
shya - m kun	- j ba n	ya mu na -	shya - ma -
0	3	X	2

page 52

ga - ga re	ga màpa pa	re ga - re	ni̱ re sa -
shya - m ga	ga n gha na	gha ta - cha	i - hai -
0	3	X	2

Antara

ga ga ga -	pa pa ni dha	sȧ - sȧ sȧ	ni rė sȧ -
sa b rang -	ga na men -	shya - m bha	lo - hai -
0	3	X	2

ni - ni dha	sȧ sȧ sȧ sȧ	ni rė gȧ rė	sȧ ni dha pa
lo - ga ka	ha ta ya ha	ba - t na	i - hai -
0	3	X	2

gȧ rė gȧ rė	ni rė sȧ -	ni dha ni dha	màdha pa -
ma da bau -	ra - ne -	lo - ga n	ki - hi -
0	3	X	2

ga - ga re	ga màpa mà	re re ga re	ni̱ re sa -
shya - m pu	ta ri ya -	ba da la ga	i - hai -
0	3	X	2

2nd and third antaras have the same melody

RAG BHUPALI

This *rag* appears to be very ancient. It is based upon a pentatonic structure which is found in many parts of the world. It is believed that the pentatonic scales; of which *Bhupali* is one, were prevalent in the middle and far East by the first millennium B.C. This scale has been in China for many centuries. It is also found in the folk music of northern Britain. Yet it is not clear whether the scale was developed independently or spread through cultural interchange. Either way, it has been around for a long time and is very popular. Common songs based upon this *rag* are *"Jyoti Kalash Chalke"* or *"Pankha Hoti To Ud Ati Re"*.

This *rag* underscores a curious weakness in the system of *thats*. It is classified under *Kalyan that*. However, *madhyam* is totaly absent. There is a related *rag* called *Deshkar* which has the same scale, yet *Deshkar* is classified under *Bilawal*. This means that the missing *madhyam* of *Bhupali* is *tivra* while the missing *madhyam* of *Deshkar* is *shuddha*. This is interesting but totaly insupportable by any objective musical criteria.

The methodology for determining the character of the missing notes is not clear. It may be an extension of an earlier tradition. Bhatkhande stated that some musicians consider this *rag* to be synonymous with *Bhup Kalyan* (Bhatkhande 1985a). However, most musicians consider *Bhup Kalyan* to be synonymous with *Shuddha Kalyan*, not *Bhupali* (Rao 1980). It may be that his decision was partly based upon the desire to support his theory of the timings of *rags*.

Such discussions are interesting but not of very great practical importance. Regardless of the reasons for the classification there is a conventional acceptance of *Bhupali's* inclusion in *Kalyan that*. We may question the methodology but we have no reason to believe that it belongs to any other *that*.

Yet there is a question which is of tremendous practical concern; the structure and definition of *Bhupali* is changing. This *rag* has been embraced by the lighter musical traditions such as *gazal*, film music, etc. Such traditions have not given prominence to the *pakard*; instead there is a simple reliance upon the modality to define the structure. Since only the scaler characteristics are used, there is a mixing of *Deshkar* and *Shuddha Kalyan*. The result is that many musicians fail to maintain clear distinctions between *Bhupali, Shuddha kalyan,* and *Deshkar*. If this practice continues it may force us to reconsider our definitions of these *rags*.

The *pakard* of *Bhupali* is: ga re - sa dha̱ - sa re pa ga- dha pa ga - re sa. Its other characteristics are:

Arohan	sa re ga pa dha sȧ
Avarohana	sȧ dha pa ga re sa
Jati	audhav-audhav
Vadi	ga
Samavadi	dha
Time	first part of night
That	Kalyan

Rag Bhupali, Tintal - Swarmalika (Bhatkhande 1985b:24)

Sthai

sȧ sȧ dha pa	ga re sa re	ga - pa ga	dha pa ga -
0	3	X	2
ga pa dha sȧ	rė sȧ dha pa	sȧ pa dha pa	ga re sa -
0	3	X	2

Antara

ga - pa dha	pa sȧ - sȧ	dha dha sȧ rė	gȧ rė sȧ dha
0	3	X	2
gȧ gȧ rė sȧ	rė rė sȧ dha	sȧ sȧ dha pa	ga re sa -
0	3	X	2

Rag Bhupali, Kaharava (Tintal) - Bhajan (Lyrics by Surdas - music by Chandrakantha Courtney)

रे मन, कृष्णनाम कहि लीजै ।	re man krishnanam kahi lijai
गुरुके बचन अटल करि मानहि,	guruke bachan atal kari manhi
साधु समागम कीजै ॥	sadhu samagam kijai
पढिये सुनिये भगति भागवत,	padhiye suniye bhagati bhagavat
और कहा कभि कीजै ।	aur kaha kabhi kijai
कृष्णनाम बिनु जनमु है,	krishnanam binu janamu hai
बिरथा जनम काहा कीजै ॥	biratha janam kaha kijai
कृष्णनाम रस ब्रह्मो जात है,	krishnanam ras bramho jat hai
तृष्णवन्त हैं पीजै ।	trushnavant hain pijai
सुरदास हरिसरन ताकिये,	surdas harisaran takiye
जनम सफल करि लीजै ॥	janam safal kari lijai

chant the name of krishna
like a sadhu you should memorize the words of the guru and consider them as permanent
one should both learn and tell the stories of krishna
without the name of krishna life has no purpose
the seekers should drink of the essence of krishna's great name
i, surdas fulfill my life by surrendering to god

Sthai

sa re ga pa	- dhasá̇ dha pa	ga re ga pa	re - sa -
re - ma n	- krisna na -	- m ka hi	li - jai --
2	0	3	X

- - - -	- gaga - ga ga	pa pa dha dha	sá̇ sá̇ sá̇ sá̇
- - - -	- guru ke -	ba cha na a	ta la ka ri
2	0	3	X

ré dha sá̇ sá̇	dha gá̇ ré gá̇	sá̇ - pa dha	sá̇ - sá̇ sá̇
ma - na hi	sa - dhu sa	ma - ga m	ki - jai -
2	0	3	X

dhasá̇ dhapa gare gapa
- - - -
2

Antara

- gaga - ga ga	pa pa dha -	sá̇ sá̇ sá̇ sá̇	- ré sá̇ sá̇
- padhi ye -	su ni ye -	bha ga ti bha	- ga va t
0	3	X	2

- dharé - sá̇ ré	sá̇ - pa dha	sá̇ - sá̇ -	- - - -
- au ra ka	ha - ka bhi	ki - jai -	- - - -
0	3	X	2

dha sá̇ sá̇ sá̇	sáré gá̇ ré gá̇	- ré - sádha	ré ré sá̇ -
kri - shna na	- m bi nu	- ja na mu	hai - - -
0	3	X	2

dha sá̇ sá̇ sá̇	dha dha pa ga	padha sá̇ - sá̇	dhasá̇ dhapa gare gapa
bir tha - ja	na ma ka ha	ki jai - -	- - - -
0	3	X	2

WORKS CITED

Bhatkhande, Vishnu Narayan

1985a   *Hindustani Sangeet Paddhati, Kramik Pustak Malika, Vol 1.* Hathras, India: Sangeet Karyalaya.

1985b   *Hindustani Sangeet Paddhati, Kramik Pustak Malika, Vol 3.* Hathras, India: Sangeet Karyalaya.

1989   *Hindustani Sangeet Paddhati, Kramik Pustak Malika, Vol 2.* Hathras, India: Sangeet Karyalaya.

Rao, B. Subba
1980   *Raganidhi: A Comparative Study of Hindustani and Karnatak Ragas, Vol. 1.* Madras, India: The Music Academy.

Singh, Lal Bahadur
1977   Rag Yaman, Tintal, *Sangeet Sagar.* Hathras, India: Sangeet Karyalaya.

CHAPTER 9.

KHAMMAJ THAT

Khammaj that is characterized by the *komal ni* (minor seventh). This *that* is known as *Harikambhoji* in the *melakarta* system of the South. Two thousand years ago in the *jati* system, it was one of the seven *shuddha jatis*, where it was known as *Madhyama jati*

Exercise 1.
Aroh   sa re ga ma pa dha <u>ni</u> sȧ
Avaroh   sȧ <u>ni</u> dha pa ma ga re sa

Exercise 2.
Aroh   sa re ga ma, re ga ma pa, ga ma pa dha, ma pa dha <u>ni</u>, pa dha <u>ni</u> sȧ
Avaroh   sȧ <u>ni</u> dha pa, <u>ni</u> dha pa ma, dha pa ma ga, pa ma ga re, ma ga re sa

Exercise 3.
Aroh   sa re ga, re ga ma, ga ma pa, ma pa dha, pa dha <u>ni</u>, dha <u>ni</u> sȧ
Avaroh   sȧ <u>ni</u> dha, <u>ni</u> dha pa, dha pa ma, pa ma ga, ma ga re, ga re sa

Exercise 4.
Aroh   sa re ga ma ga re, sa re ga ma pa dha <u>ni</u> sȧ
Avaroh   sȧ <u>ni</u> dha pa dha <u>ni</u>, sȧ <u>ni</u> dha pa ma ga re sa

Exercise 5.
Aroh   sa ga, re ma, ga pa, ma dha, pa <u>ni</u>, dha sȧ
Avaroh   sȧ dha, <u>ni</u> pa, dha ma, pa ga, ma re, ga sa

Exercise 6.
Aroh   sa re, sa re, sa re ga ma pa dha <u>ni</u> sȧ
Avaroh   sȧ <u>ni</u>, sȧ <u>ni</u>, sȧ <u>ni</u> dha pa ma ga re sa

Exercise 7.
Aroh   sa, sa re sa, sa re ga re sa, sa re ga ma ga re sa, sa re ga ma pa ma ga re sa, sa re ga ma pa
          dha pa ma ga re sa, sa re ga ma pa dha <u>ni</u> dha pa ma ga re sa, sa re ga ma pa dha <u>ni</u> sȧ <u>ni</u>
          dha pa ma ga re sa
Avaroh   sȧ, sȧ <u>ni</u> sȧ, sȧ <u>ni</u> dha <u>ni</u> sȧ, sȧ <u>ni</u> dha pa dha <u>ni</u> sȧ, sȧ <u>ni</u> dha pa ma pa dha <u>ni</u> sȧ, sȧ <u>ni</u> dha
          pa ma ga ma pa dha <u>ni</u> sȧ, sȧ <u>ni</u> dha pa ma ga re ga ma pa dha <u>ni</u> sȧ, sȧ <u>ni</u> dha pa ma ga re
          sa re ga ma pa dha <u>ni</u> sȧ

Exercise 8.

Aroh   sa - sa re ga re sa -, re - re ga ma ga re -, ga - ga ma pa ma ga -, ma - ma pa dha pa ma -,
pa - pa dha <u>ni</u> dha pa -, dha - dha <u>ni</u> sȧ - sȧ -

Avaroh   sȧ - sȧ <u>ni</u> dha <u>ni</u> sȧ -, <u>ni</u> - <u>ni</u> dha pa dha <u>ni</u> -, dha - dha pa ma pa dha -, pa - pa ma ga ma pa
-, ma - ma ga re ga ma -, ga - ga re sa - sa -

RAG KHAMMAJ

This *rag* is one of the most common in Indian music. Although it is used in the classical styles, its romantic character makes it much more common in the semi-classical and lighter styles. It is traditionally ascribed to the second part of the night. *"Kuch To Log Lahenge"* and *"Nazar Lagi Raja Tore Bungle Par"* are two well known exmples of common songs in this *rag*.

       It has a clear musical structure. It is a *shadav-sampurna rag* due to the omission of re in the *arohana*. Even in the *avarohana*, the re is *durbal* (i.e., weak). The *vadi* is ga and the *samvadi* is ni. Undoubtedly the use of *nishad* is its most defining characteristic. It is *shuddha nishad* in the *arohana* and *komal nishad* in the *avarohana*. Therefore, structures like sȧ ni sȧ <u>ni</u> dha ni sȧ are very common.

Its characteristics are:

Arohana	sa - ga ma - pa - dha ni sȧ
Avarohana	sȧ <u>ni</u> dha pa - ma ga re sa
Jati	shadav-sampurna
Vadi	ga
Samavadi	ni
Time	second part of night
That	Khammaj
Pakad	ga ma pa dha <u>ni</u> - dha - pa - dha ga ma - ga

Rag Khammaj, Swarmalika - Tintal (Bhatkhande 1985a:35-36)

<u>Sthai</u>

ga ga sa ga	ma pa ga ma	<u>ni</u> dha - ma	pa dha - ma
X	2	0	3
ga - - -	dha ni sȧ -	sȧ <u>ni</u> dha pa	ma ga re sa
X	2	0	3

<u>Antara</u>

ga ma dha ni	sȧ - ni sȧ	sȧ gȧ mȧ gȧ	ni ni sȧ -
X	2	0	3
sȧ rė sȧ <u>ni</u>	dha <u>ni</u> dha pa	dha ma pa ga	ma ga re sa
X	2	0	3
ṇi sa ga ma	pa ga - ma	<u>ni</u> dha - ma	pa dha - ma
X	2	0	3
ga - - -	dha ni sȧ -	sȧ <u>ni</u> dha pa	ma ga re sa
X	2	0	3

Rag Khammaj, Kheyal - Tintal (Bhatkhande 1985a:36-37)

पनघट मुरलिय बाजे सखी	panaghat muralia baje sakhi
सिमट जुवति जन ठाडे निचेतन	simat juvati jan thade nichetan
पुलकित सब तन मुकुलित नायन पे	pulkit sab tan mukulit nayan pe

राग खमाज सुनाय सुलच्छण   rag khammaj sunaiya sulchchan

पुलकित सब तन मुकुलित नयन पे   pulkit sab tan mukulit nayan pe

at the river bank krisna plays his flute
while all the gopis are entranced and thrilled
likewise, the beautiful sound of rag khammaj
has entranced and thrilled everyone

Sthai

			* * * sȧ
			* * * pa
			2

ni ni dhapa ma	pa ma ga ga	ma - pa ma	pa - - -
na ga t mu	ra li - ya	ba - je sa	khi - - -
0	3	X	2

sȧ ni sȧ rė	sȧ ni dha pa	ma ga ma gare	sa re nị sa
si ma t ju	va ti ja n	tha - de ni	che - ta n
0	3	X	2

nị sa ga ma	pa pa ni ni	sȧ ni sȧ rė	sȧ ni dha sȧ
pu la ki t	sa b ta n	mu ku li t	na ya n pe
0	3	X	2 (2nd time-go to start)

Antara

ga ma dha ni	sȧ - ni sȧ	ni - sȧ sȧ	ni sȧ ni dha
ra - g kha	ma - j su	na - ya su	la - chcha n
0	3	X	2

sȧ ni sȧ rė	sȧ ni dha pa	sȧ ni dha pa	ma ga re sa
- - - - - - - - - -	- - sing sargam - -	- - - - - - - - - -	- - - - - - - -
0	3	X	2

nị sa ga ma	pa pa ni ni	sȧ ni sȧ rė	sȧ ni dha sȧ
pu la ki t	sa b ta n	mu ku li t	na ya n pe
0	3	X	2

Rag Khammaj, Bhajan - Dadra Tal (Kulshreshtha 1983:13)

चरन परत, विनति करत; मानो अब कन्हाई श्याम ।   charan parat vinati karat, mano ab kanhai shyam

बाट तकत नैन थकत, रूठे क्यों कन्हाई श्याम ।   bat takat nain thakat, ruthe kyon kanhai shyam

ढूँढ़ गई हार-हार, पायो ना तुम्हारो पार;   dhundh gai har-har, payo na tumharo par

रैन कटत तारे गिनत, दरश दो मुरारी श्याम ।   rain katat tare ginat, darash do morari shyam

शरण पड़ी, द्वार खड़ी, अँसुअन की लगी झड़ी;   sharan padi, dwar khadi, ansuan ki lagi jhadi

नाम रटत, मोह मिटत, क्यों न आए प्यारे श्याम ।   *nam ratat, moh mitat, kyon na ae pyare shyam*

i fall at your feet, i plead with you, please listen now, oh shyam (krishna)
looking out for you my eyes are tired, why are you angry, oh shyam (krishna)
i have searched for you in vain, you are beyond my comprehension
please reveal yourself to me, oh shyam (krishna) in consideration of my many troubled and sleepless nights
my tears are flowing copiously, i come to you for shelter, i wait in the doorway,
i repeat your name, my love is unfulfilled, why don't you come
my beloved shyam (krishna)

Sthai

sa sa sa	ga ga ga	ma ma ma	pa dha dha	sȧ - sȧ	ni dha ma
cha ra n	pa ra t	vi na ti	ka ra t	ma - no	a b kan
X	0	X	0	X	0

pa dha ma	ga - ga	ni - ni	ni ni ni	sȧ - sȧ	sȧ pa dha
ha - i	shya - m	ba - t	ta ka t	nai - n	tha ka t
X	0	X	0	X	0

sȧ - ni	dha - ma	pa dha ma	ga - ga
ru - the	kyon - kan	ha - i	shya - m
X	0	X	0

Antara #1

ga ma ga	ma ni dha	sȧ - ni	sȧ - sȧ	pa ni ni	sȧ - sȧ
dhun - dh	ga i -	ha - ra	ha - r	pa - yo	na - tum
X	0	X	0	X	0

ni sȧ ni	dha - dha	sa - sa	ga ga ga	ma - ma	pa dha dha
ha - ro	pa - r	rai - n	ka ta t	ta - re	gi na t
X	0	X	0	X	0

sȧ sȧ sȧ	ni dha ma	pa dha ma	ga - ga
da ra sh	do - mu	ra - ri	shya - m
X	0	X	0

Antara #2

ga ga ga	ma ni dha	sȧ - ni	sȧ sȧ -	pa pa ni	ni ni -
sha ra n	pa di -	dwa - r	kha di -	an su a	n ki -
X	0	X	0	X	0

sȧ ni sȧ	ni dha -	pȧ - gȧ	mȧ gȧ gȧ	sȧ - ni	sȧ ni dha
la gi -	jha di -	na - m	ra ta t	mo - h	mi ta t
X	0	X	0	X	0

ga - ma	sȧ - ma	pa dha ma	ga - ga
kyon - n	a - e	pya - re	shya - m
X	0	X	0

Sthai Tans

1) pa dha ni	sȧ ni dha	pa ma ga	re sa -
X	0	X	0

2) ni sà gà	rè sà <u>ni</u>	dha pa ma	ga re sa
X	0	X	0

Antara Tans

1) sà <u>ni</u> dha	pa ma ga	ga ma pa	dha ni sà
X	0	X	0

2) ni sà gà	rè sà <u>ni</u>	dha pa dha	ni sà -
X	0	X	0

TILAK KAMOD

This *rag* is usually attributed to *khammaj that*. However, most subtraditions within India show a conspicuous absence of any *komal ni*. Its structure places it squarely into *Bilawal that*. It is with extreme reluctance that we bow to tradition and include *Tilak Kamod* with *Khammaj that*.

The structure of *Tilak Kamod* is quite pleasant. Some musicians maintain that the *vadi* is sa and the *samavadi* is pa. Others claim that re is *vadi*. Its *pakard* is pa ni sa re ga - sa - re pa ma ga - sa ni. It is *shadav-sampurna* due to the omission of dha in the *arohana*. It is performed in the second part of the night. Its structure is:

Arohana	pa ni sa re ga sa - re ma pa ni sà
Avarohan	sà - pa dha ma ga - sa re ga sa ni
Jati	shadav-sampurna
Vadi	sa (disputed)
Samavadi	pa (disputed)
Time	second part of night
That	Khammaj (disputed)

Tilak Kamod, Swarmalika - Tintal (Bhatkhande 1985b:288)

Sthai

ni pa ni sa	re ga ni sa	re ga re pa	ma ga ni sa
X	2	0	3

re ma pa dha	ma pa sà pa	dha ma ga sa	re ga ni sa
X	2	0	3

Antara

ma pa ni ni	sà - rè sà	rè gà rè gà	mà gà ni sà
X	2	0	3

pa ni sà rè	sà pa dha ma	ga sa re pa	ma ga ni sa
X	2	0	3

Rag Tilak Kamod, Lakshangit - Jhaptal (Bhatkhande 1985b:300)

तिलक कामोद को चतुर उद्धारे   tilak kamod ko chatur uddhare

देस सोरट विशद भेद कर न्यारे   des sorat vishad bhed kar nyare

आरोहन अध सुमत वादि सुर रिखब सुध   arohan adh sumat vadi sur rikhab sudh

वक्र गतनी को अपन्यास चितहारे   vakra gatani ko apanyas chitahare

tilak kamod is very similar to rag desh
but the learned are able to make the distinction
it is important to grasp the ascending structure
shuddha re is the vadi
It is sung in a convoluted manner

Sthai

nị pạ	nị nị sa	re -	ga sa -	re re	pa ma gare	sa re	ga sa nị
ti la	k ka -	mo -	da ko -	cha tu	r u -	ddha -	- re -
X	2	0	3	X	2	0	3

ma -	re ma -	pa pa	dha ma ma	re -	pa ma gare	sa re	ga sa nị
de -	sa so -	ra t	vi sha d	bhe -	d ka ra	nya -	- re -
X	2	0	3	X	2	0	3

Antara

ma -	pa ni ni	sá sá	ni sá sá	ré -	pá má garé	sá ré	gá ni dha
a -	ro ha n	a dha	su ma t	va -	di su r	ri kha	b su dh
X	2	0	3	X	2	0	3

sá -	pa sá sá	pa -	dha ma gare re -	pa ma gare	sa re	ga sa nị
va -	kra ga t	ni -	ko a p nya -	sa chi t	ha -	- re -
X	2	0	3	X	2	0	3

Rag Tilak Kamod, Tulsi Bhajan - Dadra tal (Bhatkhande 1985b:325)

तू दयाल, दीन हौं, तू दानि, हौं भिखारी ।   tu dayal din haun tu dani haun bhikhari

हौं प्रसिद्ध पातकी, तू पापपुंजहारी ॥   haun prasiddha pataki tu pappunjahari

नाथ तू अनाथको, अनाथ कौन मोसो ।   nath tu anathko anath kaun moso

मो समान आरत नहिं, आरतिहर तोसो ॥   mo saman arat nahin aratihar toso

ब्रमह तू, हौं जीव, तू है ठाकुर, हौं चेरो ।   bramha tu haun jiv tu hai thakur haun chero

तात, मात, गुरू, सखा तू सब बिधि हितु मेरो ॥   tat mat guru sakha tu sab bidhi hitu mero

तोहि मोहि नाते अनेक, मानिये जो भावै ।   tohi mohi nate anek maniye jo bhave

ज्यों त्यों तुलसी कृपालु, चरन-सरन पावै ॥   jyon tyon tulsi krapalu charan saran pave

i am helpless, you are helpful
i am needy, you are charitable
i am a sinner and you are a redeemer
i am vulnerable, you are the protector
no one is as helpless as i, and no one can be as great as you

i am the most afflicted and you are the ultimate remover of afflictions
you are god and we are mortals
you are our lord, you are our father, mother, and teacher
you are our friend who always looks after our wellbeing
we have various relationships of which you choose by whim
but ultimately i, tulsi, am a recipient of your grace

Sthai

ni pa pa	ni sa sa	re - ga	sa - sa	ni pa ni	sa - sa	re ma pa	dha ma -
tu - da	ya - la	dee - n	haun - tu	da - ni	haun - bi	kha - -	- - ri
X	0	X	0	X	0	X	0

ma - pa	ni sa ni	sa - ni	sa - sa	dhapa dha ma	gare ga sa	re ma pa	dha ma -
haun - pra	si - ddha	pa - t	ki - tu	pa - p	pu n ja	ha - -	- ri -
X	0	X	0	X	0	X	0

Antara

ma - pa	ni - ni	sa - ni	sa - sa	pa - ni	sa - sa	sa re ni	dha pa -
na - th	tu - a	na - tha	ko - a	na - th	kou - n	mo - -	so - -
X	0	X	0	X	0	X	0

ma - dha	dha ni pa	sa ni dha	pa dha ma	dhapa dha ma	gare ga sa	sa re ma	pa dha ma
mo - sa	ma - n	a - ra	ta na hin	a - ra	ti ha ra	to - -	- so -
X	0	X	0	X	0	X	0

(second and third antara are sung to the same melody)

WORKS CITED

Bhatkhande, Vishnu Narayan
1985a   *Hindustani Sangeet Paddhati, Kramik Pustak Malika, Vol 1.* Hathras, India: Sangeet Karyalaya.
1985b   *Hindustani Sangeet Paddhati, Kramik Pustak Malika, Vol 3.* Hathras, India: Sangeet Karyalaya.
1989   *Hindustani Sangeet Paddhati, Kramik Pustak Malika, Vol 2.* Hathras, India: Sangeet Karyalaya.

CHAPTER 10.

KAFI THAT

Kafi that is a very ancient musical mode. In Bharata's time it was known as *Shadaji jati*. In the *melakarta* system of the South it is known as *Kharaharapriya*. It is characterized by a *komal gandhar* and a *komal nishad*.

Exercise 1.

Aroh   sa re ga ma pa dha ni sȧ
Avaroh   sȧ ni dha pa ma ga re sa

Exercise 2.

Aroh   sa re ga ma, re ga ma pa, ga ma pa dha, ma pa dha ni, pa dha ni sȧ
Avaroh   sȧ ni dha pa, ni dha pa ma, dha pa ma ga, pa ma ga re, ma ga re sa

Exercise 3.

Aroh   sa re ga, re ga ma, ga ma pa, ma pa dha, pa dha ni, dha ni sȧ
Avaroh   sȧ ni dha, ni dha pa, dha pa ma, pa ma ga, ma ga re, ga re sa

Exercise 4.

Aroh   sa re ga ma ga re, sa re ga ma pa dha ni sȧ
Avaroh   sȧ ni dha pa dha ni, sȧ ni dha pa ma ga re sa

Exercise 5.

Aroh   sa ga, re ma, ga pa, ma dha, pa ni, dha sȧ
Avaroh   sȧ dha, ni pa, dha ma, pa ga, ma re, ga sa

Exercise 6.

Aroh   sa re, sa re, sa re ga ma pa dha ni sȧ
Avaroh   sȧ ni, sȧ ni, sȧ ni dha pa ma ga re sa

Exercise 7.

Aroh   sa, sa re sa, sa re ga re sa, sa re ga ma ga re sa, sa re ga ma pa ma ga re sa, sa re ga ma pa
         dha pa ma ga re sa, sa re ga ma pa dha ni dha pa ma ga re sa, sa re ga ma pa dha ni sȧ ni
         dha pa ma ga re sa

Avaroh   sȧ, sȧ ni sȧ, sȧ ni dha ni sȧ, sȧ ni dha pa dha ni sȧ, sȧ ni dha pa ma pa dha ni sȧ, sȧ ni dha
         pa ma ga ma pa dha ni sȧ, sȧ ni dha pa ma ga re ga ma pa dha ni sȧ, sȧ ni dha pa ma ga re
         sa re ga ma pa dha ni sȧ

Exercise 8.

Aroh   sa - sa re ga re sa -, re - re ga ma ga re -, ga - ga ma pa ma ga -, ma - ma pa dha pa ma -, pa
         - pa dha ni dha pa -, dha - dha ni sȧ - sȧ -

Avaroh   sȧ - sȧ ni dha ni sȧ -, ni - ni dha pa dha ni -, dha - dha pa ma pa dha -, pa - pa ma ga ma pa
         -, ma - ma ga re ga ma -, ga - ga re sa - sa -

RAG KAFI

Rag Kafi is the primary *rag* in *Kafi that*. One common song in this *rag* is *"Biraj Me, Holi Khelat Nand Lal"*. It is a *sampurna-sampurna rag* that is very straightforward in its execution. There is some disagreement concerning the *vadi* and the *samvadi*. Some suggest that the *vadi* and *samvadi* are pa and sa respectively. However, many are of the opinion that it should be ga for the *vadi* and ni for the *samavadi*. Its characteristics are:

Arohan sa re ga ma pa dha ni sȧ
Avarohana   sȧ ni dha pa ma ga re sa
Jati   sampurna-sampurna
Vadi   pa (disputed)
Samavadi   sa (disputed)
Time   evening
That   Kafi

Rag Kafi, Swarmalika-Jhaptal (Bhatkhande 1989:318)

Sthai

ga ga	re sa re	pa -	ma pa dha
X	2	0	3
ga ga	re sa re	pa -	ma pa pa
X	2	0	3
ma dha	ni sȧ ni	dha ma	pa ga re
X	2	0	3
re ga	re ma ga	re sa	re ni sa
X	2	0	3
ni dha	sȧ ni dha	ma pa	dha ga re
X	2	0	3

Antara

ma ma	pa dha ni	sȧ -	dha ni sȧ
X	2	0	3
rė gȧ	rė sȧ rė	ni sȧ	ni dha dha
X	2	0	3
pa rė	sȧ sȧ rė	ni sȧ	ni dha dha
X	2	0	3
sȧ -	ni dha ma	pa dha	ga ga re
X	2	0	3
re ga	re ma ga	re sa	re ni sa
X	2	0	3
ni dha	sȧ ni dha	ma pa	dha ga re
X	2	0	3

Rag Kafi, Lakshangit - Ektal (Bhatkhande 1989:320)

गुणि गावत काफी राग   guni gavat kafi rag
खरहरप्रीया मेल जानित   karaharapriya mel janit
कोमल ग नी उज्वल पर   komal ga ni ujval par
सुर पंचम वादी साधा   sur pancham vadi sadha
                          -
सरल स्वरुप विपश्चित   saral svarup vipashchit
मानत सब सुधाविकल   manat sab sudhavikal
अश्रय गुणि चतुर कहत   ashray guni chatur kahat

page 66

to sing rag kafi well you must know that it is from the kharaharpriya mode
komal ga ni display the brilliance of the rag
pancham is the vadi note, kafi is simple in form
it is sweet to sing and is easy
the learned classify it as a host rag

Sthai

```
padha mapa     ga -      resa re    ga -      ma pa      - pa
gu      ni     ga -      va  ta     ka -      fi  ra     - g
0              3         4          X         0          2

sà rè          sà ni     dha pa     ga -      re sa      re sa
kha ra         ha ra     pri ya     me -      la ja      ni ta
0              3         4          X         0          2

sa -           re re     ga ga      ma -      pa pa      dha dha
ko -           ma la     ga ni      u  -      jva l      pa    r
0              3         4          X         0          2

ni sà          nisà rè   sà ni      dha -     ma pa      - mapa
su ra          pan  -    cha m      va  -     di sa      - dha
0              3         4          X         0          2

padha dha
gu    ni
0
```

Antara

```
ma ma          pa pa     dha -      ni ni     sà -       sà sà
sa  ra         la sva    ru  -      p  vi     pa -       sh chit
0              3         4          X         0          2

ni sà          rè gà     rè sà      rè sà     rè ni      sà sà
ma -           na  t     sa  b      su dha    a  vi      ka la
0              3         4          X         0          2

sà -           ni dha    ma pa      ga ga     re sa      re ni
a  -           shra ya   gu ni      cha tu    ra ka      ha ta
0              3         4          X         0          2

sa -           re re     ga ga      ma -      pa pa      dha dha
ko -           ma l      ga ni      u  -      jva l      pa    r
0              3         4          X         0          2

ni sà          nisà rè   sà ni      dha -     ma pa      - mapa
su ra          pan  -    cha m      va  -     di sa      - dha
0              3         4          X         0          2

padha dha
gu    ni
0
```

Rag Kafi, Kheyal - Tintal (Kulshreshtha 1983: 26)

वंसी मधुर बजावे श्याम	vansi madhur bajave shyam
मुरलिया मधुर बजावे श्याम	muraliya madhur bajave shyam
मन मोह लिनो सुर नर मुनि को	man moha lino, sur nar muni ko
ग्वाल बाल गोपियन भुल गई	gval bal gopiyan, bhul gai

काम छोडे जब मिठी तान   kam chode jab mithi tan

गोपिन संग नित रास रचावे   gopin sang nit ras rachave

ग्वाल बाल संग गैयन चरावे   gval bal sang gaiyan charave

वंसी वाला नन्द को लाला   vamsi wala, nand ko lala

यासोद घनश्याम जाको गिरीधर है नाम   yasoda ghanshyam jako giridhar hai nam

krishna is playing his beautiful melody on the flute,
his playing has enchanted every type of person
his melodies enchant the gopis and the cowherds into oblivious surrender
krishna dances with the gopis, he tends the cows with the cowherds
vamsi wala, nand ko lala, yasoda ghanshyam, giridhar; he is known by many names.

Sthai

```
                                                              *  *  sa  ni
                                                              *  *  vam si
                                                              2
```

sa sa re re	ga - ma -	pa - pa ma	ga re sa ni
ma dhu ra ba	ja - ve -	shya - m mu	ra li ya -
0	3	X	2
sa sa re re	ga - ma -	pa - pa ma	pa dha ni sa
ma dhu ra ba	ja - ve -	shya m ma n	mo hi li no
0	3	X	2
ni dha pa ma	ga ga re -	re ni dha ni	pa dha ma pa
su r na r	mu ni ko -	gva l ba l	go pi ya na
0	3	X	2
ga ma ga pa	ma ma sa ni	sa ga re ma	ga re sa ni
bhul le ga e	ka m cho de	ja b mi thi	taan - vam si
0	3	X	2

Antara

pa - pa dha	ma pa ni sa	re ga re sa	re ni sa sa
go - pi na	san ga ni t	ra - sa ra	cha - ve -
X	2	0	3
ni - ni ni	dha ni pa dha	ni re sa re	ni dha pa pa
gva - l ba	- la san ga	ga ye n cha	ra - ve -
X	2	0	3
pa ni dha ni	pa dha ma pa	ga ma ga pa	ma - sa ni
vam si va la	nand ko la la	ya so da ghan	shya - mja ko
X	2	0	3
sa ga re ma	ga re sa ni		
gi ri dhar hai	na me vam si		
X	2		

Sthai Tans

1)	sa re <u>ga</u> ma	pa dha <u>ni</u> sȧ	<u>ni</u> dha pa ma	<u>ga</u> re sa -
	0	3	X	2
2)	sa re <u>ga</u> ma	pa ma <u>ga</u> re	sa re <u>ga</u> ma	pa dha ma pa
	0	3	X	2

Antara Tans

1)	sȧ <u>ni</u> dha pa	ma <u>ga</u> re sa	sa re <u>ga</u> ma	pa dha <u>ni</u> sȧ
	X	2	0	3
2)	sa re <u>ga</u> ma	pa ma <u>ga</u> re	sa re <u>ga</u> ma	pa dha <u>ni</u> sȧ
	X	2	0	3

RAG BAHAR

This is a very popular springtime *rag*. During the spring it may be sung at any time of the day. However, during any other season it is a night time *rag*. This *rag* has a very distinctive character. It uses both nishads; *shuddha* in the *arohana* and *komal* in the *avarohana*. Ma is the *vadi* and sa is the *samvadi*. This *rag* is not performed straight but in a *vakra* (twisted) fashion. These characteristic twists give the *rag* its form. The *pakard* is, <u>ni</u> pa - ma pa <u>ga</u> ma - dha - ni sȧ.

Its characteristics are:

Arohana	sa ma - pa <u>ga</u> ma - dha - ni sȧ
Avarohana	rė ni sȧ dha <u>ni</u> pa - ma pa <u>ga</u> ma - re sa
Jati	shadav-sampurna
Vadi	ma
Samavadi	Sa
Time	spring
That	Kafi

Rag Bahar, Geet - Kaherava Tal (Garg 1973: 26)

आज शक्ति का तांडव हो ।	aj shakti ka tandava ho
	–
युग - युग से है खप्पर खाली,	yug-yug se he khappar khali
सोच - विचार न कर अब काली ।	soch-vichar na kar ab kali
भर उसमें लोहू की लाली,	bhar usmen lohu ki lali
यही आज तव आसव हो ।	yahi aj tav asav ho
आज... ।	aj shakti ....
	–
देखें लोचन जब रतनारे,	dekhen lochan jab ratnare
टूट पड़ें अंबर के तारे,	tut pden ambar ke tare
मूर्च्छित हों निश्चर हत्यारे,	murchchhit hon nishchar hatyare
जब माँ तव रव भैरव हो ।	jab man tav rav bhairav ho
आज... ॥	aj shakti ....

let the dance of shiva show its power
for ages the bowl has been empty
awake now kali and fill it with blood so we may drink until intoxicated
let the dance of shiva show its power
with red eyes we see the stars fall from the sky
when kali makes her frightful sound the evildoers will be eliminated
let the dance of shiva show its power

Sthai

```
⌐dhani⌐ sȧ ni pa    ma pa ga ma    ma ni dha ni    sȧ rė ni sȧ    ⌐dhani⌐ sȧ ni pa    ma pa ga ma
a      - ja sha      - kti ka -     tan - da va     ho - - -       a       - ja sha      - kti ka -
X                   0              X              0              X                   0

ma ni dha ni    sȧ rė ni sȧ
tan - da va     ho - - -
X               0
```

Antara #1

```
⌐dhani⌐ sȧ ni pa    pa ma ma pa    ga - ga ma     re - sa -       sa - ma ma      ma pa ga ma
yu      ga yu ga     se - he -      kha - ppa ra   kha - li -      so - cha vi     cha - ra na
X                   0              X              0              X               0

ma ni dha ni    sȧ rė ni sȧ    gȧ gȧ gȧ gȧ    gȧ mȧ rė sȧ    ni dha dha ni    sȧ rė ni sȧ
ka ra a ba      ka - li -      bha ra u sa    man - lo -     hu - ki -        la - li -
X               0              X              0              X                0

ni pa - pa      ma pa ga ma    ma ni dha ni    sȧ rė ni sȧ    ⌐dhani⌐ sȧ ni pa    ma pa ga ma
ya hi - a       - ja ta va     a - sa va       ho - - -       a       - ja sha      - kti ka -
X  0            X              0              X              0

ma ni dha ni    sȧ rė ni sȧ
tan - da va     ho - - -
X               0
```

Antara #2

```
sȧ - ni -       pa - ma pa     ga ga ga ma    re - sa -       sa - ma ma      ma pa ga ma
de - khe -      lo - cha na    ja ba ra ta    na - re -       tu - ta pa      den - an -
X               0              X              0              X               0

ma ni dha ni    sȧ rė ni sȧ    gȧ - gȧ gȧ     gȧ mȧ rė sȧ    ni ni dha ni    sȧ rė ni sȧ
ba ra ke -      ta - re -      mu - rchchi ta hon - ni sha    cha ra ha -     tya - re -
X               0              X              0              X               0

ni ni pa -      ma pa ga ma    ma ni dha ni   sȧ rė ni sȧ    ⌐dhani⌐ sȧ ni pa    ma pa ga ma
ja ba man -     ta va ra va    bhai - ra va   ho - - -       a       - ja sha      - kti ka -
X               0              X              0              X               0

ma ni dha ni    sȧ rė ni sȧ
tan - da va     ho - - -
X               0
```

WORKS CITED

Bhatkhande. V.N.
1989   *Hindustani Sangeet Paddhati, Kramik Pustak Malika,Vol 2.* Hathras, India: Sangeet Karyalaya.

Garg, Lakshminarayan
1973   *Bal Sangeet Shiksha, Vol. 2.* Hathras, India: Sangeet Karyalaya.

Kulshreshtha, J.S.
1983   *Sangeet Kishor.* Hathras, India: Sangeet Karyalaya.

CHAPTER 11.

ASAVARI THAT

Asawari that is a very common musical mode. It was one of the ancient *jatis* mentioned by *Bharata* in the *Natya-Shastra*. In the *Natya-Shastra* it was known as *Panchami jati*. It is characterized by *komal ga, komal dha,* and *komal ni*. In the *melakarta* system of the South it is known as *Natabhairavi*.

Exercise 1.
Aroh   sa re ga ma pa dha ni sȧ
Avaroh   sȧ ni dha pa ma ga re sa

Exercise 2.
Aroh   sa re ga ma, re ga ma pa, ga ma pa dha, ma pa dha ni, pa dha ni sȧ
Avaroh   sȧ ni dha pa, ni dha pa ma, dha pa ma ga, pa ma ga re, ma ga re sa

Exercise 3.
Aroh   sa re ga, re ga ma, ga ma pa, ma pa dha, pa dha ni, dha ni sȧ
Avaroh   sȧ ni dha, ni dha pa, dha pa ma, pa ma ga, ma ga re, ga re sa

Exercise 4.
Aroh   sa re ga ma ga re, sa re ga ma pa dha ni sȧ
Avaroh   sȧ ni dha pa dha ni, sȧ ni dha pa ma ga re sa

Exercise 5.
Aroh   sa ga, re ma, ga pa, ma dha, pa ni, dha sȧ
Avaroh   sȧ dha, ni pa, dha ma, pa ga, ma re, ga sa

Exercise 6.
Aroh   sa re, sa re, sa re ga ma pa dha ni sȧ
Avaroh   sȧ ni, sȧ ni, sȧ ni dha pa ma ga re sa

Exercise 7.
Aroh   sa, sa re sa, sa re ga re sa, sa re ga ma ga re sa, sa re ga ma pa ma ga re sa, sa re ga ma pa dha pa ma ga re sa, sa re ga ma pa dha ni dha pa ma ga re sa, sa re ga ma pa dha ni sȧ ni dha pa ma ga re sa
Avaroh   sȧ, sȧ ni sȧ, sȧ ni dha ni sȧ, sȧ ni dha pa dha ni sȧ, sȧ ni dha pa ma pa dha ni sȧ, sȧ ni dha pa ma ga ma pa dha ni sȧ, sȧ ni dha pa ma ga re ga ma pa dha ni sȧ, sȧ ni dha pa ma ga re sa re ga ma pa dha ni sȧ

Exercise 8.

Aroh   sa - sa re <u>ga</u> re sa -, re - re <u>ga</u> ma <u>ga</u> re -, <u>ga</u> - <u>ga</u> ma pa ma <u>ga</u> -, ma - ma pa <u>dha</u> pa ma -, pa
              - pa <u>dha</u> ni <u>dha</u> pa -, <u>dha</u> - <u>dha</u> ni sȧ - sȧ -

Avaroh sȧ - sȧ ni <u>dha</u> ni sȧ -, ni - ni <u>dha</u> pa <u>dha</u> ni -, <u>dha</u> - <u>dha</u> pa ma pa <u>dha</u> -, pa - pa ma <u>ga</u> ma pa
              -, ma - ma <u>ga</u> re <u>ga</u> ma -, <u>ga</u> - <u>ga</u> re sa - sa -

RAG ASAWARI

Rag Asawari is considered to be the fundamental *rag* in *Asawari that*. One common song in this *rag* is *"Meri Yad Me Tum Na Ansu Bahana"*. *Asawari* is a morning *rag*. It is *audhav-sampurna* due to the omission of the ga and ni in the ascending structure. The *vadi* is dha and the *samavadi* is ga.

     There are several *rags* which share the same *that*. *Jaunpuri* and *Darbari Kanada* are two of the most common examples. Therefore, it is important to pay attention to the *pakard* to keep from impinging upon them. The *pakard* is :

re ma pa - <u>ni</u> <u>dha</u> pa - ma pa <u>dha</u> ma pa - - <u>ga</u> - re sa

Asawari's characteristics are:

Arohana	sa - re ma pa - <u>dha</u> sȧ
Avarohan	sȧ <u>ni</u> <u>dha</u> - pa - ma <u>ga</u> - re - sa
Jati	audhav-sampurna
Vadi	dha
Samavadi	ga
Time	morning
That	Asawari

Rag Asawari, Swarmalika - Tintal (J.V.S. Rao - personal interview)

Sthai

re ma pa sȧ	<u>dha</u> <u>dha</u> pa pa	ma pa <u>dha</u> pa	ga ga re sa
3	X	2	0
re sa <u>dha</u> pạ	mạ pạ <u>dha</u> sa	re ma pa <u>dha</u>	ga ga re sa
3	X	2	0

Antara

ma pa <u>dha</u> <u>dha</u>	sȧ - rė sȧ	<u>dha</u> sȧ rė gȧ	rė sȧ <u>dha</u> pa
3	X	2	0
<u>dha</u> gȧ rė sȧ	rė <u>ni</u> <u>dha</u> pa	ma pa <u>dha</u> pa	ga ga re sa
3	X	2	0

Rag Asawari, Lakshangit - Tintal (Bhatkhande 1989:358)

कान मोहे असावरी राग सुनाए	kan mohe asavari rag sunae
ग नी को अधिरोहन मे छुपाए	ga ni ko adhirohn me chupae
धैवत वादी ग समवादी	dhaivat vadi ga samvadi
मध्यम सुर ग्रह न्यास सुपंचम	madhyam sur grah nyas supancham
अवरोहन सम्पूर्ण दिखाये	avarohana sampurna dikhaye

sing rag asawari to me
ga and ni are absent while ascending
dhaivat is vadi and ga is samavadi
madhyam is the grah and pancham is nyas
all the notes are used while descending

Sthai

ma ͺpasȧ ͺ dha pa	dha ma ͺpadha ͺ mapa ͺ	ga - re sa	re ma pa -
ka na mo he	a sa va ri	ra - ga su	na - ye -
0	3	X	2

dha dha dha -	ni dha pa ͺdhama ͺ	ma pa ͺpadha ͺ mapa ͺ	ga - re sa
ga ni ko -	a dhi ro -	ha na me chu	pa - - ye
0	3	X	2

sa re ma re	ma pa dha pa	dha gȧ rė sȧ	rė ni dha pa
- - - - - - - - - - - - - - - - - - sing sargam -
0	3	X	2

Antara

ma - pa pa	dha - dha -	sȧ - sȧ sȧ	sȧ - sȧ -
dhai - va ta	va - di -	ga - sa ma	va - di -
0	3	X	2

dha - dha dha	sȧ sȧ sȧ sȧ	ͺsȧrė ͺ gȧ rė sȧ	sȧ ͺrėni ͺ dha pa
ma - dhya me	su ra gra ha	nya - sa su	pan - cha ma
0	3	X	2

ma pa sȧ -	dha pa ͺpadha ͺ mapa ͺ	ga ga re sa	re - sa sa
a va ro -	ha na sum -	pu ra na di	kha - ye -
0	3	X	2

sa re ma re	ma pa dha pa	dha gȧ rė sȧ	rė ni dha pa
- - - - - - - - - - - - - - - - - - sing sargam -
0	3	X	2

Rag Asawari, Drut Kheyal - Tintal (Kulshreshtha 1983:42)

मधुर-मधुर धुन, मुरली बजावे ।	madhur madhur dhun murali bajawe
कुँवर कन्हैया, ढीठ लँगरवा ॥	kunvara kanhaiya dhit langarawa
धुन सुन सखियाँ, रीझीं उनपर;	dhun sun sakhiyan rijhin unpar
ग्वाल-बाल भूले सब सुध तन ।	gval bal bhule sab sudha tan
मधुबन बिच जब तान सुनावे ॥	madhuban bich jab tan sunawe

prince krishna plays his sweet melody on his flute
all the cow-herders and gopis are mesmerized and enchanted
when they hear him playing in the forests of madhuban

Sthai

ma ma pa sȧ	dha pa ⌐padha⌐ mapa⌐	ga ga re sa	re ma pa -
ma dhu r ma	dhu r dhu n	mu ra li ba	ja - ve -
0	3	X	2

ga ga re sa	re - sa -	gȧ - rė sȧ	dha dha pa -
kun va r kan	hai - ya -	dhi - th lan	ga ra wa -
0	3	X	2

Antara

ma ma pa pa	dha dha dha -	sȧ - sȧ -	sȧ sȧ sȧ sȧ
dhu n su n	sa khi yan -	ri - jhin -	u n pa r
0	3	X	2

dha - dha dha	sȧ sȧ sȧ -	gȧ - rė sȧ	dha dha pa pa
gva - l ba	- l bhu -	le - sa b	su dh ta n
0	3	X	2

pa pa gȧ gȧ	rė rė sȧ sȧ	rė - sȧ sȧ	rė sȧ dha pa
ma dhu ba n	bi ch ja b	ta - n su	na - we -
0	3	X	2

Sthai Tans

1)	sa re ma pa	dha dha sȧ sȧ	ni dha pa ma	ga re sa -
	0	3	X	2
2)	ma pa dha sȧ	gȧ gȧ rė sȧ	ni dha pa ma	ga re sa -
	0	3	X	2

Antara Tans

1)	sȧ ni dha pa	ma ga re sa	sa re ma pa	dha dha sȧ -
	0	3	X	2
2)	sa re ma ma	re ma pa pa	ma pa dha dha	pa dha sȧ -
	0	3	X	2

DARBARI KANADA

There can be no doubt that *Darbari Kanada* is one of the most popular *rags* in the entire north Indian system. A few common songs in this *rag* are *"Ghunghat Ke Pat Khol Re Tohe Piya Milenge"*, *"Jhana Jhanak Tori Baje Payaliya"*, *"Mujhe Tumese Kuch Bhi Na Chahiye"*, or *"O Duniya Ke Rakhwale"*. This *rag* is also known as *Durbari, Darbari*, or *Durbari Kanada*. It is said to be invented by Tansen, who sang it in the *durbar* (court) of the emperor Akbar.

There is some difference of opinion concerning the important notes. Some suggest that re and dha are the *vadi* and *samvadi*. However, others are of the opinion that it should be ga and dha.

This is a night time *rag* that is *sampurna-sampurna* in its character. However, it is required to be performed in a *vakra* (oblique) manner in order to differentiate it from related *rags* such as *Jaunpuri, Adana*, or *Asawari*. It is especially important to emphasize the lower register (*mandra saptak*) and the lower tetrachord (i.e., *purvang*) to distinguish this *rag* from *Adana*. Its characteristics are:

Arohana	ni sa - re ga - re sa- ma pa - dha - ni sȧ
Avarohan	sȧ dha - ni - pa - ma pa - ga - ma - re sa

Jati	sampurna-sampurna
Vadi	re (disputed)
Samavadi	dha (disputed)
Time	night
That	Asawari

Rag Darbari Kanada, Swarmalika - Tintal (Bhatkhande 1985:654)

Sthai

re re sa -	ni sa re re	ga - - re	re - sa -
0	3	X	2
ni ni sa -	re ma re sa	ni sa re re	dha dha ni pa
0	3	X	2
ma pa dha ni	sa dha ni sa	- pa ma pa	ga ma re sa
0	3	X	2

Antara

ma ma pa pa	dha dha ni ni	sa - sa -	re re sa -
0	3	X	2
ni ni sa -	re re sa -	ni ni sa re	dha dha ni pa
0	3	X	2
ma pa sa -	dha dha ni pa	ma pa ga ma	re re sa -
0	3	X	2

Rag Darbari Kanada, Lakshangit - Jhaptal (Bhatkhande 1985:657)

दरबारि की सुरत हर रंग बखानत	darbari ki surat har rang bakhanat
नट भैरवी मेल कर्नाट शास्त्र मत	nat bhairav mela karnat shastra mat
-	-
वादी रिखब होत धैवत बिलमत जत	vadi rikhab hota dhaivat bilamat jat
गंधार मूर्छित रसिक जनम नहरत	gandhar murchit rasik janam naharat

darbari kanada is derived from the mode of natbhairavi of the carnatic system
rishabh is the vadi sawar
dhaivat is prolonged
the music lovers enjoy the character of komal ga

<u>Sthai</u>

re sa	<u>dha</u> <u>ni</u> pạ	sa -	<u>ni</u> sa sa
da ra	ba - ri	ki -	su ra ta
X	2	0	3

<u>ni</u> sa	<u>ni</u> sa re	<u>dha</u> <u>dha</u>	<u>ni</u> pạ pạ
ha r	ran ga ba	kha -	- na ta
X	2	0	3

mạ pạ	<u>dha</u> - <u>ni</u>	sa <u>dha</u>	<u>ni</u> sa sa
na ta	bhai - ra	vi -	me - la
X	2	0	3

ma pa	ma pa <u>ni</u>	ga ma	re re sa
ka ra	na - t	sha -	stra ma t
X	2	0	3

<u>Antara</u>

ma pa	<u>dha</u> <u>dha</u> ni	sȧ sȧ	<u>ni</u> sȧ sȧ
va -	di - ri	kha ba	ho - ta
X	2	0	3

<u>ni</u> sȧ	rė rė sȧ	<u>ni</u> sȧ	dha ni pa
dhai -	va ta bi	lu ma	ta ja ta
X	2	0	3

gȧ -	gȧ - mȧ	rė -	sȧ rė sȧ
gan -	dha - ra	mu -	ra chi ta
X	2	0	3

ma pa	sȧ sȧ sȧ	ga gama	re re sa
ra si	ka ja na	ma na	ha ra t
X	2	0	3

Rag Darbari Kanada, Kabir Bhajan - Kaherawa (lyrics by Kabir - music by C. Courtney)

तनकी धनकी कौन बड़ाई	tanki dhanki kaun badai
देखत नैनोंमें माटी मिलाई	dekhta nainomen mati milai
-	-
अपने खातर महल बनाया	apne khatar mahal banaya
आपहि जाकर जंगल सोया	aphi jakar jangal soya
हाड़ जले जैसे लकरिकी मोली	had jale jaise lakirki moli
बाल जले जैसे घासकी पोली	bal jale jaise ghaski poli
-	-
कहत कबीरा सुन मेरे गुनिया	kaht kbira sun mere guniya
आप मुवे पिछे डूब गई दुनिया	ap muve piche dub gai duniya

there is futility in attachment to material things
they will disappear before your very eyes
you built a great palace but you sleep in the forest
in the end your body will burn like wood
your hair will burn like grass
i, kabir, tell all of you learned people
that if you have attachment to the material world it will come to naught

Sthai

- nisa - re	sa	dha ni sa re	- ga - ga ma	re - sa -	- mama - ma ma	pa - pa pa
- tana ki	-	dha na ki -	- kau na ba	da - i -	- de kha ta	nai - no me
0		X	0	X	0	X

- mapa - ni pa ga ma re sa
- ma ti mi la - i -
0 X

Antara

- mama - ma -	pa - dha dha	- ni nisa ni	sa - sa sa	- ni - ni ni	sa - sa sa
- apa ne -	kha - ta ra	- ma hal ba	na - ya -	- a pa hi	ja - ka r
0	X	0	X	0	X

- nisa - re sa	dha - pa -	- mapa - ni pa	ga - re sa
- jun ga la	so - ya -	- jun ga la	so - ya -
0	X	0	X

WORKS CITED

Bhatkhande, V.N.
1985   *Hindustani Sangeet Paddhati, Kramik Pustak Malika,Vol 4*. Hathras, India: Sangeet Karyalaya.
1989   *Hindustani Sangeet Paddhati, Kramik Pustak Malika,Vol 2*. Hathras, India: Sangeet Karyalaya.

Kulshreshtha, J.S.
1983   *Sangeet Kishor*. Hathras, India: Sangeet Karyalaya.

CHAPTER 12.

BHAIRAV THAT

Bhairav is an interesting *that*. It is known as *Mayamalawagoula* in the *melakarta* system. South Indians consider it to be their *Shuddha-swar-saptak* (natural scale). Although Western music is modally impoverished, for some reason Hollywood has seized upon this scale to be used any time the background music requires an "oriental" feel. Therefore, in the West it has come to be known as "Arabic minor". It is characterized by a *komal re* and a *komal dha*.

Exercise 1.
Aroh   sa re ga ma pa dha ni sȧ
Avaroh sȧ ni dha pa ma ga re sa

Exercise 2.
Aroh   sa re ga ma, re ga ma pa, ga ma pa dha, ma pa dha ni, pa dha ni sȧ
Avaroh sȧ ni dha pa, ni dha pa ma, dha pa ma ga, pa ma ga re, ma ga re sa

Exercise 3.
Aroh   sa re ga, re ga ma, ga ma pa, ma pa dha, pa dha ni, dha ni sȧ
Avaroh sȧ ni dha, ni dha pa, dha pa ma, pa ma ga, ma ga re, ga re sa

Exercise 4.
Aroh   sa re ga ma ga re, sa re ga ma pa dha ni sȧ
Avaroh sȧ ni dha pa dha ni, sȧ ni dha pa ma ga re sa

Exercise 5.
Aroh   sa ga, re ma, ga pa, ma dha, pa ni, dha sȧ
Avaroh sȧ dha, ni pa, dha ma, pa ga, ma re, ga sa

Exercise 6.
Aroh   sa re, sa re, sa re ga ma pa dha ni sȧ
Avaroh sȧ ni, sȧ ni, sȧ ni dha pa ma ga re sa

Exercise 7.
Aroh   sa, sa re sa, sa re ga re sa, sa re ga ma ga re sa, sa re ga ma pa ma ga re sa, sa re ga ma pa dha pa ma ga re sa, sa re ga ma pa dha ni dha pa ma ga re sa, sa re ga ma pa dha ni sȧ ni dha pa ma ga re sa
Avaroh sȧ, sȧ ni sȧ, sȧ ni dha ni sȧ, sȧ ni dha pa dha ni sȧ, sȧ ni dha pa ma pa dha ni sȧ, sȧ ni dha pa ma ga ma pa dha ni sȧ, sȧ ni dha pa ma ga re ga ma pa dha ni sȧ, sȧ ni dha pa ma ga re sa re ga ma pa dha ni sȧ

Exercise 8.

Aroh   sa - sa <u>re</u> ga <u>re</u> sa -, <u>re</u> - <u>re</u> ga ma ga <u>re</u> -, ga - ga ma pa ma ga -, ma - ma pa <u>dha</u> pa ma -, pa
            - pa <u>dha</u> ni <u>dha</u> pa -, <u>dha</u> - <u>dha</u> ni sȧ - sȧ -

Avaroh sȧ - sȧ ni <u>dha</u> ni sȧ -, ni - ni <u>dha</u> pa <u>dha</u> ni -, <u>dha</u> - <u>dha</u> pa ma pa <u>dha</u> -, pa - pa ma ga ma pa
            -, ma - ma ga <u>re</u> ga ma -, ga - ga <u>re</u> sa - sa -

RAG BHAIRAV

Rag Bhairav is a very common *rag*. According to mythology it was the first *rag*. It is believed that it emanated directly from the face of *Mahadev (Shiva)*. It is very well known yet seldom heard in performances due to the fact that it is an evening *rag*. *"Mohe Bhul Gayi Sanveriya"* is a very well known song in this *rag*.

It has a very simple structure. It is *sampurna-sampurna* with dha as the *vadi* and re as the *samavadi*. Re and dha should have a heavy *undolan* to define its character. *Bhairav's* characteristics are:

Arohan	sa <u>re</u> ga - ma - pa <u>dha</u> - ni sȧ
Avarohana	sȧ ni <u>dha</u> - pa ma ga - <u>re</u> - sa
Jati	sampurna-sampurna
Vadi	dha
Samavadi	re
Time	morning
That	Bhairav

Rag Bhairav, Swarmalika - Jhaptal (Bhatkhande1985:40)

<u>Sthai</u>

sa <u>dha</u>	pa pa <u>dha</u>	ma pa	ma ga <u>re</u>
X	2	0	3
ga <u>re</u>	ga ma pa	ma ga	<u>re</u> <u>re</u> sa
X	2	0	3
ni sa	<u>re</u> <u>re</u> sa	<u>dha</u> <u>dha</u>	ni sa -
X	2	0	3
ga <u>re</u>	ga ma pa	ma ga	<u>re</u> <u>re</u> sa
X	2	0	3

<u>Antara</u>

pa pa	<u>dha</u> <u>dha</u> ni	sȧ -	<u>dha</u> ni sȧ
X	2	0	3
<u>dha</u> <u>dha</u>	ni sȧ <u>rė</u>	sȧ ni	<u>dha</u> <u>dha</u> pa
X	2	0	3
ma ga	ma pa <u>dha</u>	<u>rė</u> sȧ	<u>dha</u> <u>dha</u> pa
X	2	0	3
sȧ ni	<u>dha</u> <u>dha</u> pa	ma ga	<u>re</u> <u>re</u> sa
X	2	0	3
sa <u>dha</u>	pa pa <u>dha</u>	ma pa	ma ga <u>re</u>
X	2	0	3

Rag Bhairav - Tintal (Bhatkhande1985:41)

गुरु नाथ सबन के नित सुमरे   guru nath saban ke nit sumre

मन जीवित छिन भंगुर   man jivit chin bhangur

जो चाहे तू चतूर सुख सम्पद् jo chahe tu chatur suhkh sampad

मंगल नाम कमल मुख संवद् mangal nam kamal mukh samvad

जाकि कृपा सब पुरत काम jaki krupa sab purat kam

in the short span of human life
chant the name of the lord of the universe to attain salvation
whatever one desires, whether wit, happiness or material wealth
is attainable by continuous invocation of the lord's holy name
whoever is blessed by god can see his tasks to a successful completion

Sthai

			* * pa ma
			* * gu ru
			2

re - - sa	- re ni sa	ma - - -	re re ma ma
na - - tha	- sa ba n	ke - - -	ni t su ma
0	3	X	2

pa - pa dha	sȧ - sȧ sȧni	dha ni dha pa	ma re pa ma
re - ma n	ji - vi t	chi n bhan -	gu r gu ru
0	3	X	2

Antara

ma - pa -	dha - ni ni	sȧ sȧ sȧ sȧ	ni sȧ sȧ sȧ
jo - cha -	he - tu cha	tu r su kha	sam - pa d
0	3	X	2

dha - dha dha	ni - sȧ sȧ	rė rė sȧ sȧ	ni sȧ dha pa
mang - ga la	na - m ka	ma l mu kh	sam - va d
0	3	X	2

ga ma pa dha	sȧ - sȧ sȧni	dha ni dha pa	ma re pa maga
ja - ki kra	pa - sa b	pu ra t ka	- m gu ru
0	3	X	2

Rag Bhairav - Tintal (Bhatkhande 1985:42)

जागो मोहन प्यारे, jago mohan pyare

सांवरी सुरत मोरे मन भावे, sanvari surat more man bhave

सुन्दर श्याम हमारे । sundar shyam hamare

प्रातः भई उठ भानो उदय भयो । prathh bhai uth bhano uday bhayo

ग्वाल बाल सब भूपथ थाडे ॥ gval bal sab bhupath thade

तुम्हरे दरस के भुखे प्यासे । tumhare daras ke bhukhe pyase

उठ उठ नन्दकिशोर ॥ uth uth nandkishor

please wake up beloved mohan (krishna), I always cherish your pleasent face
oh our handsome shyam (krishna), wake up because it is daybreak
the cowheards have already started their daily activities
everyone is longing to see you, so please wake up, oh son of nanda

Sthai

ga ma dha dha	pa - dha ma	dha - ⌣pama⌣ pa	ma - ga -
ja - go -	mo - ha n	pya - - -	re - - -
0	3	X	2

ga ga ma ga	re - ga pa	ma ga ma ga	re - sa -
sa - va re	su - ra t	mo re ma n	bha - ve -
0	3	X	2

ni sa ga ma	pa dha ni sa	re - sa ni	dha pa ma ga
sun - da r	shya - m ha	ma - - -	- - re -
0	3	X	2

Antara

pa pa pa pa	dha dha ni ni	sa sa sa sa	re - sa -
pra - tah bha	i - u th	bha - no u	da y bha yo
0	3	X	2

dha dha dha -	ni ni sa sa	re - sa sa	ni sa dha pa
gva - la ba	- la sa b	bhu - pa th	tha - de -
0	3	X	2

ga ma pa dha	sa ni dha pa	ma ga ma ga	re - sa sa
tum ha re da	ra s ke -	bhu - ke -	pya - se -
0	3	X	2

ni sa ga ma	pa dha ni sa	re - sa ni	dha pa ma ga
u th u th	na n da ki	sho - - -	- - r -
0	3	X	2

Sthai Tans

1)	ni sa ga ma	pa dha sa -	ni dha pa ma	ga re sa -
	0	3	X	2
2)	ga ma pa dha	ni sa re sa	ni dha pa ma	ga re sa -
	0	3	X	2

Antara Tans

1)	sa ni dha pa	ma ga re sa	sa re ga ma	pa dha ni sa
	0	3	X	2
2)	dha ni sa re	sa ni dha pa	ma ga ma pa	dha ni sa -
	0	3	X	2

RAG KALINGADA

Rag Kalingada is very similar to *Bhairav*. Unlike *Bhairav,* this *rag* is sung in the last part of night. Its structure is very simple. It is a *sampurna-sampurna rag* sung in a very straight manner. Some say that pa and sa are the *vadi* and *samvadi* respectively. Unfortunately, there is no agreement on this point. Ga, dha, and ma have also been suggested. Its characteristics are:

Arohana	sa re ga ma - pa - dha ni sȧ
Avarohana	sȧ ni dha pa - ma ga re sa
Jati	sampurna-sampurna
Vadi	pa (disputed)
Samavadi	sa (disputed)
Time	last part of night
That	Bhairav

Rag Kalingada, Mira Bhajan - Kaharava (Bhajan ka Theka) (music by C. Courtney - lyrics by Mira)

सुनी हो मैं हरि-आवनकी अवाज़	suni ho main hari-avanaki avaz
-	-
महल चढ़-चढ़ जोऊँ मेरी सजनी	mahal chadh-chadh joun meri sajani
कब आवै महाराज	kab avai maharaj
-	-
दादर मोर पपइया बोलै	dadar mora papaiya bolai
कोयल मधुरे साज	koyal madhure saj
-	-
उभँग्यो इन्द चहू दिसि बरसे	ubhangyo ind chahun disi barse
दामणि छोडी लाज	damini chodi laj
-	-
धरती रूप नवा नव धरिया	dharati rup nava nav dhariya
इंद्र मिलाणझै काज	indra milanjhai kaj
-	-
मीरा के प्रभु हरि अबिनासी	mira ke prabhu hari abinasi
बेग मिलो सिरराज	beg milo sirraj

i hear my lord coming
I am eager for his arrival
the frogs, peacocks, cuckoos, and nightingales burst into song
and clouds pour water with his appearance
oh lord of mira, please come to me

<u>Sthai</u>

			* * * ni
			* * * su
			0

så ni <u>dha</u> pa	- ⌣gama ⌢- pa ⌣ pa	<u>dha</u> pa ga ma	ga - - *
ni ho main -	- hari a -	va na ki a	va - j *
X	0	X	0

<u>Antara</u>

- ⌣pa<u>dha</u> ⌢- pa ⌣ <u>dha</u>	ni ni så sa	- ⌣sårė ⌢- så ⌣ rė	ni ni så -
- maha l -	cha dh cha dh	- jou me ri	sa ja ni -
0	X	0	X

- ⌣såså ⌢- så ⌣ så	ni så pa <u>dha</u>	ni - så -	- - - -
- kab a -	ve - ma ha	ra - ja -	- - - -
0	X	0	X

- ⌣sårė ⌢- gå ⌣ rė	gå - gå -	- ⌣påga ⌢- rė ⌣ så	ni rė så -
- da da r	mo - re -	- papi ya -	bo - lai -
0	X	0	X

- ni ⌣- så ⌣ rė	så ni pa <u>dha</u>	ni så ni <u>dha</u>	pa - ma ga
- ko ya la	ma dhu re -	sa - ja su	ni ho mai -
0	X	0	X

WORKS CITED

Bhatkhande, V.N.
1985   *Hindustani Sangeet Paddhati, Kramik Pustak Malika, Vol 1.* Hathras, India: Sangeet Karyalaya.

CHAPTER 13.

BHAIRAVI THAT

This is a very ancient musical mode. In Bharata's time it was referred to as *Arshabi jati*. In the South it is known as *Hanumantodi*. It is characterized by a *komal re, komal ga, komal dha,* and *komal ni*.

Exercise 1.
Aroh   sa re ga ma pa dha ni sȧ
Avaroh sȧ ni dha pa ma ga re sa

Exercise 2.
Aroh   sa re ga ma, re ga ma pa, ga ma pa dha, ma pa dha ni, pa dha ni sȧ
Avaroh sȧ ni dha pa, ni dha pa ma, dha pa ma ga, pa ma ga re, ma ga re sa

Exercise 3.
Aroh   sa re ga, re ga ma, ga ma pa, ma pa dha, pa dha ni, dha ni sȧ,
Avaroh sȧ ni dha, ni dha pa, dha pa ma, pa ma ga, ma ga re, ga re sa,

Exercise 4.
Aroh   sa re ga ma ga re, sa re ga ma pa dha ni sȧ
Avaroh sȧ ni dha pa dha ni, sȧ ni dha pa ma ga re sa

Exercise 5.
Aroh   sa ga, re ma, ga pa, ma dha, pa ni, dha sȧ
Avaroh sȧ dha, ni pa, dha ma, pa ga, ma re, ga sa

Exercise 6.
Aroh   sa re, sa re, sa re ga ma pa dha ni sȧ
Avaroh sȧ ni, sȧ ni, sȧ ni dha pa ma ga re sa

Exercise 7.
Aroh   sa, sa re sa, sa re ga re sa, sa re ga ma ga re sa, sa re ga ma pa ma ga re sa, sa re ga ma pa
        dha pa ma ga re sa, sa re ga ma pa dha ni dha pa ma ga re sa, sa re ga ma pa dha ni sȧ ni
        dha pa ma ga re sa
Avaroh sȧ, sȧ ni sȧ, sȧ ni dha ni sȧ, sȧ ni dha pa dha ni sȧ, sȧ ni dha pa ma pa dha ni sȧ, sȧ ni dha
        pa ma ga ma pa dha ni sȧ, sȧ ni dha pa ma ga re ga ma pa dha ni sȧ, sȧ ni dha pa ma ga re
        sa re ga ma pa dha ni sȧ

Exercise 8.
Aroh   sa - sa re ga re sa -, re - re ga ma ga re -, ga - ga ma pa ma ga
        -, ma - ma pa dha pa ma -, pa - pa dha ni dha pa -, dha - dha ni sȧ - sȧ -
Avaroh sȧ - sȧ ni dha ni sȧ -, ni - ni dha pa dha ni -, dha - dha pa ma pa dha -, pa - pa ma ga ma pa
        -, ma - ma ga re ga ma -, ga - ga re sa - sa -

RAG BHAIRAVI

This *rag* is the main representative of *Bhairavi that*. It has traditionally been sung in the early morning hours. However, due to the fact that performances went all night, it has now become common to consider *Bhairavi* the *finale rag*. Today this *rag* is used at any time, provided it is the end of a concert. A few common songs in this *rag* are *"Babul Mora Naihar Chutohe Jai"*, *"Jyot Se Jyot Jagate Chalo, Prem Ki Ganga Bahate Chalo"*, and *"Laga Chunari Me Dag Chupaun Kaise"*.

There are two approaches to the performance of *Bhairavi; Shuddha Bhairavi* and *Sindhi (Sindhu) Bhairavi*. In *Shuddha Bhairavi*, only the notes of *Bhairavi that* are used. In *Sindhi Bhairavi* all of the *swar*, both *komal* and *tivra* are used. These are opposite extremes of philosophy. Contemporary practice tends to be somewhere in between, although the degree is strictly a question of individual artistic interpretation.

The structure is very simple and extremely flexible. The *vadi* is usually considered to be ma and the *samavadi* is sa. However ga, dha, and pa have also been suggested as the *vadi/samavadi*. The characteristics are:

Arohana	sa re ga ma pa dha ni sa
Avarohan	sa ni dha pa ma ga re sa
Jati	sampurna-sampurna
Vadi	ma (disputed)
Samavadi	sa (disputed
Time	early morning or end of concert (anytime)
That	Bhairavi
Pakad	ga ma pa dha - pa - ma ga re ga - re - sa sa ni dha pa ma ga re sa

Rag Bhairavi, Swarmalika - Tintal (Bhatkhande 1989:392)

Sthai

ma ga re sa	ni sa dha -	ni dha - ga	ma dha ma pa
0	3	X	2
ga ma ga re	sa ni dha -	dha ni sa ga	- ma dha -
0	3	X	2
ni sa - re	sa ni dha ma	pa ni dha pa	ma ga re sa
0	3	X	2

Antara

ni ni dha ni	dha pa ma ga	ma dha ni sa	dha ni sa -
0	3	X	2
ga ma ga re	sa ni dha ni	ga - sa -	re ni sa -
0	3	X	2
dha - ni ma	- dha ga -	ma ni dha pa	ma ga re sa
0	3	X	2

Rag Bhairavi, Lakshangit - Jhaptal (J.V.S. Rao - personal interview)

जयती जय रागीणी	jayati jay ragini
भैरवी नामिनि	bhairavi namin
भक्ति रस पुरिणि	bhakti ras purini
प्रातः गावत गुणि	pratah gavat guni
-	-
सप्त सुर रुपिणी	sapt sur rupini
सकल मृदु स्वैरिणि	sakal mrudu svairini

page 88

षडज संवादिनी   shadaj samvadini

पंचम सुवादिनी   pancham suvadini

hail rag bhairavi, which is full of devotion
this rag is best performed in the early morning hours
this rag uses all seven notes in a flattened form
shadj is the samavadi and pancham is the vadi

Sthai

pa dha	pa ga ma	pa ni	dhapa ga ma
ja ya	ti ja ya	ra -	gi ni -
X	2	0	3

pa dha	sáni dha pa	ga ma	pama re sa
bhai -	ra vi -	na -	mi ni -
X	2	0	3

ga -	ga ma ma	saga mapa	ma re sa
bha -	kti ra sa	pu -	ri ni -
X	2	0	3

gama pani	dha pa ga	pa ma	re sa -
pra -	ta ga -	va ta	gu ni -
X	2	0	3

Antara

ga ga	ma dha ni	sá ni	sagá rè sá
sa -	pta su ra	ru -	pi ni -
X	2	0	3

ni ni	ni sá sá	dhani sárè	sá dha pa
sa ka	la mru du	svai -	ri ni -
X	2	0	3

dha dha	ni sá -	sárè ga	rè sá -
sha da	ja sam -	va -	di ni -
X	2	0	3

sa -	ni dha pa	ga ma	pama re sa
pan -	cha ma su	va -	di ni -
X	2	0	3

Rag Bhairavi, Drut Kheyal - Tintal (Kulshreshth 1983:36-37)

डगर चलत छेड़े श्याम सखी री ।   dagar chalat chhede shyam sakhi ri

मैं दूँगी गारी, निपट अनारी ॥   main dungi gari nipat anari

पनियाँ भरत मोरी गागर फोरी ।   paniyan bharat mori gagar phori

नाहक बैयाँ मरोरी-झकझोरी ॥   nahak baiyan morari-jhakajhori

oh friend, i will tease shyam (krishna) as he walks along the path
i will scold him because he broke my pitcher full of water
and for no reason twisted my arm

Sthai

pa pa pa dha	pama pa ga ma	pa ni dha pa	ma ga re sa
da ga ra cha	la t che de	shya - m sa	khi - ri -
0	3	X	2

re - ga ma	ga - re sa	pa dha ni sa	pa dha pa -
main - dun -	gi ga - ri	ni pa t a	na - ri -
0	3	X	2

Antara

ga ma dha ni	sa sa re sa	ni - sa sa	reni sa dha pa
pa ni yan bha	ra t mo ri	ga - ga r	pho - ri -
0	3	X	2

pa - pa pa	pa dha ni sa	pa dha pa ma	ga re - sa
na - ha ka	bai - yan ma	ro - ri jha	ka jho - ri
0	3	X	2

Sthai Tans

1) | ni sa ga ma | pa dha ni sa | ni dha pa ma | ga re sa - |
|---|---|---|---|
| 0 | 3 | X | 2 |

2) | pa dha ni sa | ni dha pa ma | ga ma pa ma | ga re sa - |
|---|---|---|---|
| 0 | 3 | X | 2 |

3) | sa ni dha pa | ma pa ga ma | pa dha pa ma | ga re sa - |
|---|---|---|---|
| 0 | 3 | X | 2 |

4) | sa re ga ma | re ga ma pa | ga ma pa dha | ma pa dha ni |
|---|---|---|---|
| 0 | 3 | X | 2 |
| pa dha ni sa | sa ni dha pa | ni dha pa ma | ga re sa - |
| 0 | 3 | X | 2 |

Antara Tans

1) | sa ni dha pa | ma ga re sa | ni sa ga ma | pa dha ni sa |
|---|---|---|---|
| 0 | 3 | X | 2 |

2) | sa re sa ni | dha pa ma ga | re ga ma pa | dha ni sa - |
|---|---|---|---|
| 0 | 3 | X | 2 |

WORKS CITED

Bhatkhande, V.N.
1989   *Hindustani Sangeet Paddhati, Kramik Pustak Malika,Vol 2.* Hathras, India: Sangeet Karyalaya.

Kulshreshth, Jagdish Sahay
1983   *Sangeet Kishor.* Hathras, India: Sangeet Karyalaya.

CHAPTER 14.

PURVI THAT

Purvi that is one of the ten *thats* mentioned by Bhatkhande. It is known in the South as *Kamavardhini mela.* It is characterized by a *komal re, tivra ma,* and a *komal* dha.

Exercise 1.
Aroh   sa re ga ma pa dha ni sa
Avaroh sa ni dha pa ma ga re sa

Exercise 2.
Aroh   sa re ga ma, re ga ma pa, ga ma pa dha, ma pa dha ni, pa dha ni sa
Avaroh sa ni dha pa, ni dha pa ma, dha pa ma ga, pa ma ga re, ma ga re sa

Exercise 3.
Aroh   sa re ga, re ga ma, ga ma pa, ma pa dha, pa dha ni, dha ni sa
Avaroh sa ni dha, ni dha pa, dha pa ma, pa ma ga, ma ga re, ga re sa

Exercise 4.
Aroh   sa re ga ma ga re, sa re ga ma pa dha ni sa
Avaroh sa ni dha pa dha ni, sa ni dha pa ma ga re sa

Exercise 5.
Aroh   sa ga, re ma, ga pa, ma dha, pa ni, dha sa
Avaroh sa dha, ni pa, dha ma, pa ga, ma re, ga sa

Exercise 6.
Aroh   sa re, sa re, sa re ga ma pa dha ni sa
Avaroh sa ni, sa ni, sa ni dha pa ma ga re sa

Exercise 7.
Aroh   sa, sa re sa, sa re ga re sa, sa re ga ma ga re sa, sa re ga ma pa ma ga re sa, sa re ga ma pa dha pa ma ga re sa, sa re ga ma pa dha ni dha pa ma ga re sa, sa re ga ma pa dha ni sa ni dha pa ma ga re sa
Avaroh sa, sa ni sa, sa ni dha ni sa, sa ni dha pa dha ni sa, sa ni dha pa ma pa dha ni sa, sa ni dha pa ma ga ma pa dha ni sa, sa ni dha pa ma ga re ga ma pa dha ni sa, sa ni dha pa ma ga re sa re ga ma pa dha ni sa

Exercise 8.
Aroh   sa - sa re ga re sa -, re - re ga ma ga re -, ga - ga ma pa ma ga -, ma - ma pa dha pa ma -, pa - pa dha ni dha pa -, dha - dha ni sa - sa -,
Avaroh sa - sa ni dha ni sa -, ni - ni dha pa dha ni -, dha - dha pa ma pa dha -, pa - pa ma ga ma pa -, ma - ma ga re ga ma -, ga - ga re sa - sa -

RAG PURVI

Purvi is considered the fundamental *rag* for *Purvi that*. It is a sung around sunset *(sandhi-prakash)*. There are two philosophies to this *rag*. The first is to use only the *swar* of *Purvi that*. Unfortunately, this impinges upon *Puriadhanashri*. The second and more common philosophy is to use a touch of *shuddha ma*. We will only discuss the second approach.

The structure of *Purvi* is a bit complex. The inclusion of *shuddha ma* forces a somewhat convoluted approach. This rag is *sampurna-sampurna* with ga as the *vadi* and ni as the *samvadi*. It is based upon the *swarup;* ni - sa re ga - ma ga - ma ga - re ma ga - re ga re sa. Its characteristics are:

Arohana	sa - re ga - ma pa dha - ni sa
Avarohana	sa ni dha pa - ma ga - re ma ga - re ga re sa
Jati	sampurna-sampurna
Vadi	ga
Samavadi	ni
Time	sunset
That	Purvi
Pakad	ni sa re ga, ma ga, ma ga re ga, re sa

Rag Purvi, Swarmalika - Tintal (Bhatkhande 1985:44)

Sthai

sa dha ma pa	ga ma ga re	ma ga - re	ga ma pa -
0	3	X	2
pa dha ma pa	ga ma ga -	re ga - ma	ga re sa -
0	3	X	2
ni ni sa re	ga - ma ga	ma dha re ni	dha ni dha pa
0	3	X	2
pa dha ma pa	ga ma ga re	ma ga - re	ga ma pa -
0	3	X	2

Antara

ma ga ma dha	ma sa - sa	ni re ga re	sa ni dha pa
0	3	X	2
re ni dha ni	dha pa dha pa	ma ga - ma	ga re sa -
0	3	X	2
ni ni sa re	ga - ma ga	ma dha re ni	dha ni dha pa
0	3	X	2
pa dha ma pa	ga ma ga re	ma ga - re	ga ma pa -
0	3	X	2

Rag Purvi, Kheyal - Tintal (Bhatkhande 1985:46)

नाथ नाथ कर बोल रसना	nath nath kar bol rasana
-	-
काहे तु मन बकवाद करत है	kahe tu man bakawad kart he
कृष्ण कृष्ण काहि डोल रसना	krisna krishna kahi dol rasana
नाथ नाथ कर बोल रसना	nath nath kar bol rasana

chant the name of the lord with love
rebuking the heart for getting distracted from lord krishna's name
one is asked to take the lord's name cheerfully and reverentially

Sthai

pa - dha ma	- pama ga ma	ga - - ma	ga re sa -
na - th na	- th ka r	bo - - l	ra sa na -
0	3	X	2

ma dha ni ma	dha ma ga ma	ga - - ma	ga re sa -
na - th na	- th ka r	bo - - l	ra sa na -
0	3	X	2

ni - dha ni	re ni ma ma	ga - - ma	ga re sa -
na - th na	- th ka r	bo - - l	ra sa na -
0	3	X	2

sa dha dha ma	- pama ga ma	ga - - ma	ga re sa -
na - th na	- th ka r	bo - - l	ra sa na -
0	3	X	2

Antara

ma - ga ga	ma ma dha madha	sa - sa sa	sa re sa -
ka - he tu	ma n ba ka	va - d ka	ra ta hai -
0	3	X	2

ni re ga ni	re ni ma ma	ga - - ma	ga re sa -
kri - shna kri	- shna ka hi	do - - l	ra sa na -
0	3	X	2

ma - dha ni	re ni ma ma	ga - - ma	ga re sa -
na - th na	- tha ka r	bo - - l	ra sa na -
0	3	X	2

Sthai Tans

1)	ni re ga ga	ma ga re ga	re sa ni re	sa - sa -
	0	3	X	2
2)	ma dha ni dha	ma dha ma ga	re ga ma ga	ma ga re sa
	0	3	X	2

Antara Tans

1)	ni dha ni re	sa - sa -	ni dha ma dha	ni dha pa -
	0	3	X	2
2)	ni re ga ni	re ni ma ga	ma dha ni sa	ni re sa -
	0	3	X	2

WORKS CITED

Bhatkhande, V.N.
1985   *Hindustani Sangeet Paddhati, Kramik Pustak Malika*, Vol.1. Hathras, India: Sangeet Karyalaya.

CHAPTER 15.

MARWA THAT

Marwa is one of the lesser used *thats* in the *Hindustani* system. It is characterized by a *komal re* and a *tivra ma.* It is known as *Gamanashrama mela* in the South.

Exercise 1.
Aroh   sa re ga má pa dha ni sá
Avaroh   sá ni dha pa má ga re sa

Exercise 2.
Aroh   sa re ga má, re ga má pa, ga má pa dha, má pa dha ni, pa dha ni sá
Avaroh   sá ni dha pa, ni dha pa má, dha pa má ga, pa má ga re, má ga re sa

Exercise 3.
Aroh   sa re ga, re ga má, ga má pa, má pa dha, pa dha ni, dha ni sá
Avaroh   sá ni dha, ni dha pa, dha pa má, pa má ga, má ga re, ga re sa

Exercise 4.
Aroh   sa re ga má ga re, sa re ga má pa dha ni sá
Avaroh   sá ni dha pa dha ni, sá ni dha pa má ga re sa

Exercise 5.
Aroh   sa ga, re má, ga pa, má dha, pa ni, dha sá
Avaroh   sá dha, ni pa, dha má, pa ga, má re, ga sa

Exercise 6.
Aroh   sa re, sa re, sa re ga má pa dha ni sá
Avaroh   sá ni, sá ni, sá ni dha pa má ga re sa

Exercise 7.
Aroh   sa, sa re sa, sa re ga re sa, sa re ga má ga re sa, sa re ga má pa má ga re sa, sa re ga má pa dha pa má ga re sa, sa re ga má pa dha ni dha pa má ga re sa, sa re ga má pa dha ni sá ni dha pa má ga re sa
Avaroh   sá, sá ni sá, sá ni dha ni sá, sá ni dha pa dha ni sá, sá ni dha pa má pa dha ni sá, sá ni dha pa má ga má pa dha ni sá, sá ni dha pa má ga re ga má pa dha ni sá, sá ni dha pa má ga re sa re ga má pa dha ni sá

Exercise 8.
Aroh   sa - sa re ga re sa -, re - re ga má ga re -, ga - ga má pa má ga -, má - má pa dha pa má -, pa - pa dha ni dha pa -, dha - dha ni sá - sá -
Avaroh   sá - sá ni dha ni sá -, ni - ni dha pa dha ni -, dha - dha pa má pa dha -, pa - pa má ga má pa -, má - má ga re ga má -, ga - ga re sa - sa -

RAG MARWA

Marwa is considered the most fundamental *rag* in *Marwa that*. It is an evening *rag* that is quite popular. It is unusual in that there is a compromise in the tonality. The pa is totaly absent and the ma is *tivra*. This tonal imbalance creates a very distinctive character. Considering the tonal imbalance, the structure is surprisingly simple. Re is the *vadi* and dha is the *samavadi*. It is *shadav-shadav* due to the exclusion of pa. One well known song in this *rag* is *"Payalia banwari baje"*. Marwa's characteristics are:

Arohana	sa re - ga ma dha - ni dha sa
Avarohan	sa - re - ni dha - ma ga re - sa
Jati	shadav-shadav
Vadi	re
Samavadi	dha
Time	evening
That	Marwa

Swarmalika, Rag Marwa - Ektal (J.V.S. Rao - personal interview)

Sthai

dha ma	dha ma	ga re	ga ma	ga re	sa -
X	0	2	0	3	4
ni re	ni dha	ma dha	sa -	re re	sa -
X	0	2	0	3	4
ni re	ga ga	ma dha	ma dha	sa -	re sa
X	0	2	0	3	4
ni re	ni dha	ma dha	ni dha	ma ga	re sa
X	0	2	0	3	4

Antara

ga ga	ma dha	ma dha	sa -	ni re	sa -
X	0	2	0	3	4
ni ni	re re	ni re	ni dha	ma dha	ma ga
X	0	2	0	3	4
re re	ga ga	ma ma	ni dha	ma ga	re sa
X	0	2	0	3	4
ni re	ni dha	ma dha	ma ga	ma ga	re sa
X	0	2	0	3	4

Marwa, Kheyal - Tintal (Bhatkhande 1989:287)

जगत जननी जगदंबा भवानी	jagat janni jagadamba bhavani
कृपा करनि दुख हरनि सुख करनि	krupa karani dukha harini sukha karani
प्रणत जन शरनि भव जलधि तरनि	pranat jan sharini bhava jaladhi tarani
मैं पतीत सेवक चरनन को	main patit sevaka charanan ko
मुझ पर कृपा दृष्टि अब की जे	mujh par krupa drushti ab ki je
महा माय जोगनी शिवनी	maha maya jogani shivani
प्रणत जन शरनि भव जलधि तरनी	pranath jan sharani bhav jaladhi tarani

hail goddess jagadamba (durga)
she is the mother of the world
the great forgiver

remover of misery and giver of fortunes
i am your humble servant
so keep a forgiving eye on me
goddess durga
consort of lord shiva

Sthai

ni ni re ga	ga ga ma dha	sa - ni ni	ma dha ma ga
ja ga ta ja	na ni ja ga	dam - ba bha	va - - ni
0	3	X	2

ma ga - re	re sa sa sa	dha dha dha ma	dha sa sa sa
kru pa - ka	ra ni du kha	ha ra ni su	kha k ra ni
0	3	X	2

ni ni re ga	ga ga ma dha	ni ni dha ma	ga re sa sa
pra na ta ja	na sha ra ni	bha va ja la	dhi ta ra ni
0	3	X	2

Antara

ma - dha sa	- sa sa -	sa sa sa sa	sa re sa -
main - pa ti	- t se -	va ka cha ra	na n ko -
0	3	X	2

ni ni re re	ni ni re ni	- re ni dha	ma dha ma ga
mu jha pa ra	kru pa - dru	- shti a b	ki - je -
0	3	X	2

ma re - ga	- ga ma dha	ma ga - ma	ga re sa -
ma ha - ma	- ya jo -	ga ni - shi	va - ni -
0	3	X	2

ni ni re ga	ga ga ma dha	ni ni dha ma	ga re sa sa
pra na ta ja	na sha ra ni	bha va ja la	dhi ta ra ni
0	3	X	2

Sthai Tans

1)	ni re ga ma	dha ni dha ma	ga re ga ma	ga re ni sa
	0	3	X	2
2)	ga ma dha ni	re ni dha ma	ga ma dha ma	ga re sa -
	0	3	X	2
3)	ni re ga ma	re ga ma dha	ga ma dha ni	ma dha ni re
	0	3	X	2
	dha ni re ga	re ni dha ma	ga re ga ma	ga re ni sa
	0	3	X	2

Antara Tans

1)	ma dha ni sa	ni dha ma ga	ma dha ni sa	ni re sa -
	0	3	X	2
2)	ga ma dha ni	sa ni re sa	ni dha ma ga	ma dha ni sa
	0	3	X	2

RAG LALIT

Lalit is a relatively common *rag*. The basic notes are simple: sa, *komal* re, ga, both mas, dha, and ni. One well known song in this *rag* is *"Tu Hai Mera Prema Devata"*. There is some disagreement concerning dha because various usages of *shuddha* and *komal* have been proposed The absence of pa makes it *shadav-shadav* in its *jati*.

This is one of the most curious *rags* in the *Hindustani* tradition. Normally *rags* which use both *madhyams* show a clear "either / or" philosophy. One may use either the *shuddha ma* or a *tivra ma* in a passage. But, one does not place both *madhyams* together unless they are linked by a well defined *pakard*. *Lalit* is different because it considers both *madhyams* as distinct notes; therefore, it is common to see both *madhyams* side by side. It is this chromatic approach which has caused some scholars to conclude that this is a *"komal pancham"* (Jairazbhoy 1971)

The concept of a *komal pancham* is a very controversial. Present musical theory and practice clearly precludes this. However, *komal pa* was a characteristic of the old *Dhaivati jati* in the *Natya-shastra*. The conservative approach is to ignore the concept of *komal pancham*.

Accepting the concept of two *madhyams* does not automatically simplify our job of classifying *Lalit*. The equal weight of both *madhyams* creates some questions. If we give importance to *tivra madhyam*, *Lalit* falls into *Marwa that*. However, if we give importance to the *shuddha madhyam*, it falls into the *Suriyakantha mela*. Giving importance to *shuddha* ma makes a lot of sense when one considers that it is the *vadi*.

The characteristics of *Lalit* are:

Arohana	ni re ga ma - m'a ma ga - m'a dha sa
Avarohana	re ni dha - m'a dha - m'a ma - ga re - sa
Jati	shadav-shadav
Vadi	ma
Samavadi	sa
Time	midnight to mid-morning
That	Marwa

Lalit, Kheyal - Tintal (Bhatkhande 1989:464)

बलि बलि जाऊं मुख अरबिंद के	bali bali jaun mukh arbind ke
सुंदर की छबि मोरे मन बस गई	sundar ki chhabi more man bas gai
का कहूं अपने आंनद को पार	ka kahun apne anand ko par
मोर मुकुट मकारा कृत कुंडल	mor mukat makara kruta kundal
गल बैजंती सोहत माला	gal baijanti sohat mala
शंख चक्र और गदा पदमासन	shank chakra aur gada padmaasan
हर रंग ललित सरुप अपार	har rang lalit sarup apar

i look at krishna's face and i love him dearly
his beautiful image has entered my heart
i feel boundless joy
his various ornaments are so beautiful
his various symbols are infinitely beautiful

Sthai

nị re̲ ga re̲	sa - ga ma	ma - ma ma	- ma̍ ma ga
ba li ba li	ja - un mu	kha - ra bin	- da ke -
0	3	X	2

- dha ma̍ dha	sȧ - sȧ sȧ	nị re̲ ni dha	ma̍ dha sȧ sȧ
- sun da ra	ki - chha bi	mo re ma na	ba sa ga i
0	3	X	2

sȧ - sȧ sȧ	re̲ ni dha dha	ma̍ - dha ma̍	dha ma̍ - maga
kaa - ka hun	aa pa ne aa	nan - da ko	- paa - ra
0	3	X	2

Antara

- dha ma̍ dha	sȧ sȧ sȧ sȧ	sȧ - sȧ sȧ	re̲ - sȧ sȧ
- mo ra mu	ka ta ma ka	raa - kru ta	kun - da la
0	3	X	2

sȧ sȧ sȧ -	ni - dha -	ma̍ - dha ni	ma̍ dha ma̍ ma
ga la bai -	jan - ti -	so - ha ta	ma - - la
0	3	X	2

ma - ma ga	- ga ni ni	ma̍ ga - ma̍	ga re̲ sa sa
shan - kha cha	- kra o ra	ga da - pa	da ma sa ma
0	3	X	2

nị re̲ ga ga	ma̍ dha sȧ sȧ	ni - dha ma̍	dha ma̍ - maga
ha ra ran ga	la li ta sa	ru - pa a	- pa - ra
0	3	X	2

WORKS CITED

Bhatkhande, V.N.
1989   *Hindustani Sangeet Paddhati, Kramik Pustak Malika,Vol 2.* Hathras, India: Sangeet Karyalaya.

Jairazbhoy, N.A.
1971   *The Rags of North Indian Music.* Middletown CT: Wesleyan University Press.

CHAPTER 16.

TODI THAT

Todi that is characterized by *koma re, komal ga, tivra ma,* and *komal dha.* It is called *Shubhapantuvarali mela* in the South.

Exercise 1.
Aroh sa re ga m'a pa dha ni sa
Avaroh sa ni dha pa m'a ga re sa

Exercise 2.
Aroh sa re ga m'a, re ga m'a pa, ga m'a pa dha, m'a pa dha ni, pa dha ni sa
Avaroh sa ni dha pa, ni dha pa m'a, dha pa m'a ga, pa m'a ga re, m'a ga re sa

Exercise 3.
Aroh sa re ga, re ga m'a, ga m'a pa, m'a pa dha, pa dha ni, dha ni sa
Avaroh sa ni dha, ni dha pa, dha pa m'a, pa m'a ga, m'a ga re, ga re sa

Exercise 4.
Aroh sa re ga m'a ga re, sa re ga m'a pa dha ni sa
Avaroh sa ni dha pa dha ni, sa ni dha pa m'a ga re sa

Exercise 5.
Aroh sa ga, re m'a, ga pa, m'a dha, pa ni, dha sa
Avaroh sa dha, ni pa, dha m'a, pa ga, m'a re, ga sa

Exercise 6.
Aroh sa re, sa re, sa re ga m'a pa dha ni sa
Avaroh sa ni, sa ni, sa ni dha pa m'a ga re sa

Exercise 7.
Aroh sa, sa re sa, sa re ga re sa, sa re ga m'a ga re sa, sa re ga m'a pa m'a ga re sa, sa re ga m'a pa dha pa m'a ga re sa, sa re ga m'a pa dha ni dha pa m'a ga re sa, sa re ga m'a pa dha ni sa ni dha pa m'a ga re sa
Avaroh sa, sa ni sa, sa ni dha ni sa, sa ni dha pa dha ni sa, sa ni dha pa m'a pa dha ni sa, sa ni dha pa m'a ga m'a pa dha ni sa, sa ni dha pa m'a ga re ga m'a pa dha ni sa, sa ni dha pa m'a ga re sa re ga m'a pa dha ni sa

Exercise 8.
Aroh sa - sa re ga re sa -, re - re ga m'a ga re -, ga - ga m'a pa m'a ga -, m'a - m'a pa dha pa m'a -, pa - pa dha ni dha pa -, dha - dha ni sa - sa -
Avaroh sa - sa ni dha ni sa -, ni - ni dha pa dha ni -, dha - dha pa m'a pa dha -, pa - pa m'a ga m'a pa -, m'a - m'a ga re ga m'a -, ga - ga re sa - sa -

RAG MIAN-KI-TODI

Todi, also known as *Mian-ki-Todi*, is a very common morning *rag* in *Todi that*. There is disagreement as to its structure. According to some, all seven notes are used, so it is *sampurna-sampurna* in its character. However according to others pa is absent in the *aroh* so it is *shadav-sampurna*. We will show the *sampurna-sampurna* version because it is easier for a beginner. There is also disagreement as to the vadi and samavadi. Some consider the *vadi* to be dha while others consider it to be ma. The *samavadi* is ga. Its structure is:

Arohana	sa re ga ma pa dha ni sa (disputed)
Avarohana	sa ni dha pa ma ga re sa
Jati	sampurna- sampurna (disputed)
Vadi	dha (disputed)
Samavad	ga
Time	morning
That	Todi
Pakad	dha dha pa ma ga - re sa

Rag Mian-ki-Todi, Swarmalika - Tintal (Bhatkhande 1985:63)

Sthai

dha dha pa pa	ma ma pa dha	ma ga - re	ga ma pa -
0	3	X	2
ga ma pa dha	ni dha pa ma	ga ma pa ma	ga ga re sa
0	3	X	2
ni sa ga ga	ma ga ma dha	ni dha re ni	dha ni dha pa
0	3	X	2

Antara

ma ga ma dha	ni ni sa -	dha ni sa ga	re sa ni dha
0	3	X	2
ga ga re sa	re ni dha dha	ma dha ni dha	ma ga re sa
0	3	X	2
ni sa ga ga	ma ga ma dha	ni dha re ni	dha ni dha pa
0	3	X	2

Rag Mian-ki-Todi, Kheyal - Tintal (Bhatkhande 1989:438)

लँगर काँकरिय जिन मारो	langar kankariya jin maro
लँगर काँकरिय जिन मारो	langar kankariya jin maro
मोरे अँगवा लग जाये लँगर	more angva lag jaye langar
-	-
सुनपावे मोरी सास नंनदिया	sunpave mori sas nanadiya
दौरि दौरि घर आवे	dauri dauri ghar ave
लँगर काँकरिय जिन मारो	langar kankariya jin maro

krishna struck me with a pebble
krishna struck me with a pebble
i wished that he would embrace me
i hope that my mother-in-law and sister-in-laws will hear
and that the one who embraces me will come scurrying home

Sthai

- re sa sa	pa - pa pa	m'a - pa dha	m'a ga - re
- lan ga r	kan - ka ri	ya - ji na	ma - - ro
3	X	2	0

ga re sa sa	dha - pa pa	m'apa, dha dha ni	m'a ga - re
- lan ga r	kan - ka ri	ya - ji na	ma - - ro
3	X	2	0

ga re - sa	ni re ga -	m'a - pa dha	m'a - ga re
- mo - re	an ga va -	- - la g	ja - - -
3	X	2	0

ga re sa sa
ye lan ga r
3

Antara

pa pa ga -	m'a - dha dha	ni - sa ni	sa sa sa -
su na pa -	ve - mo ri	sa - sa n	na di ya -
X	2	0	3

sa re, ga re ni	- ni sa re	ni dha ni dha	- pa ga m'a
dau - ri dau	- ri gha r	a - - ve	- lan ga r
X	2	0	3

dha - dha ni	m'a - pa dha	m'a ga - re	ga re sa sa
kan - ka ri	ya - ji na	ma - - ro	- lan ga r
X	2	0	3

Sthai Tans

1) ni re ga m'a	dha ni sa ni	dha pa m'a ga	re ga re sa
X	2	0	3

2) dha ni sa ni	dha pa m'a ga	re ga m'a ga	re sa ni sa
X	2	0	3

Antara Tans

1) sa ni dha pa	m'a ga re sa	re ga m'a dha	ni sa re sa
X	2	0	3
2) ni re ga ga	re sa ni dha	m'a dha ni sa	dha ni sa -
X	2	0	3

RAG GUJARI TODI

This is a very common morning *rag* in *Todi that*. The pa is omitted so it is *shadav-shadav* character. The *vadi* is Dha, however some suggest that the *samavadi* should be ga while others say it should be re. Its *pakard* is m'a dha ni dha - m'a ga re sa. Its structure is :

Arohana	sa re ga m'a dha ni sa
Avarohana	sa ni dha m'a ga re sa
Jati	shadav-shadav
Vadi	dha
Samavad	ga (disputed)
Time	morning
That	Todi

Rag Gujari Todi, Lakshangit - Jhaptal (J.V.S. Rao Personal Interview)

पंचम वरज किये तोरी में जबहिं   pancham varaj kiye tori men jabhin

उपजे राग गुजरि षाडव बनाईये   upje rag gujari shadaj banaiye

रे ग ध कोमल करत तीव्र म   re ga dha komal karat tivra ma

नि ध ग प्रमुख रामरंग रे बहुत्व   ni dha ga pramukh ramarang re bahutv

गुनिजन विचारिचे   gunijan vichariche

pancham is absent in gujari todi
it is characterized by being shadav jati.
re, ga, and dha are komal in gujari
madhyam is tivra
the notes ni, dha and ga are important
this has astutely been documented by ramarang

Sthai

dha m'a	dha sa sa	sa sa	sa dha -
pan -	cha ma va	ra ja	ki ye -
X	2	0	3

m'a dha	ni dha m'a	re ga	re sa sa
to -	- ri -	men -	ja ba hin
X	2	0	3

sa dha	sa - sa	re ga	re sa sa
u pa	je - ra	- ga	gu ja ri
X	2	0	3

sa re	ga m'a dha	dhani sani	dham'a gare sa
sha -	da va ba	na -	i ye -
X	2	0	3

Antara

re ga	dha dha -	m'a m'a	ni dha dha
re ga	dha ko -	ma la	ka ra t
X	2	0	3

sȧ ni	ḍha m̐a ni	ḍha ga	m̐a ḍha ḍha
ti va	ra ma ni	dha ga	pra mu kha
X	2	0	3

sa re̱	ga m̐a ḍha	re̱ ga	m̐a ḍha ni
ra -	ma ran g	re -	ba hu tva
X	2	0	3

ga m̐a	ḍha ni sȧ	dhani sȧni	ḍham̐a gare̱ sa
gu ni	ja na bi	cha -	ri che -
X	2	0	3

WORKS CITED

Bhatkhande, Vishnu Narayan

1985   *Hindustani Sangeet Paddhati, Kramik Pustak Malika, Vol 1*. Hathras, India: Sangeet Karyalaya.

1989   *Hindustani Sangeet Paddhati, Kramik Pustak Malika, Vol 2*. Hathras, India: Sangeet Karyalaya.

CHAPTER 17.

CHAKRAVAKA MELA (THAT)

Chakravaka mela (that) is a very old that. It has been in use by musicians for centuries. Although Bhatkhande acknowledges the existence of this scale, he did not incorporate it into his system. *Chakravaka* is characterized by a *komal re* (minor second) and a *komal ni* (minor seventh). Here are some exercises in this *that*.

Exercise 1.
Aroh   sa re ga ma pa dha ni sá
Avaroh   sá ni dha pa ma ga re sa

Exercise 2.
Aroh   sa re ga ma, re ga ma pa, ga ma pa dha, ma pa dha ni, pa dha ni sá
Avaroh   sá ni dha pa, ni dha pa ma, dha pa ma ga, pa ma ga re, ma ga re sa

Exercise 3.
Aroh   sa re ga, re ga ma, ga ma pa, ma pa dha, pa dha ni, dha ni sá
Avaroh   sá ni dha, ni dha pa, dha pa ma, pa ma ga, ma ga re, ga re sa

Exercise 4.
Aroh   sa re ga ma ga re, sa re ga ma pa dha ni sá
Avaroh   sá ni dha pa dha ni, sá ni dha pa ma ga re sa

Exercise 5.
Aroh   sa ga, re ma, ga pa, ma dha, pa ni, dha sá
Avaroh   sá dha, ni pa, dha ma, pa ga, ma re, ga sa

Exercise 6.
Aroh   sa re, sa re, sa re ga ma pa dha ni sá
Avaroh   sá ni, sá ni, sá ni dha pa ma ga re sa

Exercise 7.
Aroh   sa, sa re sa, sa re ga re sa, sa re ga ma ga re sa, sa re ga ma pa ma ga re sa, sa re ga ma pa dha pa ma ga re sa, sa re ga ma pa dha ni dha pa ma ga re sa, sa re ga ma pa dha ni sá ni dha pa ma ga re sa
Avaroh   sá, sá ni sá, sá ni dha ni sá, sá ni dha pa dha ni sá, sá ni dha pa ma pa dha ni sá, sá ni dha pa ma ga ma pa dha ni sá, sá ni dha pa ma ga re ga ma pa dha ni sá, sá ni dha pa ma ga re sa re ga ma pa dha ni sá

Exercise 8.
Aroh   sa - sa re ga re sa -, re - re ga ma ga re -, ga - ga ma pa ma ga -, ma - ma pa dha pa ma -, pa - pa dha ni dha pa -, dha - dha ni sá - sá -
Avaroh   sá - sá ni dha ni sá -, ni - ni dha pa dha ni -, dha - dha pa ma pa dha -, pa - pa ma ga ma pa -, ma - ma ga re ga ma -, ga - ga re sa - sa -

AHIR BHAIRAV

This is an old *rag*. It is characterized by a *komal re* and a *komal ni*; therefore, it belongs to *Chakravaka mela (that)*. It is an early morning *rag* that uses ma as the *vadi* and sa as the *samvadi*. It is very well known through old film songs like *"Pucho Na Kaise"* and *"Meri Veena Tum Bin Roye Sajana"*. There are two approaches to this *rag* (Rao 1980). The first type omits ni in the *arohana*; it is therefore *shadav-sampurna*. The second type contains all of the notes; it is therefore *sampurna-sampurna*.

The *shadav-sampurna* version has the structure:

Arohana sa re ga ma pa dha sa

Avarohana   sa ni dha - pa - ma - pa ga - re sa

The *sampurna - sampurna* version is more common; its structure is:

Arohana sa re ga ma pa dha ni sa

Avarohana   sa - ni dha pa ma - ga re - ni re - sa

Other characteristics are:

Vadi	ma
Samavadi	sa
Time	early morning
That	Chakravaka (disputed)

Ahir Bhairav, Bhajan - Kaharava (Dhavan 1970:148)

दर्शन दो बनवारी ! आस लगाए आए द्वारे,   darshan do banwari as lagae ae dvare

करो कृपा असुरारी !   karo krupa asurari

पन्थ निहारत नैना हारे, कहाँ छुपे हो मोहन प्यारे,   panth niharat naina hare kahan chupe ho mohan pyare

मन-मन्दिर की ज्योति जगाओ, गोवर्धन-गिरिधारी !   man-mandir ki jyoti jagao govardhan - giridhari

भक्तन के तुम हो रखवारे, टेर सुनो ब्रजराज दुलारे,   bhaktan ke tum ho rakhaware ter suno brajaraj dulare

नैया हमरी पार लगाओ, घट-घट कुंज-बिहारी !   naiya hamari par lagao ghat-ghat kunja-bihari

संकटमोचन नाम तिहारो, जग के बिगड़े काज सँवारो,   sankatmochan nam tiharo jag ke bigade kaj samvaro

तुझ बिन अपना कोई नहीं है, नटवर कृष्ण मुरारी !   tujh bina apna koi nahin hai natvar krishna murari

lord bless me with your divine presence, for i have come to your door with great expectation
my eyes have grown tired in waiting for you, where are you hiding oh beloved mohan (krishna)
please light a candle in the temple of my heart, please listen to me, oh brijraj (krishna)
for you are known to take care of your devotees, please allow the boat of my life to sail smoothly
you are aptly named sankatmochan because you remove all problems
oh natvar krishna murari without you i have nobody

Sthai

*	nisa	- sa	re	gama	ga	- re	sa	sa - sa -			- -	resa	ni
*	dara sha	na		do	-	ba na	va - ri -				- - -	-	-
X				0				X				0	

```
-  nisa  - sa  re        gama  - ga  re sa      sa - sa -           - - - -
-  dara sha na           do   -   ba na          va - ri -          - - - -
X                        0                       X                  0

- ma  - pa  ma           re - ni re             -  sare  - ma  ga    ma - ma -
-  a   sa  la            ga - e -               -   a    e -          dva - re -
X                        0                       X                    0

-  madha  - dha  dha     dha ni sa re           sa - sa -           nire  sani  dhapa  ma
-  karo   kru   -        pa - a su              ra - ri -           -    -    -     -
X                        0                       X                   0

-  gapa  - ga  re        sa ni ni re   sa - sa -      - - sare  sare   ni
-  karo  kru  -          pa - a su     ra - ri -      - -   -    -     -  (darashan do banwari)
X                        0             X              0                X
```

Various Antaras (only the first shown)

```
*  ma  - dha  ni         sa - sa sa              - re - re           resa  nire  sa sa
*  pan  tha  ni          ha - ra ta              - nai - na          ha   -    - re
X                        0                       X                   0

- ni sa -                - - - -                 ni ni sa ni         dhani  dha  padha  pa
- a - -                  - - - -                 - a - -             -    -    -     -
X                        0                       X                   0

ma ma  - dha  ni         sa - sa sa              - re - re           resa  nire  sa sa
-  pan tha  ni           ha - ra ta              - nai - na          ha   -    - re
X                        0                       X                   0

ni  ma dha ni            sa - sa --              re  - re  re        resa  nire  sa sa
-  ka han chu            pe - ho -               -  mo ha na         pya  -    - re
X                        0                       X                   0

-  sare  - ga  re        sa sa  nidha  padha     -  nidha  - pa  ma   ma - pama - pa  -
-  mana man -            di ra  ki     -         -   jyo   ti   ja    ga -   o    -
X                        0                       X                    0

ga  gapa  - ga  re       sa ni ni re             sa - sa re          re ga ga ma
-   go   va   r          dha na gi ri            dha - ri -          - - - -
X                        0                       X                   0

pa  gapa  - ga  re       sa ni ni re             sa - sa -           - - resa  ni
-   go   va   r          dha na gi ri            dha - ri -          - - -    -
X                        0                       X                   0

-
- (darshan do
X
```

(repeat with various antaras)

WORKS CITED

Rao, B. Subba
1980   *Raganidhi - A Comparative Study of Hindustani and Karnatak Ragas* -Vol. 1. Madras, India: Music Academy.

Dhavan, Devakinandan
1970   "Pad". *Bhakti Sangit Ank.* (edited by Lakshminarayan Garg). Hathras, India: Sangeet Karyalaya.

CHAPTER 18.

HARMONIUM

The harmonium is the most popular keyboard instrument in India. Over the last 150 years it has become inextricably linked to Indian vocal music. The harmonium is a secondary instrument for the vocalist: it is never played by itself. It is used to give depth and color to the performance. The harmonium echoes the vocalist in such a way that it reinforces the melodic concepts which are being conveyed. Furthermore, when the main vocalist wishes to rest, the harmonium takes over and provides the needed respite. This is important because Indian classical performances can be very long. This alternation also keeps the performance varied and interesting.

There are several things which we will cover in this chapter. We will briefly discuss the history, technique and parts of the harmonium. This is a vocal book so it will not be practical to go into great depth about the technique. However, we shall go into greater detail concerning theoretical and conceptual aspects of the instrument, especially aspects which concern the vocal student.

HISTORY OF THE HARMONIUM - We must go back 200 years to the *tawaif* tradition to begin the story of the harmonium. The word *tawaif* means a prostitute in common parlance, but this is not entirely correct. The *tawaifs* were traditional female entertainers similar to the *geishas* of Japan. It was an honored profession and demanded the highest standards of artistry and manners. The *tawaifs* specialized in a variety of entertainment including dance and music. Much of what we consider classical music was refined by them.

Our story about the Indian harmonium now shifts to the other side of the world. It was in 1810 that Grenié developed the *orgue expressif* (Randel 1978). This instrument was based upon reeds which gave an impressive control over the musical dynamics. This degree of control was never practical with the pipe organs. The principal of the *orgue expressif* was refined and in 1848, Alexandre F. Debain of Paris patented the first real harmonium (Diagram Visual Information 1976).

The advent of the harmonium was very important for the popularization of the organ in the West. Pipe organs were the major form of organ prior to the 19th century; but they could not be manufactured inexpensively or made small enough to be practical in the home. The free-reed nature of the harmonium meant that now an organ could be made smaller and more economically. The harmonium immediately became very popular. In the last century there were all manner of harmoniums manufactured, everything from small portable versions to large free-standing ones the size of large cabinets.

We must now turn to events back in India. In 1856-1857 the British were consolidating their interests within the Indian subcontinent. The most noteworthy was the annexation of the princely state of Avadh (Oudh) and its capital city of Lucknow. It was under the Wazid Ali Shah that Lucknow had become the major center of arts and culture. His dethronement meant the loss of patronage for a large number of *tawaifs* and other artists.

British control over India created greater opportunities for Christian missionaries. Part of their activity was directed at the nonchristian population, and part was for the British military and administrative personal which were stationed there. Christian missionaries needed a small organ for their ministries. The large pipe organs common in European churches were clearly impractical, so the harmonium was a natural replacement. Thus the harmonium was introduced.

These events were having a profound effect upon Indian society. The British presence was creating a new middle class. This middle class had familiarity with the English language and a different set of world views. In many ways they were closer to the European bourgeoisie than to the courtiers of princely India. One characteristic was a Victorian system of values which greatly frowned upon the *tawaif*.

The consequences of the various political and social events spelled the death of the *tawaif* tradition. Some of the greatest patrons were removed from power and replaced with new rulers who were subject to the crown. They were either ambivalent or hostile to the entire institution. The *tawaif* gradually became less educated, less skilled, and less well mannered until the institution degenerated into simple prostitution.

This shift in social *mores* had tremendous effect on the musical genres associated with the *tawaif*. The singing of *kheyal* shifted from women to men. The *kathak* dance style acquired a stigma which survives even today. The stigma behind playing the *tabla* has only been eliminated in the past 20 years. Undoubtedly the greatest sufferer was the *sarangi*.

The *sarangi* is a bowed instrument (fig. 4.16). It is made of a single block of wood approximately 20 inches long with a bridge placed in the middle of stretched parchment. It was an instrument ideally suited to musical accompaniment. It is incredibly flexible and had a tone which was remarkably similar to a woman's voice. Unfortunately it is incredibly difficult to play. The difficulty of the instrument coupled with the stigma, are considered by many to be the reason for the demise of this instrument (Bor 1986,1987). Today there are only a few masters of the instrument left.

The demise of *sarangi* created a musical void. A style of performance had been created which required a secondary instrument. Another instrument had to be found to take the *sarangi's* place. The harmonium was a convenient replacement.

The harmonium was able to take over the position of *sarangi* due to a number of reasons. The harmonium was easy to play. It had no social stigma attached to it. Quite the contrary, it had a very respectable connotation since it was associated with the new *"Gaura Sahibs"*(i.e., the British). Although it was incapable of producing the nuances of Indian music it did have a good sustain which was a requisite for musical accompaniment. It could also be manufactured as easily as the *sarangi*. The harmonium also had a few technical advantages. The key *(shruti)* could be changed instantly. *Sarangi* on the other hand required a replacement of the main playing strings and a complete retuning of the sympathetics. The large number of strings involved made this a difficult undertaking. Another problem of the *sarangi* came from its use of animal skin. Skin became loose in high humidity and adversely effected the sound of the instrument. In contrast the harmonium was impervious to climatic changes.

These factors pushed the harmonium to large degree of acceptance. It obtained its foothold in Bengal but by the latter part of the 19th century it had spread to the other parts of the country. One of the pioneers of the instrument was Bhaiya Ganpat Rao. By the time he died in 1924, he had helped raise the art to a level where the harmonium had gained wide acceptance among classical musicians.

The harmonium's acceptance was not without reservation. The instrument is tuned to the Western scale, not the Indian. It is also incapable of producing the ornaments which are an essential part of the music. These limitations have continually raised questions about its suitability to Indian music. Even its strongest proponents could not recommend it without reservation. One example is Krishna Dhan Banerjee, the author of *"Harmonium Shiksha"* (1899) who felt that it was unsuitable for *Hindustani* music (Bor 1986,1987:110). Even in recent times the harmonium was banned from all India radio for many years (Neuman 1980:184-186).

We may summarize the rise of harmonium in just a few words. It was developed in France in the early part of the 19th century. It has come to India only within the last 150 years. It established itself by pulling an artistic *coup-d'eta* against an instrument known as *sarangi*. Although it is well established now, the harmonium's limitations have given it many detractors. Regardless of the ups and downs, it is firmly a part of Indian music today.

TYPES OF HARMONIUMS - There are two types of harmoniums in common use: the scale changing and the fixed scale. Each has certain advantages and disadvantages.

The fixed scale version has each key fixed to a particular pitch. Ideally these pitches should be international tuning (i.e., A=440 Hz). Normally one finds two to three sets of reeds. Therefore, depending upon which stops are pulled, each key may control one, two, or three reeds. The fixed scale harmonium has several advantages. Its simple construction makes it easy to produce and sell inexpensively. It is also very rugged. One disadvantage is that it requires an exceptionally advanced knowledge of scales in order to handle the various keys. Another disadvantage is that fixed-scale harmoniums are often made of substandard materials in order to keep the cost low.

The scale changer is a harmonium where each key may be assigned a different pitch. It has a keyboard which rests upon a sliding tray. This tray shifts the keys up or down with respect to the underlying reeds. Most scale changers also have a control which allows the lower octave to be automatically engaged. Scale changers have the advantage of a rich smooth sound. Their prime advantage is that they are easy to play because one only has to learn to play in a single key. However there are several disadvantages. It is ironic that the *raison d'etre* of the scale changer is also a pedagogic disadvantage. It promotes an intellectual laziness. A musician who plays only on a scale changer seldom has as well developed sense of *murchana* and scale structure. Conversely, a musician who plays only on a fixed-scale version usually has a well-developed sense of scale and key. Another disadvantage of the scale changer is that it is very expensive. Finally the greatest disadvantage is that it is extremely delicate. For anyone who buys a scale changer, expensive maintenance is going to accompany it. This is a major consideration in the United States where there is a shortage of skilled repairmen.

PARTS OF THE HARMONIUM - It is necessary for us to become acquainted with the parts of the harmonium. The harmonium is classed as a free reed aerophone in Western music and as *sushir* in the Indian system. It is based upon the passage of air around metal reeds which vibrated because of small turbulences of air. This is the same principal behind its closest relatives, the harmonica and the accordion. Most of the activity is located deep within the body of the instrument. Since these parts would only be of interest to the repairman we will confine our discussion to the externally accessible parts. Figure 18.1 illustrates these parts. We are most concerned with only three things: the keys, bellows and stops.

The keys are the most important part of the harmonium. A key is a small valve which, when pressed, allows air to pass around the reeds. Harmoniums may have any number of keys, but 35-45 is a typical number. The first thing that anyone notices is that there are black keys and white keys. These keys are in repeating patterns of 12. Each group of twelve is called a register. The start of any register may be found by identifying the two black keys, then coming down to the next white key (fig. 18.2).

There are three systems of nomenclature for the keys in India. These are shown in figure 18.2. One of the most common counts the black keys from one to five, then separately counts the white keys from one to seven. This is very common among north Indian musicians. It is shown in figure 18.2. in English but it is just as likely to be expressed in Hindi or some other north Indian language (e.g. *safed ek, kali ek,* etc.). There is another approach which is common in the South. In this method one simply numbers all of the white keys from one to seven. The black keys are designated by halves. At first the two systems appear to be the same but they are not. For example, black-three in the north Indian approach would be called 4 1/2 in the south Indian system. Finally, there is the Western nomenclature. In this method, the white keys are designated as C, D, E, F, G, A, and B. The black keys have two names each. Each black key may be thought of as either a flattened form of the higher note or a sharpened form of the lower note.

The stops are another thing that must be attended to. There are two kinds of stops on the harmonium. The first type channels the air into the various chambers. There are two to three chambers, each containing a different set of reeds. One of these stops has an unusual construction and provides a *tremolo* effect. Some stops do not channel air into any chambers at all but instead control a drone. It is common to have five drones which are typically tuned to C#, D#, F#, G# and B#. The drones are an Indian addition for they are not found in the European models.

Some times there are other controls. The most important ones are associated with scale changing harmoniums. On scale changers there is a lever located in the front of the instrument which allows the entire keyboard to be shifted up or down with respect to the underlying reeds. This is the mechanism by which the scale changer operates. There is also a small knob located on one side of the keyboard. This knob allows a series of levers to become active which automatically engage the keys of the lower octave.

The bellows are used to pump the air. This allows a certain degree of control over the

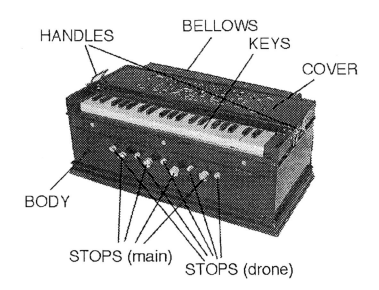

Figure 18.1. Parts of the Harmonium

dynamics of the harmonium. If one pumps hard, the sound will be come louder; if one pump less, the sound is quieter.

In summary we may say that there are really only a few external parts of the harmonium that concern us. These parts are the bellows for pumping the air, the keys for playing the music, and the stops for channeling the flow of air. Let us now look at some conceptual problems created by the harmonium.

CONCEPTUAL PROBLEMS AND THE HARMONIUM - The application of the harmonium to Indian music has received much criticism. It is unsuccessfully trying to apply Western concepts of scale to Indian music. To be blunt, it is out of tune and incapable of conveying the nuances which are the foundation of the *rag*.

Consider the nature of the Indian scale. Any musical note will have a certain frequency. The intervals of the Indian scale *(saptaswar)* are determined by simple mathematical relationships between these frequencies. This is called just-intonation. Table 18.1 shows some of the important intervals of this scale. It must be remembered that the intervals of just-intonation are derived from psychoacoustic rather than ethnic processes.

The scales on the harmonium are different. Originally European music used just-intonation, but this was abandoned after the Renaissance. It was abandoned because it was inconvenient for instrumentalists. Just-scales have intervals which are staggered and of unequal size (see fig. 18.3)(Jairazbhoy 1971), therefore any instrument tuned to this scale could play only in the key to which it was set. Instrumentalists were forced to have different instruments for each key. This might have been practical for something as small as a flute, but it was clearly impractical when dealing with large instruments such as clavichords, harpsichords or other keyboard instruments. Over the years a number of tuning schemes were experimented with, but ultimately the solution was found in a system called equal temperament. The tempered-scale works by taking the intervals of just-scales and slightly detuning them so that all of the intervals become the same. This produces the chromatic scale that we think of for Western music today. The difference between the Indian scale and the Western tempered-scale is graphically shown in figure 18.3. This is what we mean when we say that the harmonium is out of tune!

If the tempered-scale offered advantages to Western musicians wouldn't it offer the same advantages to Indian musicians? The answer is both yes and no. It is convenient to have one harmonium be able to accompany anyone in any key. Yet we must remember that a change of key within a single piece is common for Western musicians, but is never done in Indian music. From this standpoint it offers no advantage. Let us look at the concept of key a little closer.

The key is an area where there is a difference between Indian concepts and those inherent to the harmonium. The harmonium merely provides a series of absolute pitches; there are even engineering tables which show the exact frequency of each key on the keyboard. Therefore the concept of key is very important because any change in key produces drastic changes in the fingering. The entire Western concept of scale is grounded in the key. This is not the case with Indian music. The concept of key is merely a practical matter to be determined at the time of performance.

There is another problem with the harmonium; it is inflexibile. The harmonium is incapable of representing the nuances of Indian music because it is impossible to play the microtones which lay between the keys.

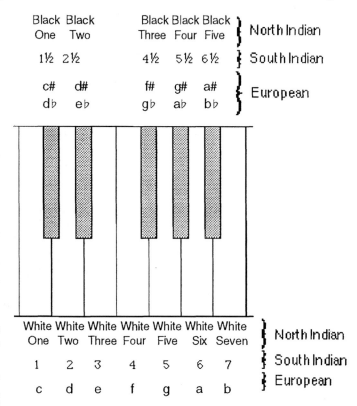

Figure 18.2. Names of the Keys.

Table 18.1. Perfect Intervals		
Western Name	Interval	Ratio of Hz
Octave	sa-sȧ	2/1
Perfect 5th	sa-pa	3/2
Perfect 4th	sa-ma	4/3
Perfect 3rd	sa-ga	5/4
Perfect Minor 3rd	sa-ga̲	6/5

Many *rags* are actually defined by the use of certain *meends* (slides), *andolan* (slow shakes) and *gamaks* (*vibrato*). If a musician acquirers their concepts from the harmonium, these very important features of Indian music will be missed. We have encountered many young vocal students who through excessive use of the harmonium, were unable to sing in anything other than "*kat*" notes (i.e., notes which have no ornamentation).

In this section we covered many undesirable concepts that can be acquired from using the harmonium. Yet there are a few advantages to using the harmonium in pedagogic and performance situations.

PROPER CONCEPTS AND THE HARMONIUM - Strength and weakness are but two sides of the same coin. It is paradoxical that harmonium's weaknesses are also its sources of strength.

The pitch of the harmonium is very stable. The reeds hold their tuning and do not require to be retuned. Unlike many other instruments you cannot play a "sour" note. Interestingly enough this is the same mechanism which makes the harmonium inflexible. Many classical vocalist prefer harmonium over *sarangi* because the harmonium does not drift up or down. One criticism leveled at the *sarangi* is that it becomes unclear when played very fast. The keys of the harmonium will play the same whether the instrument is played fast or slow. Furthermore a good harmonium (i.e., A=440Hz) is a reliable gauge for determining the absolute value for any key. This facilitates communication between the various artists.

Murchana is a musical concept which is easily taught on the harmonium. *Murchana* is illustrated in figure 18.4. If we play all of the white keys of a harmonium starting with C, we will get the notes of *Bilawal that*. However if we play all of the white keys, but begin our scale from D, we get the notes of *Kafi that*. Any seven note scale may produce six additional scales simply by shifting the tonic *(sa)*. By the same token any five note scale may produce an additional four scales. It should be noted that the scales produce by *murchana* are not necessarily valid musical scales. The last *murchana* in figure 18.4 is not valid because it uses a *komal pa*. It is up to the musician to determine the suitability of any scale produced in this manner.

The harmonium is particularly suited to teaching *murchana*. First of all, the keys are a graphic illustration of the relationship between the notes. Additionally the fact that the keyboard uses equal temperament means that after modulation there is no need to retune the scale. The entire 22 *shruti* system was merely a normalization process to correct the tuning of ancient musical instruments after the process of *murchana*.

The harmonium, if properly used can help a beginning student get an easy grasp of the position of the notes. This would at first appear to be a contradiction to what was said in the last section where we pointed out that the harmonium is inherently out of tune. It is true that the harmonium is out of tune, but it is also true that many beginners have such a poor concept of proper intonation that just to get anywhere near the correct note is a challenge. The harmonium can bring the student into the vicinity of the correct note with little effort. If used with discretion it can be a great aid for the beginner.

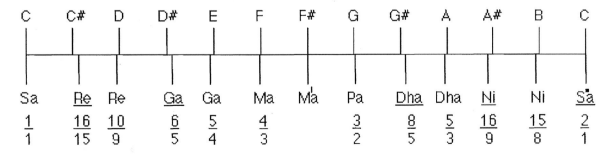

Figure. 18. 3 Western and Indian scale

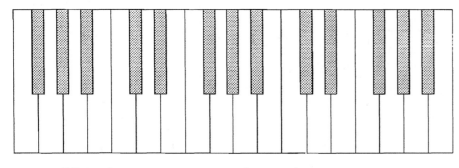

Bilawal Sa Re Ga Ma Pa Dha Ni Sa

Kafi Sa Re G̲a̲ Ma Pa Dha N̲i̲ Sa

Bhairavi Sa R̲e̲ G̲a̲ Ma Pa D̲h̲a̲ N̲i̲ Sa

Kalyan Sa Re Ga Ma' Pa Dha Ni Sa

khammaj Sa Re Ga Ma Pa Dha N̲i̲ Sa

Asavari Sa Re G̲a̲ Ma Pa D̲h̲a̲ N̲i̲ Sa

-Nonexistant- Sa R̲e̲ G̲a̲ Ma P̲a̲ D̲h̲a̲ N̲i̲ Sa

Figure. 18.4.   Murchana

We have shown that the harmonium may have an advantage in teaching certain important musical concepts. The equal-temperament and graphic representation of the relationship between the notes make the concept of *murchana* easy to grasp. It is also a good tool for teaching a particularly challenged student the position of the notes. It maintains good stability when accompanying a performer, even at high speeds. Undoubtedly the most practical strength is that it is a good reference for absolute pitch that allows various musicians to communicate in matters concerning key. We can now turn our attention to the technique of harmonium.

TECHNIQUE OF THE HARMONIUM - This book is devoted primarily to vocal music so it is not practical to go into any great detail on the technique of harmonium. However, we will try to give a few basic tips and some useful information.

The first thing is to learn a proper sitting position. Virtually any position is acceptable for the harmonium, but the standard one is shown in figure 18.5. A right-handed person will pump with the left hand and use the right hand to play the keys. A left handed person will reverse the whole thing (fig. 4.7).

Play the keys with the tips of the fingers! (see fig. 18.6) It has become customary among some players to play with the flat part of the fingers. This is exceptionally bad because it tremendously hampers the freedom and flexibility of the hands, especially the thumb. When you play with the flat part of the fingers you have interfered with the thumb's ability to reach under. This reaching under is important when one is playing a long ascending sequences of notes.

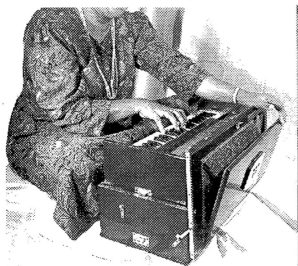

Figure 18.5.   Sitting position

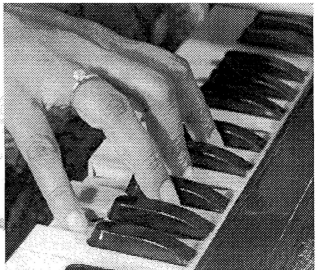

Figure 18.6.   Proper Hand Position

Try to avoid playing any black key with the thumb. Playing a black key with the thumb makes it difficult to reach over with the rest of the fingers. This is necessary when playing long descending sequences of notes.

Use the little finger. Many players develop the habit of not using their little finger. This is pointless because it is an option which one should keep open.

There is no such thing as "Sa" on the keyboard! Many Indian teachers of harmonium teach the instrument in such a way that certain keys are referred to as Sa, Re, Ga, etc. The harmonium has no Sa, Re, Ga, it has only C, D, E, etc. Any key may be assigned to Sa.

We must admit that we have only touched upon the technique of the harmonium. Space does not allow us to go into any greater depth. There are any number of books on piano which are an excellent source of information on keyboard technique. We strongly recommend a study of piano for any one wishing to go into harmonium in any depth.

HARMONIUM AND VOCAL INSTRUCTION - A proper use of the harmonium must stem from a knowledge of the strengths and weaknesses of the instrument. The first step in determining the correct use of the harmonium is to determine what ones goals are. The harmonium is very much analogous to training wheels on a bicycle. If ones goal is to move easily from place to place, then training wheels are the thing to do. However if ones goal is to learn how to ride a bicycle, then this will never happen as long as the training wheels are in place. In a similar manner if one merely wishes to sing *kirtan* in the *mandir* once a week, then the use of the harmonium is fine. However if one is wishing to become a serious vocalist, then the extensive use of the harmonium is a great impediment. Let us now go over some of the uses of the harmonium for pedagogic purposes.

We will proceed from the presumption that one is wishing to become a vocalist. Therefore we wish to use the harmonium as little as possible to avoid crippling the student. If one is desiring great proficiency in the harmonium then the approach would be different; one should use the harmonium as much as possible. With this in mind we can proceed.

One good use of the harmonium is to provide the shruti (drone) for the vocalist. It just so happens that the intervals for sa, ma, and pa in the Western tempered-scale are basically correct. Therefore one simply holds down the keys which correspond to sa and pa, (or sa and ma). This provides a very good drone. One may then sing the various exercises and songs. If the student gets totally lost and does not know where a note should be, then the appropriate key may be temporarily played. This will provide a hint of where the correct note should be. Remember, this is only a hint.

One may also practice using the harmonium to play the interludes. Indian music, especially the lighter forms, have interludes which are already composed and part of the music. The harmonium is acceptable for providing these interludes.

SUMMARY - We have covered many things about the harmonium in this chapter. We showed how it is a European instrument which became popular in India the last century. It became popular by displacing a traditional bowed instrument known as *sarangi*. Its European origins have made its application to Indian music questionable. It uses equal temperament which is different from Indian music and it is incapable of producing the microtones which are the life of the music. However, if correctly used the harmonium can be a valuable aid to the beginner. It is ideally suited towards conveying the concept behind the *murchana* and if correctly used it can aid the beginner by getting them near the correct note.

WORKS CITED

Diagram Visual Information ltd.
1976   *Musical Instruments of the World*. New York: Facts on File Publications.

Jairazbhoy, N. A.
1971   *The Rags of North Indian Music*. Middletown CT :Wesleyan University Press.

Neuman, Daniel M.
1980   *The Life of Music in North India*. Detroit: Wayne State University Press,

Randel, Don Michael
1978   *Harvard Concise Dictionary of Music*. Cambridge Mass: Belknap Press of Harvard University Press.

CHAPTER 19.

TANPURA

The *tanpura* (fig. 19.1) is a stringed instrument which is used to provide the drone. It is an indispensable part of the classical Indian performance. We will look at this instrument and familiarize our self with it. This will include the history, playing, tuning, parts of the instrument, as well as a brief discussion of the psychoacoustics of the instrument.

HISTORY OF THE TANPURA - No one knows the age of the *tanpura*. The scarcity of evidence makes it very difficult to make any firm statements concerning the development of this instrument. However we can use linguistic and archaeological evidence to make a conjecture.

Etymology is the study of the origins of words. In many cases finding where the word for an instrument comes from gives evidence as to where the instrument itself came from. But in the case of *tanpura* this yields only more unanswered questions.

According to most people, the word *tanpura* is a combination of two different words: *tan* (तान) and *pura*

(पुरा). The word *tan* implies a musical run, while *pura* means complete. This is the standard answer that most Indian musicologists will give when questioned about the etymology of the word. Unfortunately this becomes doubtful under closer examination. The doubt stems from the relationship between the terms *tanpura* and *tamboura*. For this we need to know something about the shifting of sounds.

There are general patterns which words follow when they pass from Sanskrit into contemporary north Indian languages. One very common one is a shift from the labial "*m*" to the dental or nasal form of "*n*". This is most evident in the letter अं. It is likely that the word *tanpura* is a recent corruption of the more ancient *tamboura*.

There is additional evidence to the antiquity of the term *tamboura*. The word "*tambura*", "*tambur*", or other variations are used through out the middle-East and Eastern Europe to denote a variety of folk lutes (Diagram Visual Information 1976). Forms of the word *tambura* are spread throughout a very wide geographical area while the word *tanpura* is not as common.

The word is probably not of Indo-Aryan origin. The tendency in the older Indo-Aryan languages is to look at stringed instruments in terms of the generic "*vina*". Thus we find terms like "*rudra vina*", "*saraswati vina*", etc. Occasionally the more generic term *vadhya* (instrument) is used (e.g., *gotuvadhyam*). There are of course many stringed instruments whose names are not expressed in terms of *vina* or *vadhya*, but these are usually traceable to Persian (e.g., *sitar, dilruba*), Arabic (e.g., *sarod*) or some other non-Indo-Aryan source.

We find that in recent centuries Indian languages tend not to look at stringed instruments in terms of vina. *Sarangi* is one example. However if the term tamboura developed in modern India it raises questions about whether this gives enough time for for the word to spread throughout the middle east. It is also questionable as to whether it gives enough time for the shift from the "*m*" to the "*n*".

If the etymology of the word *tanpura* does not lead us to an Indo-Aryan source then where does it come from. It could be Indo-Iranian, Semitic, or Elamo-Dravidian. I have absolutely no idea.

Etymology is interesting, but what of the various instruments themselves? If we look at the tamburs which are spread across the middle East this may shed light on the origins of the *tanpura*.

There are similarities and differences between the various *tamburs* of the middle-east and India. In almost every case *tamburs* are long-necked lutes where the

Figure. 19.1.   Tanpura

neck flows into the body of the resonator (fig. 19.2). This is in contrast to the ancient Indian tendency of having a resonator as a distinct entity from the neck. However one interesting difference between the Indian *tanpura* and the *tamburs* of the middle East is that the middle eastern versions have frets and play complete melodies. In contrast, the Indian *tanpura* has no frets and is a mere drone. Another interesting difference is that the North Indian *tanpura* is based upon a gourd. Gourds have been popular with Indian instrument makers for thousands of years.

This leads us to a discussion of the musical function of the *tanpura*. If we look at when the function of the *tanpura* developed, then this can shed some light on what timeframe the *tambur* may have developed. Documents as early as the *Natya Shastra* (circa 200 BC) clearly indicate that the music of ancient India was modal. Modal music is unclear unless there is some mechanism, like a drone, to give it a firm foundation. It is certainly possible and likely that drones based upon other classes of instruments (such as wind instruments) have been used, but the technological simplicity of the stringed instrument suggests that stringed instruments may have been common. From the *Natya Shastra* we may infer that some type of drone was in use as early as 200 BC.

The instruments of folk musicians may also shed some light on the early prototypes of the *tanpura*. Drone instruments are common in Indian folk music. There are instruments called *ektar* and *dotar* which are simply gourds which have been penetrated by sticks of bamboo (fig. 19.3). Crude pegs fashioned from bamboo or other materials are used to effect the tuning. In the North, there is a skin stretched over an opening in the gourd. This gives a sound similar to the banjo. This skin is often absent in south Indian versions. It is unlikely that these folk instruments have changed much over the last few thousand years.

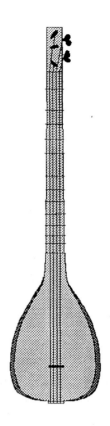

Figure 19.2. Irani Tambur

Ancient stringed musical instruments are inherently delicate and are not likely to survive the ravages of time; yet temple carvings can give us brief glimpses as to their form. Drawing inferences from temples is risky. Exposure to the elements can remove important details. Furthermore the artists who carved the reliefs were probably not musicians so may have been unaware of subtle yet musically important details of the instruments. However, musical instruments are clearly visible which may have been the ancestors of the modern *tanpura*.

One version of an ancient drone instrument is shown in figure 19.4. This photograph is a relief taken from the the Sun Temple at Konark in the Eastern state of Orissa. This temple was built by king Langula Narasimha Dev in the 13th century (Mishra 1979). In this particular relief we find a statue of a musician carrying and playing an instrument which is remarkably similar to the *dotar* shown in figure 19.3. It is unclear how many strings are on the instrument. We know that it is a drone because it is only played with one hand. One interesting point is that it is held with the resonator on top. Ancient carvings and paintings indicate that this was a common playing position. Most contemporary musicians play the *ektar* or *dotar* with the resonator at the bottom although in Pakistan and parts of northern India it is played sideways.

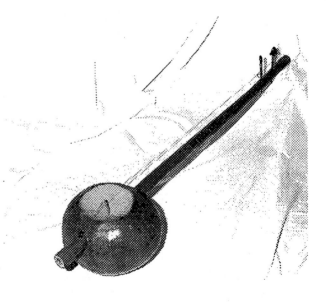

Figure 19.3. Dotar

Figure 19.4.   Ancient Stringed Instrument

A type of *dotar* is referred to in the *Ain-i-Akbari*. This publication is a veritable time capsule of day-to-day life in northern India during the 16th century. It goes into great detail about a large number of matters. (If you ever wish to know the proper way to inject oil into the nostrils of your camel, this is the place to go.) This work refers to an instrument called *adhati*. This source tells us only that it has two wires and one gourd. We do not know much about it, but it may be just another name for the *dotar* shown in figure 19.3.

The etymology, archaeology and history may not clear, but we can put the clues together to come up with a hypothesis. It appears that simple drone instruments made of bamboo and gourd were used from the earliest times in ancient India to provide a musical drone. At some time in Indian history the instrument began to merge with a non-Indo-Aryan *tambur*. The gourd was fused to a neck in the manner similar to the *tamburs* of the middle East: the term *tamboura* was also adopted. It was at this point that the *tanpura* in the modern sense was developed. This is admittedly mere conjecture; the absence of any firm evidence makes it impossible to develop a clear picture.

PARTS OF THE TANPURA - The *tanpura* is simple in its construction; even then, there are a number of parts with which we should acquaint ourselves. The major parts of the *tanpura* are shown in figure 19.5.

There are two styles of *tanpura* made in India: a north Indian and a south Indian. Both have four strings and are tuned in the same way. Yet there are differences in construction. We will confine discussion in this section to the north Indian version.

The neck is referred to as *dan* (दान), *dand* (डांड) or *dandi* (दांडी); it is hollowed out of a single piece of wood with a wooden plate glued to the front.

The strings are referred to as *tar* (तार). Most *tanpuras* have four strings, but occasionally one finds five, six, or even seven strings. The inner string is usually made of brass, bronze, or copper, and is tuned to *shadj* in in the lower register. The two middle strings are made of steel and tuned to *shadj* in the middle register. The outer string is usually made of steel, but in some cases it may be made of brass, bronze or copper. It is tuned to *pancham* or *madhyam* of the lower register. Due to the extreme variation in size and pitch it is impossible to make any statement concerning the correct gauge.

There is a compound bridge at the upper end of the *tanpura*. These two bridges are made of camel bone, wood or ivory. There is a lack of agreement as to the terminology. Many people call the uppermost bridge *tardan* (तारदान). The strings pass through holes in this piece so it is not really a bridge in the traditional (fig. 19.7). The major bridge is referred to as *ati* (अटी) or *atti* (अट्टी). Some people reverse these terms.

The main bridge is referred to as *ghodi* (घोड़ी), *gurj* (गुर्ज), *ghurch* (घुर्च) or *javari* (जवारी). This bridge is usually made of camel bone but in some cases it is made of wood (fig. 19.5). Notice that this bridge has a spherical shape. This slight contour is essential for the proper sound. When pieces of thread, called *taga* (तागा) (fig 19.5), are placed at the proper position, it will resound with the characteristic overtones which distinguish this instrument.

The faceplate is known as *tabali* (तबली). The *tabali* should be free of defects and be of a proper thickness because it is very important to the sound of the instrument. A thin *tabali* has a strong sound but a very poor sustain. Conversely a thick *tabali* has a good sustain but usually a weak sound. One hunts for that rare instrument which has a correct thickness, a good strong sound, and a good sustain.

The back part of the main resonator is called either *tomba* (तोंबा), or *tumba* (तुम्बा), or *kaddu* (कद्दू). This *tumba* forms the resonating chamber. It is usually made of a gourd and is decorated with wooden leaves.

The strings attach at the end to a block of wood called a *chota* (चोटा).

Each string has two places for tuning. The major job of tuning is performed by the tuning pegs, called *khunti* (खूंटी). The fine tuning is performed by moving the tuning beads. These beads are known as *manka* (मनका).

We briefly mentioned that there is also a south Indian version of the *tanpura*. This is functionally identical to the north Indian version but there are slight differences in construction. The nomenclature is completely different. This is to be expected since the south Indian languages are drastically different from the north Indian languages. We will not delve into that here. The construction is different in several ways. To begin with there is a hollowed out wooden bowl used instead of a gourd. Also, the front plate (*tabali*) is totally flat and does not have the distinct convex that is seen in the north Indian *tanpura*.

TUNING THE TANPURA

- The *tanpura* must be correctly tuned before it can be of any use, unfortunately this is very difficult to do. It is difficult because it requires a well developed sense of pitch (*swar gnyan*). This ability may be normal for an advanced performer but it is usually beyond that of a rank beginner.

The first step in tuning the *tanpura* is to find out what key you need. For a vocalist this involves finding ones range, then establishing the middle octave for this range. One rule of thumb is to take the lowest note that you can sing and establish that note as *mandra pancham* (low Pa).

The next step is to make sure that the strings of *tanpura* are appropriate for the desired tuning. If one buys a *tanpura* at random (which is almost always the case) there is only a slim chance that the strings will support the desired tuning. It is therefore necessary to change the strings to the necessary gauge. Unless you are in possession of a large variety of strings you will probably wish to seek the services of an experienced technician. A simple cut-and-try approach can become expensive if you have to keep going out to buy strings.

There are a number of variables that determine the type of string to use. The length, tension, gauge, and material all determine the pitch and tone of the instrument. The length is determined by the size of the instrument and is not under anyone's control. The gauge is an important factor; a thicker string will tune to a lower pitch

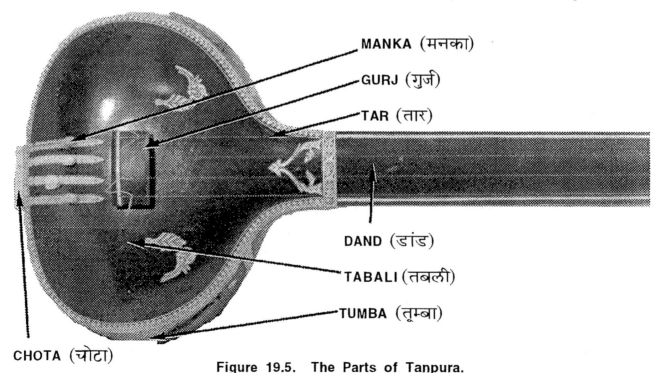

Figure 19.5. The Parts of Tanpura.

MANKA (मनका)
GURJ (गुर्ज)
TAR (तार)
DAND (डांड)
TABALI (तबली)
TUMBA (तुम्बा)
CHOTA (चोटा)

page 122

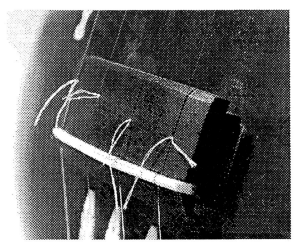 

Figure 19.6.   Tanpura Bridge and Threads **Figure 19.7.   Ati and Tardan**

while a thinner string will tune to a higher pitch.   The material is also important; brass, bronze and copper will tune lower than steel. If one is dealing with very thick strings, it is advisable to use a wrapped string rather than a solid wire; this produces a much more pleasant tone.

The actual job of tuning is performed at three places; the pegs (*khunti*), beads (*manka*), and the threads (*taga*).   The first step is to tune the tuning pegs as close to the desired note as convenient; the pegs serve as a coarse tuner.   Then one slides the beads up and down until the right pitch is obtained; this serves as a fine tuner. Finally, one slides the threads up or down until the right location is found. It is only in a small place that the full rich sound of the *tanpura* will be heard.

All of this presumes that you know what intervals you wish to tune to.   In almost every case one will tune to low Pa, Sa, Sa, low Sa; beginning with the outermost string (fig.19.5). However one must understand the nature of the *rag*. If there is no Pa AND the Ma is *shuddha*, then retune the Pa string to low Ma. This is common for *rags* such as *Chandrakauns* and *Malkauns*. There are rare cases such as *Marwa*, where there is no Pa, and the Ma

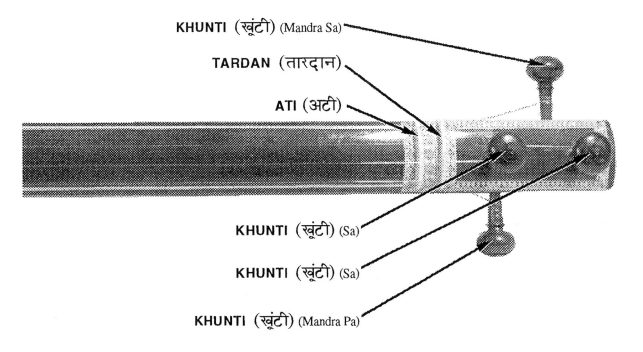

KHUNTI (खूंटी) (Mandra Sa)

TARDAN (तारदान)

ATI (अटी)

KHUNTI (खूंटी) (Sa)

KHUNTI (खूंटी) (Sa)

KHUNTI (खूंटी) (Mandra Pa)

Table 19.1. Tuning of the Tanpura.				
1st string		2nd String	3rd String	4th String
Pa - or - Ma		Sa	Sa	Sa
Low G	Low F	C	C	Low C
Low G#	Low F#	C#	C#	Low C#
Low A	Low G	D	D	Low D
Low A#	Low G#	D#	D#	Low D#
Low B	Low A	E	E	Low E
Low C	Low A#	F	F	Low F
Low C#	Low B	F#	F#	Low F#
Low D	Low C	G	G	Low G
Low D#	Low C#	G#	G#	Low G#
Low E	Low D	A	A	Low A
Low F	Low D#	A#	A#	Low A#
Low F#	Low E	B	B	Low B

is *tivra*; in these cases it is usually advisable to tune to the default low Pa, Sa, Sa, low Sa. There are no rules for such situations and sometimes it is better to tune the Pa string to Dha, Ni or some other note.

There are three methods of tuning the *tanpura*; this is the use of the keyboard or pitchpipe, use of an electronic tuner, and by ear. Let us look at these in greater detail.

A keyboard or pitchpipe are easy tools to help a novice tune the *tanpura*. It is a quirk of the tempered scale that the fourth and the fifth are basically correct. Therefore one can tune the *tanpura* by sounding the appropriate pitch and tuning the corresponding strings. The relationship between the strings and the pitches is shown in table 19.1.

Electronic tuners have also emerged as an easy-to-use tool for tuning the *tanpura*. There are many tuners on the market, but a general purpose chromatic tuner is a good choice. One point to remember when using an electronic tuner is to move the threads (*taga*) to a position where there are minimum overtones. Overtones can sometimes confuse a tuner. The strings will be tuned to the same notes that is shown in table 19.1.

Tuning by ear is another way to tune the *tanpura*. One simply tunes one of the Sa strings to the desired pitch. The other strings are then tuned in reference to the first on tuned.

There is an easy trick which can be done with the *tanpura*. In a concert it is sometimes necessary to make a quick change in the key to accommodate certain songs. One can raise the pitch of the *tanpura* a perfect fourth simply by retuning one string. If one takes the pa string and brings it down one step. This then becomes the Sa of the perfect fourth. Therefore the new tuning is Low Sa, Pa, Pa, low Pa. This is an unconventional tuning, but its effect is the same. Nobody in the audience ever realizes that there is anything unusual. This approach also has the advantage that the tabla also does not need to be retuned. If the original tuning of the *tabla* was Sa, then the

Figure 19.8. Standard Sitting Position

tabla becomes pa without having to retune at all. The net result of this trick is that a drastic change of key can be performed with an absolute minimum of retuning, only one string!

PLAYING THE TANPURA - There are three ways to hold the *tanpura*. There is a north Indian vertical position, a north Indian horizontal position, and a south Indian position. These are shown in figures 19.8-18.10.

The common vertical position is shown in Figure 19.8. This is the most common position used by north Indian vocalists. In this position the right knee helps support the instrument. This position has the advantage of allowing the artist to hear the sound very clearly. Unfortunately after a long time this position can become uncomfortable. This position also can obstruct the view of the *tabla* player, thus compromising communication on the stage.

The horizontal placement (fig.19.9) is also quite common. It has the advantage of giving the artist a clear view of the audience, and an unobstructed view of the accompanists. It also has the advantage of being very

Figure 19.9.   Alternative Sitting Position.

comfortable over long periods of time.   Unfortunately stage acoustics are such that it is sometimes difficult to hear the sound with this position. It also takes more room on stage.

Figure 19.10 shows a position which is very popular among south Indian musicians. It is also rising in popularity in the North. In this position the tanpura is resting on the right knee. This is an especially comfortable position when using small *tanpuras*. A small *tanpura* is sometimes called a "*tamburi*".

Figure 19.10.   South Indian Position.

The position of the thumb is important when playing *tanpura*. Notice that in figures 19.8-19.11, the thumb is held firmly against the edge of the neck. This forms an anchor for the hand. From this basic position every string may be accessed.

The plucking of the

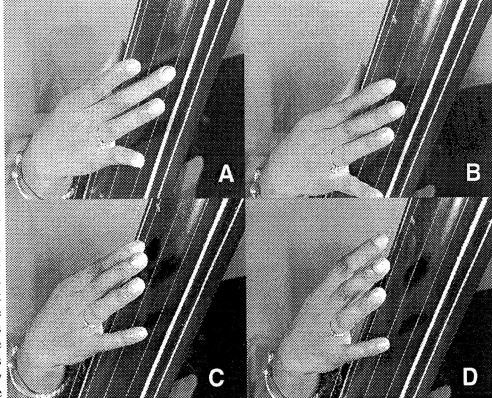

Figure 19.11.   Plucking the Tanpura.
A. Low Pa/Ma.   B. Sa.   C. Sa.   D. Low Sa.

strings is performed with the index and middle fingers only. The Pa string is plucked with the middle finger (fig. 19.11.A); the Sa string is plucked with the index finger (fig. 19.11.B): the next Sa string is also plucked with the middle finger (fig. 19.11.C); finally the low Pa string is plucked with the index finger (fig. 19.11.D). In each case it is important that the string be plucked downwards so that the string gently rolls off the side of the finger. There is a tendency for beginners to pluck the strings sideways. This is bad because it tends to pull the strings out of tune. It is also important that there be no rhythm in the plucking. Generally the procedure is: Low Pa, short pause; Sa, Sa, low Sa, long pause, repeat. The plucking should be done slowly with an easy arrhythmic quality.

Try not to look at the strings when you play the tanpura. You should let your own kinesthetic senses tell you where all of the strings are located.

This pretty much covers the playing of the tanpura. Refer to the figures to refresh yourself about the sitting position and technique of the instrument.

MUSICAL AND PSYCHOACOUSTIC FUNCTION

The function of the drone may not be clear to a beginning student of Indian music. Therefore it is proper that we devote some time to the musical and psychoacoustic function of the drone. The characteristics of the *tanpura* are especially relevant here.

The drone is very important to Indian music. The modal character of the music is very complex. We saw in the last chapter that through a process of *murchana*, a number of scales are indistinguishable without a clear drone to define the tonic. It is for this reason that many melodic instruments have a drone built into them. The *sitar* has a group of strings known as *chikari* which continuously sound the drone. The harmonium has a series of stops which when pulled sound the drone. The *saraswati vina* has a series of strings, known as *thalam*, which give the drone. However, the human vocal chords are not set up to sing and sound a drone at the same time. Therefore the classical vocalist must rely on an external instrument such as the *tanpura*.

Yet how does a vocalist rely on the *tanpura*? Musicians have always said that all of the notes of Indian music may be heard in the sound of the *tanpura*. At first, one would tend to dismiss this statement as mere fancy because only two notes are used in the tuning. We will see that through some rather complex psychoacoustics the above statement is correct[1].

Let us begin our discussion with a review of some basics of sound. Any musical sound consists of a repeating pattern of rarefactions and compressions of air. If these patterns come 100 times in a second then it is said to have a frequency of 100 Hertz. Hertz is a unit which equals one cycle per second, and is usually abbreviated as Hz. These rarefactions and compressions will be perceived as having a musical pitch. If the frequency increases to 150 Hertz then the pitch will be higher. Conversely if the frequency of drops to 90 Hz, then the pitch will be lower. Therefore pitch may be see as being tied to the frequency.

One of the foundations of music is the concept of consonance. If somebody plucks a *tanpura* string which is tuned to Sa and a vocalist sings Sa, one can immediately feel a sense of peace and repose; this is called consonance. Conversely if the singer is not good and the two sounds do not match, one will immediately feel a strong grating sensation; this is called dissonance. From a psychoacoustic standpoint consonance and dissonance are nothing more than the nature of the mathematical relationships between the two notes. Therefore if both singer and *tanpura* are both producing a sound at 100Hz the ratio is 1/1. This is considered the simplest mathematical ratio and corresponds to the greatest consonance. Let us say that the singer is singing at 105Hz then the ratio is 21/20. This is a more complex interval and corresponds to a great degree of dissonance.

We have confined our discussion so far to simple pure tones, but in the real world musical instruments are a mixture of different frequencies. There is a general tendency for there to be a base frequency, referred to as the fundamental, and overtones. These overtones will tend to be in some integral relationship to the fundamental. Therefore if our fundamental is 100 Hz, then the overtones will tend to be at 200Hz, 300Hz, 400Hz, 500Hz, etc. A sound which has this characteristic is referred to as a harmonic spectrum. The musical pitch generally corresponds to the frequency of the fundamental.

Musical consonance is not just felt at the level of the fundamental (i.e., the lowest frequency) but also at

---

[1] Psychoacoustics is a very complicated subject. We are making a desperate, and perhaps hopeless effort to tackle this difficult subject. This is only a small section of one chapter in a book devoted to Indian vocal. Out of necessity we must avoid large bodies of study and utilize gross oversimplifications. This is done in the effort of making the layman appreciate some of the marvelous mechanisms which are at work in the tanpura. We must apologize for the very cursory treatment which is dealt to the subject here and recommend that the reader go to any of a number of fine works on the subject, some of which are cited at the end of this chapter.

the overtones. Therefore tremendous consonance will be felt if one is singing at 300Hz and the *tanpura* is set at 100 Hz. It is consonant for two reasons. One is that there is a 1/1 relationship between the vocalist (300Hz) and the third harmonic (100, 200, **300**, 400, etc.). Another reason for this consonance is that the ratio of the fundamentals is 3/1 which is also considered to be a very simple mathematical ratio.

Overtones imply certain other musical notes. For instance the series of harmonics 100Hz, 200Hz, 300Hz, 400Hz, 500Hz, implies the musical notes Sa, Sa, Pa, Sa Ma. This is all from only a single string! Furthermore we must remember that there may be many more than 5 harmonics. Even a single string of the *tanpura* seems capable of defining virtually all of the notes of Indian music (Carterette, et al 1989). When the overtones of the strings of the *tanpura* interact, this further strengthens the ability of the *tanpura* to define the notes of Indian music (Jairazbhoy 1971).

The bottom line is that the *tanpura*, although relatively simple in its construction, performs a very important psychoacoustic function. The air itself is actually calibrated into the various intervals of Indian music.

CONCLUSION

We have seen that the *tanpura* is inextricably linked to vocal music in India. We have no idea as to when or where the *tanpura* developed. It has no inventor. It has no master musicians. It is one of the humblest of musical instruments, yet it works by some of the most complex psychoacoustic mechanisms. This instrument forms the musical foundation upon which the performance is based. As any stupendous edifice can only be as strong as its foundation, so too the strength and beauty of Indian vocal is based upon the *tanpura*.

WORKS CITED

Allami, Abul Fazl
1989   *Ain-i-Akbari* Vol. II (translated by H.S. Jarrett) New Delhi: New Taj Office

Carterette, Edward C, K.Vaughn, and N.Jairazbhoy
1989   Perceptual, Acoustical, and Musical Aspects of the Tambura Drone. *Music Perception*. Berkeley: University of California Press. Winter 1989, Vol.7, No 2, 75-108.

Diagram Visual Information ltd.
1976   *Musical Instruments of the World*. New York: Facts on File Publications.

Mallory, J.P.
1989   *In Search of the Indo-Europeans: Language, Archeology and Myth*. London: Thames & Hudson Ltd.

Mishra, Balaram
1979   *Konark*. Bhubaneshwar: Bibarani Prakashani.

Jairazbhoy, N. A.
1971   *The Rags of North Indian Music*. Middletown CT: Wesleyan University Press.

Randel, Don Michael
1978   *Harvard Concise Dictionary of Music*. Cambridge Mass: Belknap Press of Harvard University Press.

CHAPTER 20.

CONCLUSION

There is a curious contrast between a book and a musical performance. You are presently holding in your hand a book, a physical thing which has words frozen in time. If you come back to this page in another ten years it will still have the same words on it; it transcends time. This is in stark contrast to the musical performance. The performance exists only in the moment. The moment you hear it, it is gone; it is history; it is finished. It is strange that one can read or write a book on music when the two endeavors occupy such totally different domains.

I am reminded of the great German intellectual, Heinrich Heine (1797-1856). Although we remember him as a writer and poet, his words have been taken as lyrics by such great composers as Schumann and Schubert. As we put down this book let us remember his words when he said:

"Where words leave off music begins."

APPENDIX 1
SOURCES OF TANPURA AND HARMONIUM

Ali Akbar College of Music
215 West End
San Rafael, CA 94901-2645
(415) 454 0581 (tel)
(415) 454 9396 (fax)
(800) 74 TABLA
aacm@ix.netcom.com
http://pomo.nbn.com/home/aacm/

Bazaar of India Imports
1810 University Ave.
Berkeley, CA 94703
(510) 548 4110 (tel)
(800) 261 7662 (tel)
(510) 548 1115 (fax)

Encinitas Imports
Box 419T
Encinitas, CA 92024
(619) 436 9589

Gulmohar Imports
10195 S.W. Beaverton
Hillsdale Highway
Beaverton, OR 97005
(503) 629 5501 (tel)
(800) 603 6538 (tel)
(503) 690 6831 (fax)
buyindia@aol.com

Khazana
1032 Nicollet Mall
Minneapolis, MN 55403
(612) 339-4565 (tel)
(800) 576-4565 (tel)
(612) 854-1770 (fax)
khazana@winternet.com
http://www.winternet.com/~khazan
a/

Lark in the Morning
Box 1176
Mendocino, CA 95460
(707) 964 3762
(707) 964 5569 (orders)
(707) 964 1979 (fax)
larkinam@larkinam.com
http://www.larkinam.com

Lark in the Morning
1411 First Ave.
Seattle, WA 98101
(206) 623 3440 (tel)

Little Market
3062 North Andrews Ave.
Ft. Lauderdale, FL 33311
(954) 561 8606 (tel)
(954) 561 2183 (fax)

Mid-East Imports Mfg. Inc.
7694 Progress Circle
West Melbourne, FL 32904
(407) 724 1477
(407) 952 1080 (fax)
stevek@mid-east.com
http://www.iu.net/mid-east

Roma Enterprises
3163 Brinton Trail
Cincinnati, OH 45241
(513) 769 5363 (tel)
(513) 769 3163 (tel)

Santos
1188 Montague Ave
San Leandro, CA 94577
(510) 357 0277 (tel)
(510) 357 1462 (tel)
(510) 357 4241 (tel)
(510) 357 1637 (fax)

Sheru Music
attn. Rudy Rampersaud
861 N.E. 125 Street
N. Miami, FL 33161
(305) 895 8861 phone

Simla House
Box 1229
Woodstock, NY 12498
(914) 679 4490

Taj Mahal Imports
1612 Woodcliff Dr.
Atlanta, GA 30329
(404) 321 5940
(404) 325 8896 (fax)

Taj Mahal Imports of Dallas
26-C Richardson Heights Village
Richardson, TX 75080
(214) 644 1329

Voyager's Dream
1306 W. Hickory
Denton, TX 76201
(817) 381 2769

APPENDIXES

APPENDIX 2

COMMON THATS IN THE KEY OF SAFED EK (C)

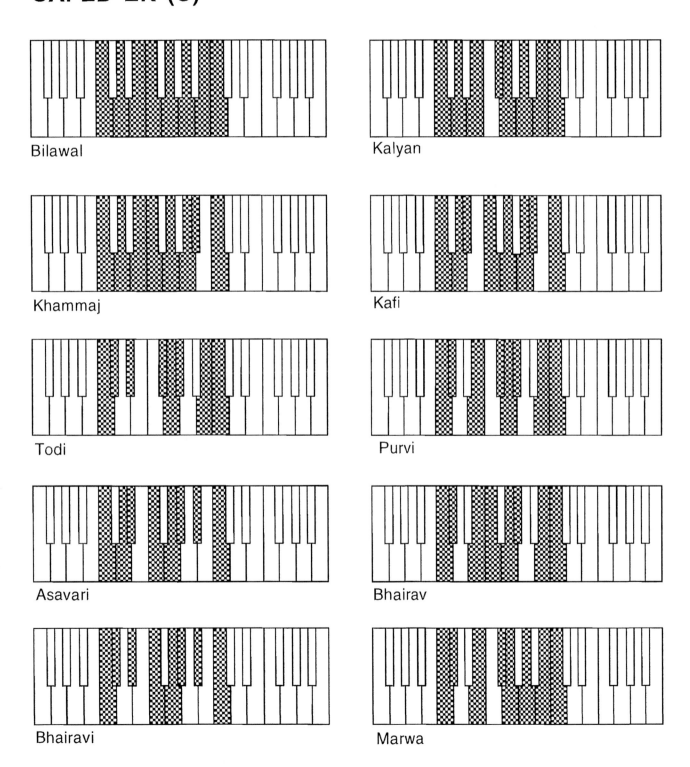

Bilawal

Kalyan

Khammaj

Kafi

Todi

Purvi

Asavari

Bhairav

Bhairavi

Marwa

COMMON THATS IN THE KEY OF
KALI EK (C#)

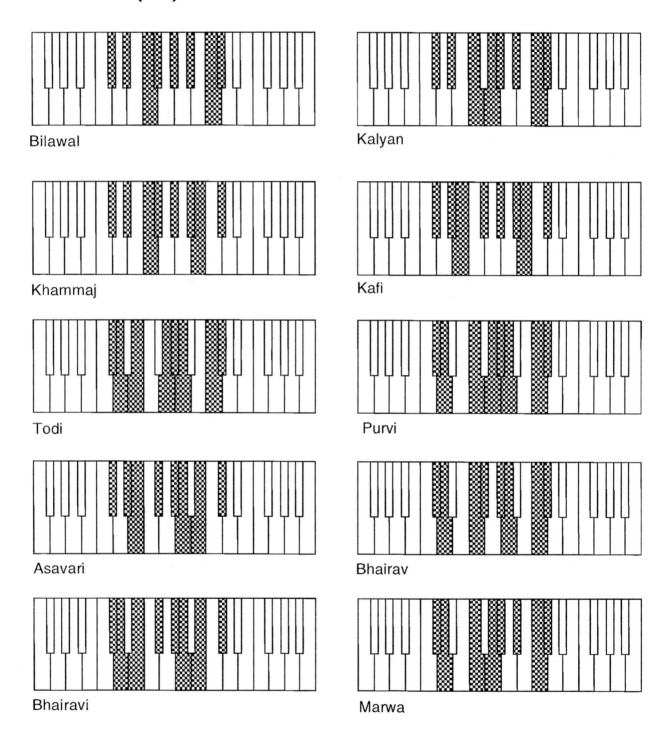

Bilawal

Kalyan

Khammaj

Kafi

Todi

Purvi

Asavari

Bhairav

Bhairavi

Marwa

COMMON THATS IN THE KEY OF SAFED DO (D)

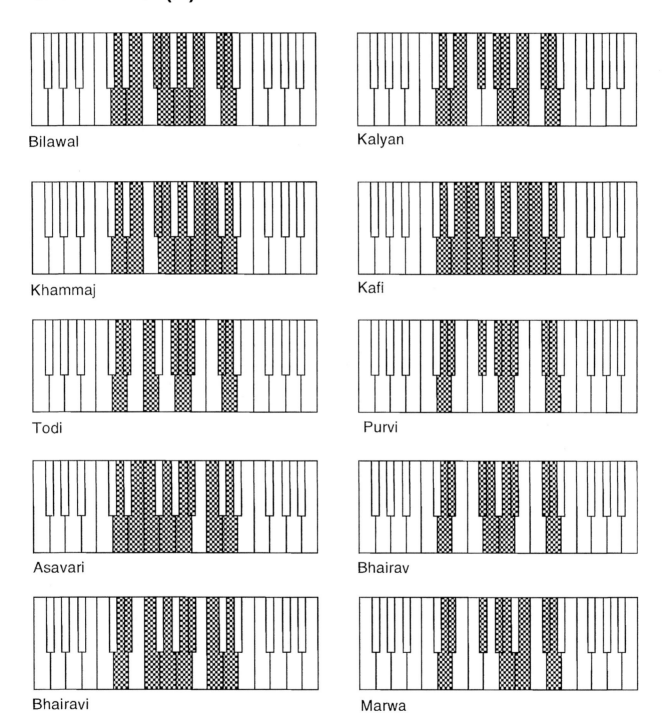

Bilawal

Kalyan

Khammaj

Kafi

Todi

Purvi

Asavari

Bhairav

Bhairavi

Marwa

COMMON THATS IN THE KEY OF
KALI DO (D#)

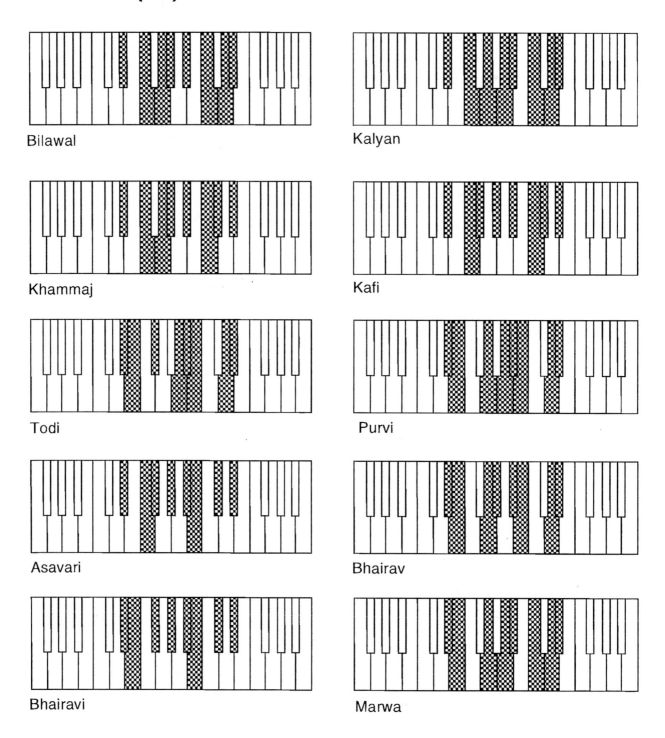

Bilawal

Kalyan

Khammaj

Kafi

Todi

Purvi

Asavari

Bhairav

Bhairavi

Marwa

COMMON THATS IN THE KEY OF SAFED TEEN (E)

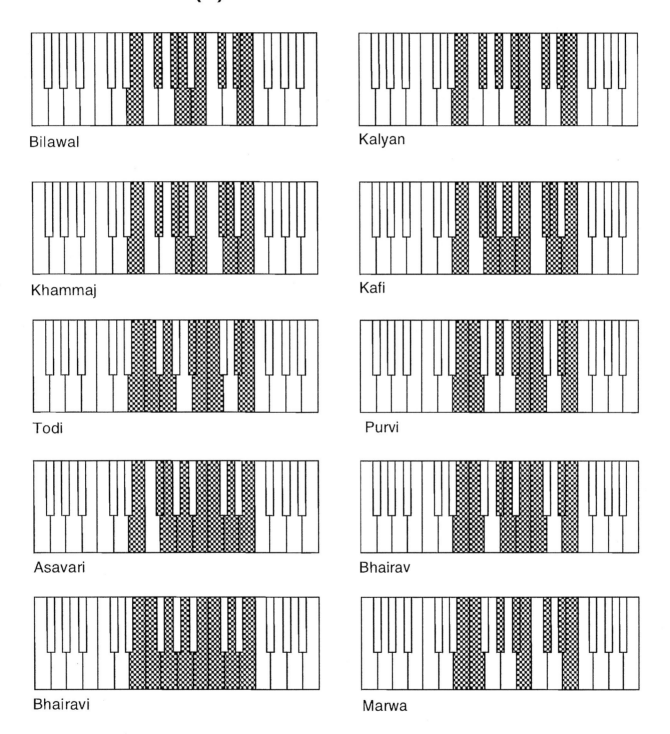

Bilawal

Kalyan

Khammaj

Kafi

Todi

Purvi

Asavari

Bhairav

Bhairavi

Marwa

COMMON THATS IN THE KEY OF SAFED CHAR (F)

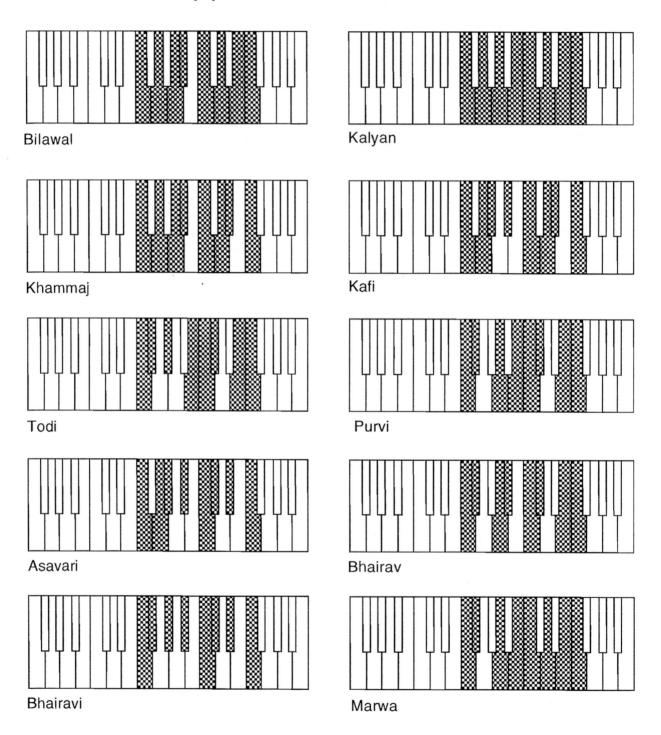

Bilawal

Kalyan

Khammaj

Kafi

Todi

Purvi

Asavari

Bhairav

Bhairavi

Marwa

COMMON THATS IN THE KEY OF
KALI TEEN (F#)

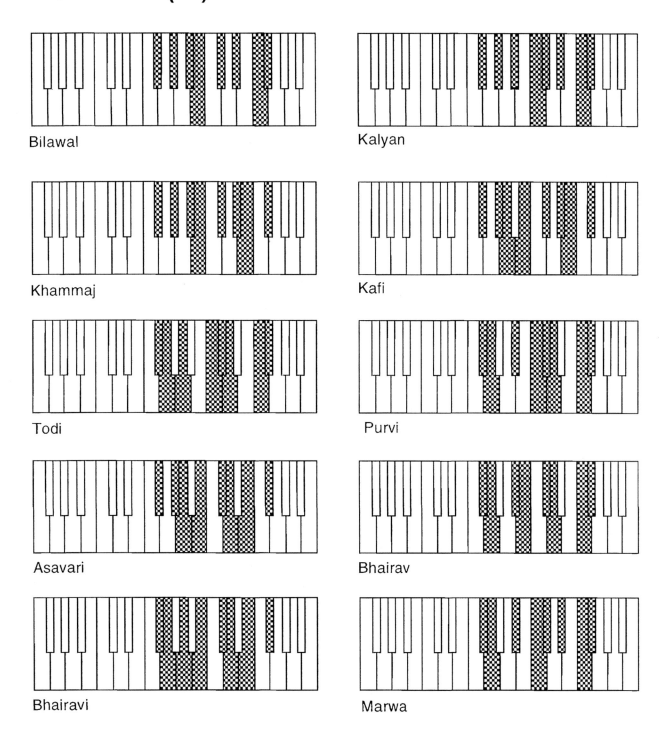

Bilawal

Kalyan

Khammaj

Kafi

Todi

Purvi

Asavari

Bhairav

Bhairavi

Marwa

COMMON THATS IN THE KEY OF SAFED PANCH (G)

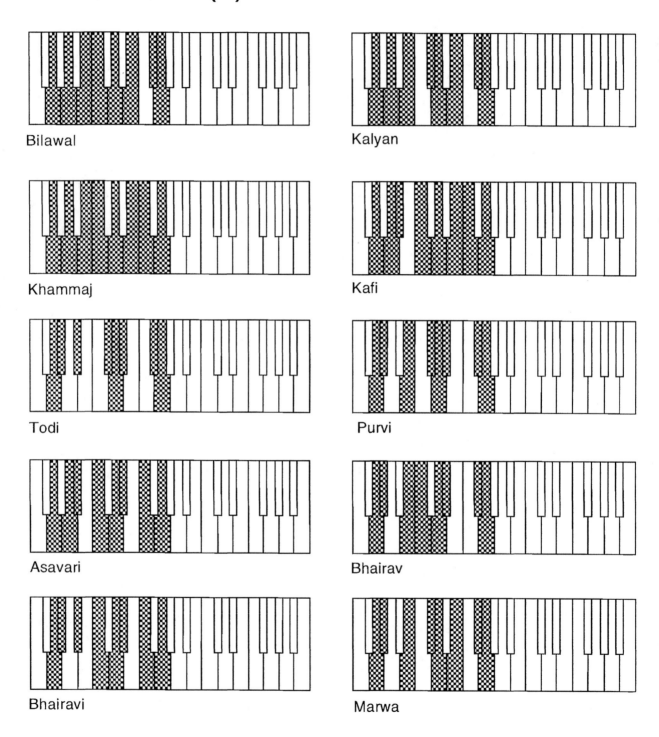

Bilawal

Kalyan

Khammaj

Kafi

Todi

Purvi

Asavari

Bhairav

Bhairavi

Marwa

COMMON THATS IN THE KEY OF KALI CHAR (G#)

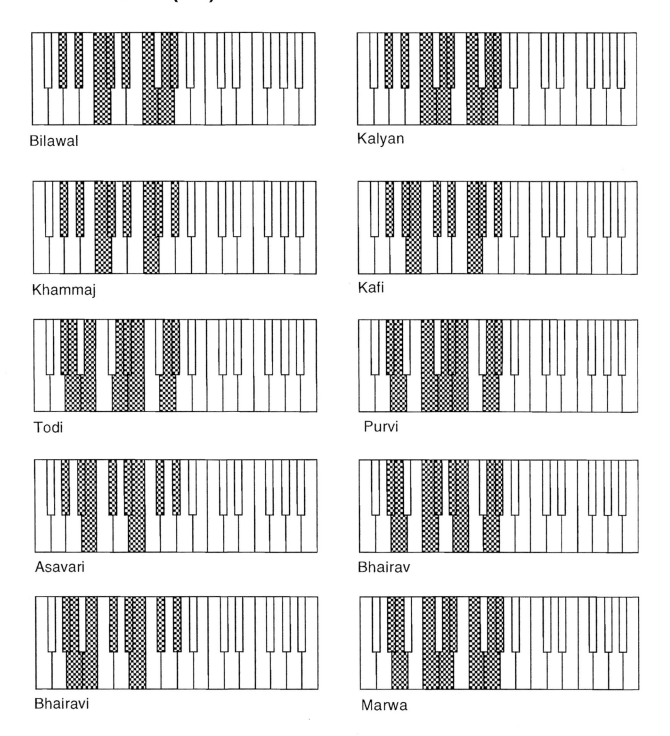

Bilawal

Kalyan

Khammaj

Kafi

Todi

Purvi

Asavari

Bhairav

Bhairavi

Marwa

COMMON THATS IN THE KEY OF SAFED CHE (A)

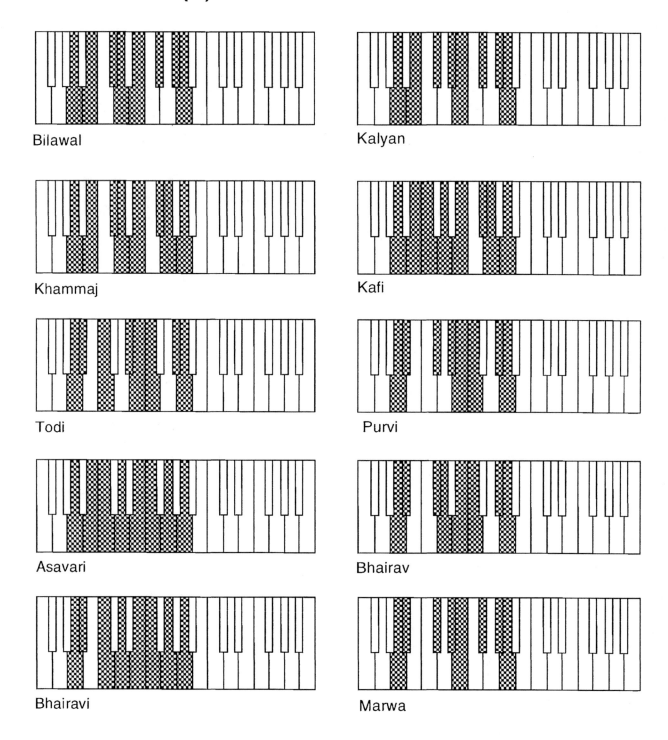

Bilawal

Kalyan

Khammaj

Kafi

Todi

Purvi

Asavari

Bhairav

Bhairavi

Marwa

COMMON THATS IN THE KEY OF KALI PANCH (A#)

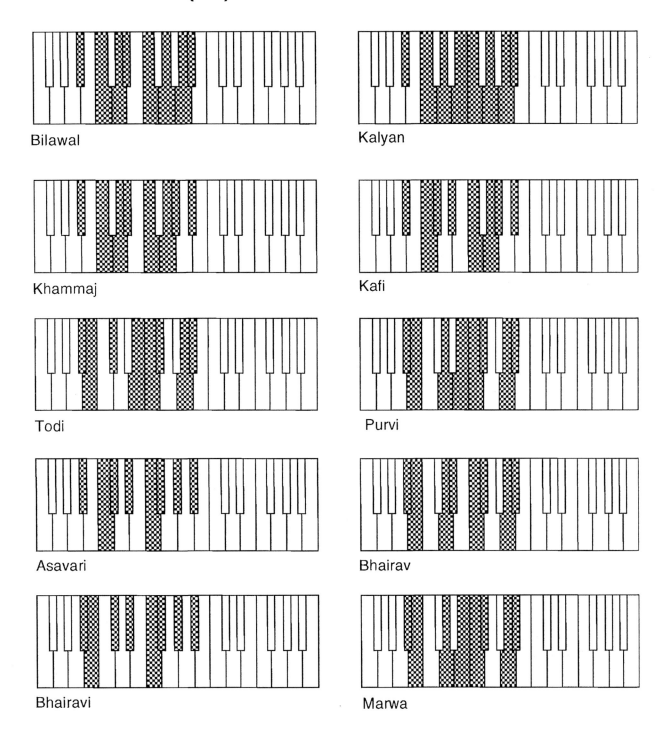

Bilawal

Kalyan

Khammaj

Kafi

Todi

Purvi

Asavari

Bhairav

Bhairavi

Marwa

COMMON THATS IN THE KEY OF
SAFED SATH (B)

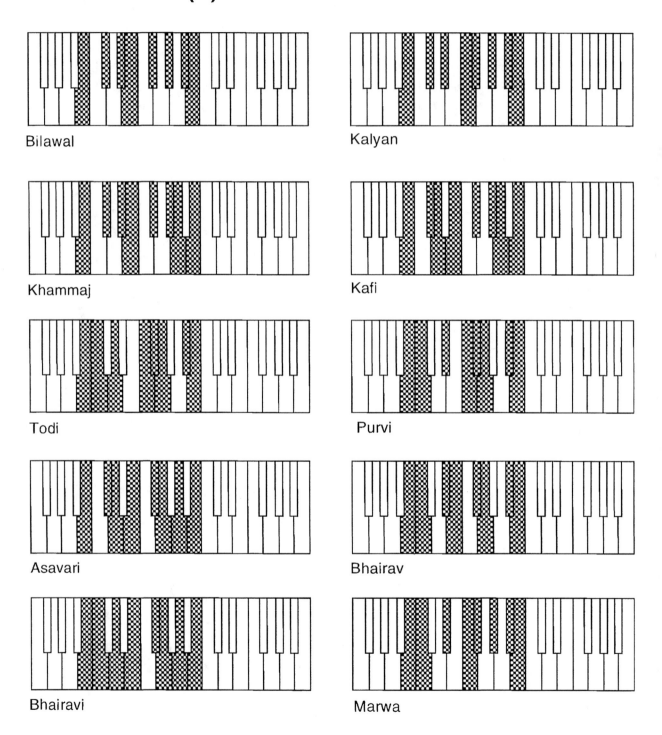

Bilawal

Kalyan

Khammaj

Kafi

Todi

Purvi

Asavari

Bhairav

Bhairavi

Marwa

GLOSSARY

aakar आकार - To sing without words and only use the vowel "A" (as in father).

abhang अभंग - Marathi devotional song.

abhay अभय - fearless

abhog अभोग - Derived from the word *Bhuj* which means to fulfill. The tertiary theme of a *dhrupad*.

abhyas अभ्यास - Practice. See *riyaz*.

achala अचल - Immovable notes (i.e., sa and pa).

adachartal आड़ाचारताल - See *adachautal*.

adachautal आड़ाचौताल - A common 14 beat *tal*.

addha tal अद्धा ताल - A *tal* of 16 beats.

adha अध - Half.

adi lay आड़ी लया - In a four unit time, one plays six units per beat. (i.e. 1 $^1/_2$ time, or *tisra jati*).

adi rag आदि राग - The primordial *rag*, said to be *Bhairav* (*mayamalavagaula*) in some mythology.

adi tal आदिताल - A south Indian *tal* of 8 beats, similar to both *tintal* and *kaherava*.

Agra आगरा - 1) A city south of Delhi. 2) A vocal *gharana* of the same place.

ahat nad आहत नाद् - Lit. "struck sound". The physical vibrations which compose sound.

ahir bhairav अहीर भैरव - A common *rag*.

ajpal अचपल - Constant, immovable, fixed, firm.

Ajrada अजराड़ा - A village near Meerat.

ajrada baj अजराड़ा बाज - A style of *tabla* playing originating from Ajrada.

akshar अक्षर - A character or letter of the alphabet. A syllable.

alakh अलख - A lock of hair, a curl.

alankar अलन्कार - An ornamental phrase.

alap आलाप - A rhythmless exposition of the *rag*.

alapini karuna आलापिनी करुणा - The 14th *shruti* (microtone).

alhaiya bilaval अल्हैयाबिलावल - A common *rag*, similar to the Western natural scale.

amad आमद् - A *kathak* piece used to make an entry onto the stage. A *tabla* or *pakhawaj* composition used for such an entry.

anagat (grah) अनागत - The process of ending a composition before the *sam*.

anagat tihai अनागत तिहाई - A *tihai* which ends before the *sam*.

anahat nad अनाहत नाद् - Lit. "unstruck sound". A metaphysical resonance which is behind the entire universe.

anand bhairav आनंद भैरव - A *rag*.

anavarat अनवरत - Always, continuously.

andolan आंदोलन - A slow vibrato.

ang अंग - (lit. limb, or section) A measure, or *vibhag*.

angushtana अंगुश्ताना -*Tabla tukadas* which concentrate on the fingers.

ansh अंश - The starting note of a *murchana*.

antara अन्तरा - The secondary theme of a classical song.

anudrut अणुद्रुत - See *ati drut*.

anupam अनुपम - Unequaled, incomparable, most excellent

anuvadi अनुवादी - The notes of the *rag* other than the *vadi* and *samavadi*.

apne अपने - Ones own.

ardhya tal अर्ध्य ताल - An obscure *tal* of 27 beats.

arjun tal अर्जुन ताल - An obscure *pakhawaj tal* of 20 beats.

aroh आरोह - The ascending structure of the *rag*.

arohana आरोहन - see *aroh*.

asavari आसावरी - 1) A *that*. 2) A common *rag*.

ashta अष्ट - Eight.

ashta-jam अष्ट जाम - 24 hours a day.

ashtapadi अष्टपदी - A lyrical form made famous by Jaidev in his *Gita Govinda*. It acquired its meaning because of the 8 line format.

ashuddh अशुद्ध - Incorrectly performed music.

ati drut अति द्रुत - ultra fast tempo.

ati tar saptak अति तार सप्तक - Two octaves above the middle register.

ati vilambit अति विलंबित - Ultra slow tempo.

atit (grah) अतति - The process of ending a *tihai* after the *sam*.

avanaddh अवनद्ध - A membranous percussive instrument (e.g., *tabla, dholak, mridang*, etc.)

avaroh अवरोह - 1) The descending structure of a *rag*. 2) The second half of a *lom-vilom gat*.

avarohana अवरोहन - See *arohana*.

avartan आवर्तन - A cycle.

ave आवे - Come.

avrati आवृत्ति - See *avartan*.

bada kheyal बड़ा खयाल   - The slow portion of the *kheyal*.

badal बदल - Change.

bageshri बागेश्री - A common *rag*.

bahar बहार - A common *rag*.

Baiju Bavra बैजु बावरा - A famous musician of the 16th century.

baj बाज - A style of *tabla* playing, originally from Delhi.

baj ka tar बाज का तार - Main playing string on *sarod, sitar,* or *sarangi*.

bakhan बखान - Description, praise.

bala बला - Pressure, stress, strength.

banarasi baj बनारसी बाज - A style of *tabla* playing originating in Benares, often considers synonymous to *purbi baj*.

band बन्द - Lit "closed". Non-resonant strokes such as te, ka, kat, tak, etc.

bandhe बंदे - A prisoner.

bandish बंदिश - A composition or fixed musical piece.

banmali बनमाली - A forester.

bansuri बंसुरी - A bamboo flute.

banti बाँटी - Another name for *kaida*.

banya बायाँ - The large metal left hand drum of the *tabla* pair.

barva बरवा - A rare *rag*.

basant बसंत - A common *rag*, generally associated with spring.

basi बसी - dwell, reside.

bat बात - 1) Words, talk. 2) A matter for discussion, an affair, an event, an incident.

baurane बौरान - Those who are confused, mad, or insane.

bedumdar tihai बेदमदार तिहाई - A *tihai* in which each section is not separated by a pause.

beenkar बीनकार - *Gharana* that has tradition of playing the *bin (vina)*.

beguni बेगुणी - Unskillful, unvirtuous, untrained.

Benares बनारस - 1) A city in north India. 2) A *tabla gharana* from that city (see *Banarasi baj*).

besur बेसुर - Out of tune.

betal बेताल - Out of rhythm.

bhagavan भगवान - God, Supreme being, Vishnu, prosperous, glorious.

bhai भई - Form of address indicating familiarity.

bhairav भैरव - 1) A *that*. 2) A common morning *rag* associated with Siva.

bhairavi भैरवी - 1) A *that*. 2) A common *rag* generally played at the end of performances.

bhaj भज - Pray.

bhajan भजन - A Hindu religious song, prayer, worship.

bhala भला - Good, well, trim, gentle, noble, excellent.

bhalo भलो - Good, well, gentile.

bharan भरन - A filler. Something used to fill up a certain number of beats.

bhari भरी - Lit. "full", clapped, see *tali*.

bhatiyar भटियार - A common *rag*.

bhatkat भटकत - Mislead, deceive.

Bhatkhande भातखन्डे - See Vishnu Narayan Bhatkhande.

Bhatkhande paddhati भातखन्डे पद्धति - The theoretical and notational system developed by Bhatkhande.

bhayanak भयानक - The emotion of fear. One of the nine principal emotions *(nava ras)*.

bhed भेद - 1) Secret. 2) Difference.

Bhendi Bazaar Gharana भेंड़ी बज़ार घराना - Bhendi bazaar is a place in Bombay. Some consider this to be a *gharana*, some do not. Its antiquity cannot be traced back further than the turn of the century.

bhimpalasi भिमपलासी - A common *rag*.

bhola भोला - Simple, innocent.

bhupal todi भूपाल तोड़ी - A *rag*.

bhupali भूपाली - A common *rag* of five notes, similar to the Western pentatonic scale.

bhushan भूषण - An ornament, an embellishment, jewel.

biadi lay बिआड़ी लय - In a four unit time one plays seven units per beat.

bihag बिहाग - A common *rag*.

bihagada बिहागड़ा - A *rag*.

bilaskhani todi बिलासखानी तोड़ी - A *rag*, attributed to Bilas Khan.

bilawal बिलावल -1) A *that*. 2) A common *rag*. 3) The natural scale.

bin बिन - 1) A *Rudra Vina*. 2) Without.

binat बीनत - Entreaty, an earnest request.

bol alap बोल अलाप - *Alap* which uses the words of the song.

bol bant बोल बांट - Division of the lyrics in the *dhrupad* style.

bol बोल - 1) The mnemonic syllables of *tabla, pakhawaj, sitar, or sarod*. 2) Referring to words (e.g., *bol tan, bol paran*, etc.).

bol paran बोल परण - A type of *tabla* or *pakhawaj* composition whose syllables are actually words.

bol tan बोल तान - A *tan* based upon the words of the song.

Brahma ब्रह्म - The supreme creator (God).

brahma-chhabi ब्रह्म-छबि - Beauty of the eternal spirit.

brindavani sarang बृन्दावनी सारंग - A common *rag*, reminiscent of the land of Krishna.

Carnatic Sangeet कर्नाटक संगीत - See *carnatic sangeet*.

chachar tal चाचर ताल - See *dipchandi*.

chai छई - Reflection, image, shadow.

chaiti चैती - A folk song from Uttar Pradesh, concerning the month of *Chait* (March or April).

chakradar चक्रदार - A *tihai* in which each phrase is a *tihai* in itself.

chal चल - Literally "move", A note which is movable, (i.e., re, ga, ma, dha, or ni)

chala चाला - See *chalan*.

chalan चलन - 1) A *tabla* composition. Some consider this to be similar to *peshkar* while some consider it to be similar to *laggi* or *ladi*. 2) The manner in which the *rag* progresses.

champak tal चंपक ताल - See *adachautal*.

chanchar चाँचर - See *dipchandi*.

chandovati madhya छंदोवती मध्य - The first *shruti*.

chandra चंद्र - Moon.

chang चंग - A musical instrument in which the musical portion is enclosed in a frame. In Persian and Urdu it is a harp; in common Hindi it is a large tambourine (*duf*); sometimes it is used for the jew's harp (*murchang*)

chant चाँट - See *chat*.

charan चारण - 1) The feet, usually of the *guru*, saint, or other great personality. 2) A bard, common in Rajasthan.

chart चार्ट - See *chat*

chartal चारताल - See *chautal*.

chat चाट -*Kinar*, the outer section of the *tabla* skin.

chati चाटी - *Kinar*, same as *chat*.

chatur चतुर - Expert, wise.

Chatur Pandit चतुर पंडित - *Nom de plume* of Vishnu Narayan Bhatkhande.

chaturai चतुराई - Ingenuity, wisdom, tact.

chaturstra jati चतुरस्त्र जाति - Any rhythm composed of 2, 4, 8, 16, 32, etc. beats.

chaugun चौगुन - A *layakari* of 4:1. (i.e., quadruple time.)

chaupalli चौपल्ली - 1) A *tabla* composition, the same as *tipalli* except with four sections. 2) A *tabla*
　　composition revolving around a quadruple repetition of a single *bol* (e.g.,. . . .धा धा धा धा . .)

chautal चौताल - An old 12 beat *pakhawaj tal*.

chaya छाया - Resemblance of one *rag* found in another.

chayanat छायानट - A common *rag*.

chikari चिकारी - The drone strings on a *sitar* or *sarod*.

chinh चिन्ह - Notational elements.

chiz चीज़ - A classical composition. See *bandish*.

choti savari tal चोटी सवारी ताल - Considered by most to be synonymous to *pancham savari*.

chutta छुट्टा - The cushioned rings which support the *tabla*.

ḍa ड - A *tabla bol*.

ḍa द - A *tabla bol* of *pakhawaj* origin.

dadra दादरा - A very light style of singing, very similar to *thumri*.

dadra tal दादरा ताल - A common 6 beat *tal* used in light and semi classical music.

daf डफ - A large tambourine.

dafli डफली - A small tambourine.

dagga डग्गा - The large metal left hand drum of the *tabla* pair.

damaru डमरू - An hour-glass shaped drum associated with shiva.

damdar tihai दमदार तिहाई - A *tihai* in which each section is separated by a pause.

dan दान - Assurance of protection, safety, or amnesty.

danya दायाँ - The small wooden right hand drum of the *tabla* pair.

daras दरस - Seeing, sight.

darbari दरबारी (also called *Darbari Kanada* दरबारी कान्हड़ा) - A common *rag* ascribed to Tansen.

dayak दायक - Bestower, giver.

dayavati karuna दयावती करुणा - The second *shruti* (microtone).

dekhiye देखिए - Look (polite form).

dekho देखो - Look.

Delhi - See *Dilli*.

desh देश - A common *rag*.

deshi देशी - An old *rag*.

deshkar देशकार - A *rag* similar to *Bhupali*.

devan देवन - Gods.

dha ध - 1) An uncommon *bol* of *tabla*. 2) *Dhaivat*.

dha धा - A fundamental *bol* of both *tabla* and *pakhawaj*.

dhaivat धैवत - The sixth note of the scale.

dhamar tal धमार ताल - See *dhammar tal*.

dhammar धमार - 1) An old style of singing, similar to *dhrupad*, generally associated with the spring
season. 2) A 14 *matra tal* associated with that style of singing

dhanashri धनाश्री - A *rag*.

dhi धि or धी - A fundamental *tabla bol*.

dhin धिं or धीं - A fundamental *tabla bol*.

dholak ढोलक - A crude folk drum characterized by a cylindrical wooden shell covered with skin on both
sides.

dhrupad धुपद् - Old classical style of singing

dhruvapad ध्रुवपद - See *dhrupad*.

dhumali tal धुमाली ताल - A variation of *kaherava tal*.

dhyan ध्यान - Concentration.

dhyavat ध्यावत - Chanting.

di दि or दी - a *tabla bol* of *pakhawaj* origin.

dikhan दीखन - To look, to appear, to see.

Dilli baj दिल्ली बाज - The style of playing *tabla*, originally from Delhi, characterized by extensive use
of the middle finger and strokes on the rim of the *tabla*.

Dilli दिल्ली - The present capitol of India.

dilruba दिलरूबा - A bowed instrument with frets like a *sitar* but a body like a *sarangi*.

din दिं - A *bol* of *tabla* and *pakhawaj*.

din दिन - Day.

dipak दीपक - A rare *rag*, associated with fire.

dipchandi tal दीपचंदी ताल - A common 14 beat *tal*.

diya-sikha दीप-सिखा - The flame of a lamp.

doha दोहा - A couplet in Hindi.

dohatthu दोहत्थु - A *tabla* composition where both hands are played on the same drum.

dotar दोतार - A simple two stringed lute.

drut द्रुत - Fast tempo.

dugdugi डुगडुगी - A *damaru*.

duggi डुग्गी - An extremely small kettle drum.

dugun दुगुन - A *layakari* of 2:1 (i.e., double time).

dupalli दुपल्ली - A type of *gat* where a phrase repeats twice.

durga दुर्गा - A common *rag*, similar to the Western pentatonic scale.

dval द्वाल - The *tasma* or lacing of the *tabla*.

ek एक - One, a, an, single.

ekaki vadan एकाकी वादन - Instrumental solo.

ekgun एकगुन - A *layakari* of 1:1 (i.e., single time).

ekhatthi एकहत्थी - See *ekhatthu*.

ekhatthu एकहत्थु - A *tabla* or *pakhawaj* composition which can be played with a single hand.

ektal एकताल - A common *tal* of 12 beats.

ektali एकताली - See *iktali*.

ektar एकतार - A simple one stringed lute.

farmaishi paran फरमाइशी परण - Any *tabla paran* which is used for a *farmaish* (encore).

farodast tal फरोदस्त ताल - An old and obscure *tal* of 7 or 14 beats.

Farukhabad फरुखाबाद - 1) A place in north India. 2) The *tabla gharana* from this place.

firat फिरत - Wandering, returning, going around, something rejected or returned .

fuljhadi फुलझड़ी - (lit. a type of fireworks, a sparkler), a type of *tabla gat* characterized by sudden changes in the overall speed.

ga ग - *Gandhara*.

gagan गगन - Sky.

gahe गहे - To hold

gai गई - Gone, done, happened.

gajara गजरा - The braid of the *tabla pudi*. (Lit. a small string of flowers in a women's hair.)

gamak गमक - A fast ornamentation of the note.

gandhara - गंधार - The third note of the scale.

gandharva गांधर्व - The celestial beings.

gandharva veda गांधर्व वेद - The science of classical music.

Ganesh गणेश - The elephant headed god who removes obstacles.

gara गारा - A common *rag*.

gat गत - 1) A fixed composition for instrumental styles; similar to *sthai*. 2) A compositional type common in the *purbi* style of *tabla* playing.

gat kaida गत कायदा - A *tabla gat* which is performed to a strict *kaida* format.

gatani गतनी - Past.

gatta गट्टा - The wooden dowels in the lacing of *tabla*.

gaud malhar गौड़ मल्हार - A common *rag*.

gaud sarang गौड़ सारंग - A common *rag*.

gaur गौर - A rare *rag*.

gauri गौरी - A *rag*.

gavat गावत - Singing, praising.

gave गावे - Sing.

gayan गायन - Vocal music. One of the three aspects of sangeet.

gaz गज़ - Bow of *sarangi*, violin, *dilruba* or *esraj*.

ge गे - A *tabla bol* for the left hand.

geet गीत - Any song.

gha घ - A basic *tabla bol* of the left hand.

ghan घन - 1) A non-membranous percussion instrument (e.g., bells, *manjira, jal tarang,* etc.) 2. Great

ghar घर - A house.

gharana घराना - A particular subtradition or "school" (lit. "house".)

ghata घटा - A gathering of clouds.

ghazal ग़ज़ल - A musical style of poetic recitation.

ghe घे - A *tabla bol* for the left hand.

ghi घि or घी - A *tabla bol* for the left hand.

ghin घिं - A *tabla bol* for the left hand.

gi गि or गी - A *tabla bol* for the left hand.

gin गिं or गीं - A *tabla bol* for the left hand.

gnyan ज्ञान - Wisdom, understanding, a visceral sense.

Gopal Nayak गोपाल नायक - A great musician and contemporary of Amir Khusru.

grah ग्रह - (Literally "house"). 1) The method of handling *sam*. There are four types: *sam, visham, atit,* and *anagat.* 2) The starting note of the *rag* (i.e., Sa).

Gujari Todi गुर्जरी तोड़ी - A common *rag*, similar to *Miyan ki Todi* except there is no pa.

gun गुण - Quality, attainment.

gunijan गुणिजन - Experts, virtuous and talented people.

guniyan गुणियन - Same as *gunijan.*

gunkali गुणकली - A *rag.*

gunkari गुणकरी - A *rag.*

guru bahin गुरु बहिन - Female fellow disciples of the *guru.*

guru bhai गुरु भाई - Male fellow disciples of the *guru.*

guru गुरु - A teacher.

guru-mukha-vidhya गुरु मुख विद्य - Knowledge which must be learned directly from the *guru.*

guru-shishya parampara गुरु शिष्य परम्परा - The lineage of teacher to disciple.

Gwalior ग्वालियर - 1) A place in Northern India. 2) The *gharana* from this place.

hamir हमीर - A common *rag*, similar to *Kedar.*

hamsadhwani हंसध्वनि - A common *rag*, originally from the South but today found in the North.

har हर - Every.

Hari हरि - brown, yellow, Vishnu, Indra, Shiva, Krishna, Ram, name of mountain.

Haridas Swami हरिदास स्वामी (circa late 15th or early 16th century) - A saint of old who was said to be the guru of Tansen.

harmonium हारमोनियम - A small hand pumped reed organ, originally of European origin but today common in the Indo-Pakistan subcontinent.

hathodi हथौड़ी - The small hammer used to tune the *tabla*.

Haveli Sangeet हवेली संगीत - A *Vaishnava* devotional song usually performed in a *dhrupad* style.

he है - Is.

hem kalyan हेम कल्यान - A *rag*.

hi ही - Only, solely, none other.

hindol हिण्डोल - A common *rag*.

Hindustani sangeet हिंन्दुस्तानी संगीत - North Indian classical music.

ho हो - To be, exists, become.

hoga होगा - Happen.

hriday हृदय - Heart.

indri ईंडरी - The cloth and fiber ring cushions upon which the *tabla* rests (see *chutta*).

jab जब - When, at whatever time.

jag जाग - A sacrifice.

jagat जगत - World.

Jaipur जयपुर - 1) A city in Northern India. 2) The vocal *gharana* from Jaipur.

jait kalyan जैतकल्याण - A *rag*.

jaitshri जैतश्री - A *rag*.

jaladhi हृदय - Ocean.

jaldhar kedar जलधर केदार - A rare *rag*.

jaltarang जलतरंग - A set of bowls tuned with water, hit with small wooden sticks.

jam जाम - A period of 3 hours.

jana जाना - To go.

janat जानत - Knowing.

jap जप - The muttering of a *mantra* or prayer.

jati जाति - 1) A class of rhythm. 2) The number of notes present in a *rag*. 3) An ancient modal form of singing.

jaunpuri जौनपुरी - A common *rag*.

jayjayvanti जयजयवन्ती - A common *rag*.

jhala झाला - A very fast instrumental style based upon the constant droning of the *chikari* strings.

jhaptal झपताल - A common *tal* of 10 matras.

jhinjhoti झिंझोटी - A common *rag*.

jhumra tal झूमरा ताल - A *tal* of 14 matras, used primarily in *kheyal*.

jit जित - Victory.

jiya जिया - Life, heart, soul.

jo जो - Who, which, that.

jod जोड - A rhythmic style of free improvisation.

jog जोग - 1) A common *rag*. 2) Fit for, on account for, capable.

jogia जोगिया - A common *rag*.

jori जोड़ी - The *tabla* pair.

jugalbandhi जुगलबंदी - Duet between two similar instruments or vocalists.

ka क - A *tabla bol* of the left hand.

Kabir कबीर - A famous saint-musician of the 15th century.

kafi काफी - 1) A *that*. 2) A common *rag*.

kahat कहत - Say.

kahe काहे - Why? What for? With what aim?

kaherava tal कहरवा ताल - A common 8-beat *tal*.

kaida कायदा - A highly formalized approach to a *tabla* solo.

kaida peshkar कायदा पेशकार - A *tabla* peshkar whose variations adhere strictly to the *kaida* format.

kaida rela कायदा रेला - A *tabla* rela performed in a strict *kaida* format.

kaise कैसे - How? Like what?

kal काल - The entire concept of time and musical timing.

kala कला - Art.

kalingada कालिंगड़ा - A *rag*.

kalyani कल्याणी - 1) a musical mode (*mela*) of the the South which corresponds to the north Indian
    Kalyan that. 2) A south Indian *rag* similar to *Kalyan*, 3) Auspicious, beautiful, happy.

kamali paran कमाली परण - A *paran* which is constructed in a highly unusual yet fascinating manner.

kamod कामोद् - A common *rag*.

kanth कंठ - Throat.

kar कर - 1) To do, or perform, 2) Duty. 3) Hand.

karat करत - The distance to which a gunshot can reach.

Karnatic Sangeet कर्नाटिक संगीत - See *carnatic sangeet*.

karo करो - Do.

kashttarang काष्टतरंग - A wooden xylophone.

kat कत् - A *tabla bol*.

kathak कथक - A common north Indian style of classical dance.

kawali कव्वाली - A style of Islamic devotional song.

kawali tal कव्वाली ताल - A *tal* of 8 beats similar to *kaherava*.

kdan कडां or कडान् - A powerful *bol* of both *pakhawaj* and *tabla*.

ke के - 1) A *tabla bol* of the left hand. 2) The inflected form of का which is used before substantives in
    the plural number.

kedar केद्गर - A common *rag*.

kerva tal केरवा ताल - See *kaherava*, a common 8 beat *tal*.

Keshav केशव - An epithet of Shiva, Krishna.

khali खाली - Literally "empty", a measure which is defined by a wave. (opposite of bhari or tali).

khambavati खंबावती - A *rag*.

khammaj खमाज - 1) A common *rag*. 2) A *that*, characterized by a flattened 7th.

khand jati खण्ड जाति - Any rhythm based upon $2^1/_2$, 5, 10, etc. beats.

khat खत - A *rag.*

khayal खयाल - See *kheyal.*

khemta tal खेमटा ताल - A fairly common yet amorphous *tal* variously described as 6 or 12 beats.

kheyal खयाल - The most prominent style of classical vocal today.

khol खोल - A folk drum of northeast India.

khula खुला - Lit. "open". Resonant *tabla* strokes such as ga, thun, etc.

khyal खयाल - See *kheyal.*

ki कि or की - A *tabla bol* of the left hand.

ki की - The feminine form of "of".

kinar किनार - Lit. "edge". The *tabla chat.*

Kirana किराना - 1) A small town in northern India. 2) A *gharana* (subtradition) of *kheyal.*

kirtan कीर्तन - A group devotional song.

ko को - Who, which, the case termination of the accusative and dative in Hindi.

komal कोमल - A note which is flat. When applied to ma it means the natural fourth.

krishna कृष्ण - An incarnation of lord Vishnu.

krodha ayata क्रधा आयता - The sixth *shruti* (microtone).

kshiti mrudu क्षिति मंदु - The 11th *shruti* (microtone).

kshobhini madhya क्षोभिणी मध्या - The 19th *shruti* (microtone).

kuadi lay कुआड़ी लय - In a four unit time, one plays five units.

kuch कुछ - Some, somewhat, a little.

kumudvati ugra कुमुद्वती उग्रा - The 21st *shruti* (microtone).

kundal कुण्डल - The small ring at the bottom side of both *tabla* used for the lacing.

kunj-ban कुंज-बन - A crane-like bird.

kuri कूड़ी - The shell of the *banya.*

ladi kaida लड़ी कायदा - A *tabla kaida* created by having a *ladi* follow a strict *kaida* format.

ladi लड़ी - A *tabla* composition similar to *laggi.*

laggi kaida लग्गी कायदा - A *laggi* constructed upon a strict *kaida* structure.

laggi लग्गी - A fast lively style of *tabla* playing, similar to *rela*, used in light styles of playing, particularly with *bhajans, thumris, gazal*, etc.

lahara लहरा - A simple, repetitive melody used to accompany *tabla* solos and kathak dance. Sometimes (incorrectly) referred to as *naghma.*

lakadi लकड़ी - Lit. wood. The wooden shell of the *tabla.*

lakhnowi baj लखनवी बाज - The style of *tabla* playing originating from Lucknow.

lakshan git लक्षण गीत - A style of singing where the lyrics are a description of the *rag.*

Lakshmi लक्ष्मी - Goddess of wealth.

lalit ललित - A common *rag.*

lalitpancham ललितपंचम - A rare north Indian *rag*.

lalkila paran लालकिला परण - A *tabla* composition, specifically a *dohatthu* which is inspired from *nagada*.

lasya लास्य - A feminine interpretation of dance.

lav लव - *Maidan*; the *sur*; the part of the *tabla*'s playing surface between the *chat* (*kinar*) and the *syahi*.

lay लय - Tempo.

layakari लयकारी - The relationship between the performed pulse of a composition and the theoretical beat.

log लोग - People.

logan लोगन - People.

lom-vilom लोम-विलोम - A novel *tabla* structure which is composed of two parts. The first part being a mirror image of the second. Therefore, the composition is the same whether it is read backwards or forwards.

Lucknow लखनऊ - 1) A city in northern India. 2) The *gharana* from this area.

mad मद् - Help, support.

madanti karuna मदंती करुणा - The 15th *shruti* (microtone).

madhur मधुर - Sweet.

madhuvanti मधुवंती - A common *rag*.

madhya lay मध्य लय - Medium tempo.

madhya saptak मध्य सप्तक - The middle octave.

madhyam मध्यम - 1) The fourth note of the scale. 2) Middle, between.

madhyamad sarang मध्यमाद् सारंग - A *rag*.

maha महा - Great, large, very, most.

maha tal महा ताल - A non-standard name for *tintal*.

mahaadi lay महाआड़ी - Double tempo of *adi lay*.

mahabiadi lay महाबिआड़ी लय - Double tempo of *biadi lay*.

mahakuadi lay महाकुआड़ी - Double tempo of *kuadi lay*.

mai मई - Filled.

makta मक्ता - Last line of a *gazal's* couplet.

malgunji मालगुंजी - A *rag*.

maligaura मालीगौरा - A rare *rag*.

malkauns मालकौंस - A common *rag*.

malkosh मालकोश - See *malkauns*.

malshri मालश्री - A rare *rag*.

man मन - The heart, soul, or mind.

mand मांड - A common *rag*.

manda mrudu मंदा मृदु - The 22nd *shruti* (microtone).

mandra saptak मन्द्र सप्तक - The lower octave.

mane माने - Meaning, purport.

manjira मञ्जीरा - Small cymbals.

Mansingh Tomar मानसिंह तोमार - A king who was famous for his devotion to music (1486-1518).

margi sangeet मार्गी संगीत - Literally a "path". A music which is based upon a spiritual path, as opposed to a music which is for mere sensual enjoyment.

marjani madhya मार्जनी मध्या - The 10th *shruti* (microtone).

marubihag मारूबिहाग - A common *rag*.

marwa मारवा - 1) A common *rag*. 2) A *that*.

masitkhani gat मसीतखानी गत - A type of slow *gat* played on *sitar* or *sarod*.

matla मत्ला - The first verse of a *gazal*.

matra मात्रा - The beat.

matt tal मत्त ताल - An obscure *pakhawaj tal* of 9 or 18 beats.

me मे - In, within.

me में - In, within.

meend मीन्ड - A slow *glissando*.

megh malhar मेघ मल्हार - A *rag*.

meghranjani मेघरंजनी - A *rag*.

mela मेल - A *that*, usually of the south Indian tradition.

mela मेला - 1) Assemblage, gathering of people, fair, congregation. 2) A musical mode, or *that* of the south Indian system.

mira malhar मीरा मल्हार - A rare *rag*.

Mira मीरा - A famous devotee and composer of *bhajans* (1559-1620).

mirasi मिरासी - 1) A caste of musicians. 2) A prostitute.

mishra jati मिश्र जाति - Any rhythm based upon $1\frac{3}{4}$, $3\frac{1}{2}$, 7, 14, etc. beats.

mishra rag मिश्र राग - A *rag* which is performed in such a way as to mix unrelated *rags*.

miyan ki malhar मियां की मल्हार - A common *rag*.

miyan ki sarang मियां की सारंग - A common *rag*.

mizrab मिज़राब - A plectrum for *sitar* or *vina*, worn on the fingers.

mo मो - Me, myself.

mohani मोहनि - Charming.

mohar मोहर - 1) Face. 2) A gold coin.

mohara मोहरा - A *tabla* piece. A short structure, similar to *mukhada*, which ends on *sam*.

mridang मृदंग or मृदङ्ग - Any two headed barrel shaped drum of the *pakhawaj* variety.

mridangam मृदङ्गगम - A south Indian *mridang*.

mrigamad मृगमद् - Musk.

mudra मुद्र - (literally a "stamp") The hand signals which represent certain actions or things, used extensively in dance.

mukhada मुखड़ा - A very small phrase or composition ending on *sam*. The important section of a *kheyal*.

multani मुलतानी - A common *rag*.

murat मूरत - An idol.

murchana मूर्छना - 1)The process of modal progression (i.e., creating a new scale by taking the old one and shifting the tonic to another note). 2) An exercise based upon sequentially shifting the pattern up and down the scale.

murchang मुरचंग - A jew's harp.

na ना or न - 1) A fundamental *tabla bol*. 2) No, not, the negation of something.

nad नाद् - Sound.

nadaswaram नादस्वरम - A very large double reed instrument of southern India, similar to an oboe.

nagada नगाड़ा - A pair of kettle drums played with sticks.

naggada नग्गाड़ा - See *nagada*.

nagma नग्मा - A *bandish*, or piece of music.

nahak नाहक़ - Improperly, unjustly, in a useless manner.

nahi नही - No, not.

nai नई - New.

nam नाम - Name.

namaskari paran नमस्कारी परन - An unusual *tabla* piece which incorporates a *namaskar* into the structure, usually into the *tihai*.

nand नंद् - A common *rag*.

nar नर - Man, men.

Narad नारद् - See Narada.

Narada नारद् - 1) A famous sage, son of Vishvamitra, who is responsible for the introduction of music and dance to the world. 2) A troublemaker.

Naradamuni नारदमुनी - See Narada.

narayan नारायण - Vishnu, God.

nari नारी - Woman.

nartan नर्तन - Dance and mime. One of the aspects of *sangeet*.

nat bilawal नट बिलावल - A *rag*.

nat नट - A *rag*.

navaras नवरस - The nine principal emotions out of which all art forms.

nilakanth नीलकंठ - 1) A bluejay. 2) Shiva.

nishad निषाद् - The 7th note of the scale.

nohakka नवहक्का - A type of *tihai* in which the *bol* "dha" comes nine times.

nom-tom नोम तोम - A style of *alap* found in *dhrupad*, *dhammar* and a few styles of *kheyal*.

nrtya नृतय or नृत्य- Dance.

nyare न्यारे - Unique, queer, idiosyncratic, distinctive.

nyas न्यास - Resting notes of a *rag*.

Om ॐ - *Nad Brahma*, the primordial sound.

padhati पद्धति - A school or theoretical system.

padmanabh पद्मनाभ - An epithet of lord Vishnu.

pahadi पहाड़ी - A common *rag*.

pakad पकड़ - The characteristic movement of a *rag*.

pakhawaj पखावज - A barrel shaped drum with playing heads on both sides.

palta पलटा or पल्टा - A passage of a *tabla* kaida.

paluskar पलुस्कर - See Vishnu Digambar Paluskar.

panang पनंग - Snake.

pancham पंचम - The 5th note of the scale.

pancham savari tal पंचम सवारी ताल - a rare *tal* of 15 beats.

par पर - On, on top.

paraj परज - A *rag*.

parameshwar परमेश्वर - The Almighty, the supreme being.

parampara परम्परा - A lineage, or continuum (e.g., *guru-shishya-parampara*)

parampurush परमपुरुष - Lord Vishnu.

paran परण or परन - A type of composition on *tabla* or *pakhawaj*.

parayan पारायन - End, completion

parda परदा - (literally "curtain") The fret of *sitar*, *vina*, or similar instrument.

Parvati पार्वती - The goddess Durga, wife of Shiva.

pashtu परतो - A *tal*. Some consider this to be mere *prakar* of *rupak* while others consider this to be a distinctly separate 7 beat *tal*.

patadip पटदीप - A common *rag*.

Patiyala पटियाला - 1) A place in the Punjab. 2) A vocal *gharana* from Patiyala.

peshkar kaida पेशकार कायदा - A *tabla* kaida produced by having a *peshkar* follow a strict *kaida* format.

peshkar पेशकार - A *tabla* composition. An introductory movement similar to *kaida* but with a different system of permutation.

pilu पीलू - A common *rag*.

pital पीतल - Lit. brass, the brass shell of the *banya*.

prabhand प्रबंध - 1) A totally fixed composition. 2) A fixed composition formally used in the ancient dramas.

prabhat प्रभात - A *rag*.

prahar प्रहार or प्रहर - 1) A period of three hours. 2) The time that a *rag* should be rendered.

prakar प्रकार - Different varieties of *tabla theka*.

prasarini ayata प्रसारिणी आयता - The eighth *shruti* (microtone).

prastar प्रस्तार - 1) Permutation upon the note, used in the creation of *tans* and the elaboration of the *rag*. 2) An approach to *tabla*. Permutations upon a *kaida* or given theme.

pratap प्रताप - Dignity, glory, splendor, majesty.

pratham प्रथम - First, beginning.

pritit mrudu प्रीति मृदु - The ninth *shruti* (microtone).

pudi पुड़ी - A *tabla* head.

Punjab पंजाब - 1) An area along the border between India and Pakistan. 2) The *tabla gharana* from this area.

punjabi पंजाबी - (Lit. From Punjab) A 16 beat *tal* similar to *tintal*.

purbi पूरबी - (lit. "Eastern") The style of *tabla* playing in the Farukhabad, Lucknow, and sometimes Benares traditions.

puriya पूरिया - A *rag*.

puriyadhanashri पूर्याधनाश्री - A common *rag*.

purvang पूर्वांङ् -The lower tetrachord.

purvi पूर्वी - A common *rag*.

putriya पुतरिया - Pertaining to a son.

ra ड़ - A *tabla bol*.

ra र - A *tabla bol*.

rabab रबाब - An instrument found in northern India, Pakistan, and Afghanistan.

rag राग - The Indian musical modes.

ragi रागी - A *shabad* singer singer in a *Sikh gudwara*.

ragmala रागमाला - A musical piece based upon a string of several *rags*.

rahat रहत - Continuing, lasting.

rain रैन - Night.

rakhle राखले - Savior, protector.

rakta madhya रक्ता मध्या - The 12th *shruti* (microtone).

Ram राम - Lord *Ram*, *Ram Chandra*, son of *Dasaradha*.

raman रमण - Cupid, husband, handsome.

ramkali रामकली - A *rag*.

Rampur रामपुर -1) A place in northern India. 2) The *gharana* from Rampur which is an offshoot of the Gwalior *gharana*.

ramya madhya रम्या मध्या - The 17th *shruti* (microtone).

rang रंग - Colour.

rangan रंगन - Colours.

rangila gharana रंगीला घराना - The Agra *gharana*.

ranjani madhya रंजनी मध्या - The third *shruti* (microtone).

ras रास - A folk dance common in Gujarat.

ras रस - The essence or emotion of a *rag*.

rassi रस्सी - The rope lacing on the *dholak*.

rat रात - Night.

ratika mrudu रतिका मृदु - The fourth *shruti* (microtone).

raudri dipta रौद्री दीप्ता - The fifth *shruti* (microtone).

ravindra sangit रवीन्द्र संगीत - A semi-classical style of music popular in Bengal. This style was created by Rabindranath Tagore.

Razakhani gat राज़ाखानी गत - A type of fast instrumental gat.

re रे - 1) The second note of the Indian scale. 2) A vocative.

rekhab रेखब - *Rishabh.*

rela रेला - A very fast manipulation of small *tabla* structures.

ri री - A *tabla bol.*

ridhi रिधी - Prosperity, good fortune.

rijhave रिझावे - Happiness.

rijhit रीझत - Pleasure.

rishabha ऋषभ - The 2nd note of the scale.

riyaz रियाज़ - Practice.

rohini ayat रोहिणी आयता - The 16th *shruti* (microtone).

rudra vina रुद्र वीण - A very ancient instrument made of bamboo and gourds (i.e., been)

rupak tal रूपक ताल - A common 7 beat *tal* with uncommon variations of 5, 6, 9, or 11 beats.

sa सा - Similar, equal.

sab सब - All, whole, every, entire.

sabko सबको - Everybody, whole.

sada सदा - Constantly, always, continually.

sadhana साधना - A lifestyle of practice and devotion to music.

sahayak सहायक - A helper, supporter, a friend.

sakal सकल - All, whole, entire, every.

sakhi सखि - Friend.

sam सम - The first beat of a cycle.

samajh समझ - To know, to understand, to realize, to comprehend.

samavadi संवादी - The second-most important note of a *rag.*

samay समय - Time.

sampurna jati संपूर्ण - A *rag* which contains all seven notes.

sanchari संचारी - The quaternary theme

sandipani ayata संदीपनी आयता - The 13th *shruti* (microtone).

sangati संगति - Accompaniment.

sangeet संगीत or सङ्गीत - Music and dance.

sankadik सनकादिक - The sons of Brahma and so forth.

sankirna jati संकीर्ण जाति - A rhythm of 4 $1/2$, 9, 18, etc. beats.

santur सन्तूर - A hammered dulcimer.

saptak सप्तक - The gamut or scale. (i.e, Sa, Re, Ga, Ma, Pa Dha, and Ni)

sarangi सारंगी - A fretless bowed instrument with numerous strings.

saras सरस - Beautiful, attractive, charming, passionate.

Sarasvati सरस्वती - Hindu goddess of music, arts, and learning.

sargam सरगम - The syllables of the scale (i.e., Sa, Re, Ga, Ma, Pa, etc.)

sarod सरोद - A classical stringed instrument derived from *rabab*.

sath साथ - A class of compositions found in the *pakhawaj* styles.

sath sangat साथ संगत - A style of playing where beat-for-beat the *tabla* follows the main artist.

shadav षाड़व - A *rag* with only six notes.

shadj षड्ज - The base note of the scale.

shai शाई - Vernacular of *syahi*. (see syahi)

shakti शक्ति - Energy, force, power.

Shankar शंकर - Lord Shiva.

shankara शंकरा - A common *rag*.

shankh शङ्ख - A conch shell horn.

shastriya sangeet शास्त्रीय संगीत - Classical music.

shehnai शहनाई - An Indian oboe.

shishya शिष्य - A student, or disciple.

Shiva शिव - The Hindu god of destruction, movement, rhythm, dance, sexuality, etc.

shri kalyan श्री कल्यान - A *rag*.

shri श्री - 1) A common *rag*. 2) Lakshmi, wife of Vishnu, Saraswati. 3) A lotus. 4) Sandalwood.

shruti श्रुति - Lit. "to be heard." 1) The drone. 2) A microtone. 3) The key. 4. Holy scriptures.

shuddha kalyan शुद्ध कल्याण - A *rag* similar to *Bilawal*.

shuddha sarang शुद्धसारंग - A common *rag*.

shuddha शुद्ध - 1) A note which is natural. 2) A *rag* which is performed in its fundamental style.

shukl bilawal शुक्ल बिलावल - A *rag*.

shultal शूलताल - see *soolfak tal*.

shyam श्याम - (Literally "the dark one") An epithet of Krishna.

sidha सीधा - The small wooden right hand drum of the *tabla*.

sidhi सिधी - Success, fulfillment, accomplishment.

sindura सिंदूरा - A *rag*.

sit सित - White, clear, shining, bright.

sitar सितार - A common long necked fretted instrument.

sitarkhani सितारखनी - A 16 beat *tal* which according to some is the same as *addha* and according to others is the same as *Punjabi*.

soch सोच - Think, meditation, consideration.

sohani सोहनि or सोहनी - 1) Beautiful. 2) A common *rag*.

sool tal सूल ताल - See *soolfak tal*.

soolfak tal सूलफाक ताल - An old *pakhawaj tal* of 10 matras.

sorath सोरठ - A *rag*.

sthai स्थायी - The primary theme of a classical song.

stuti स्तुति - (lit. prayer, praise of God) 1) A *bol paran*.

sudha सुध - See *shuddha*.

suha सूहा - A *rag*.

sujan सुजान - Intelligent, wise, clever, learned, polite.

sul tal सूल ताल - See *sool tal*.

sumat सुमत - Concord.

sumiran सुमिरन - Recollect.

Sundar सुंदर - beautiful, handsome.

sur malhar सूर मल्हार - A *rag*.

sur सुर - 1) The pitch, note, melody (see swar). 2) The key (see *shruti*).

sur सूर - Sun.

Surat सूरत - Face.

surbahar सुरबहार - A bass *sitar*.

Surdas सुरदास - A musician saint who composed many *bhajan*s (1535-1640).

surmandal सुरमंडल - A small harp used to provide the drone.

sushir सुषिर - A musical instrument characterized by blowing air (flute, *shehnai*, harmonium, etc.)

svarlipi स्वरलिपि - Musical notation.

swar स्वर - A musical note.

syahi स्याही - The black application on the heads of the *tabla*.

ta ट - Fundamental *tabla bol*.

ta ता - Fundamental *tabla bol* of the right hand.

tab तब - Then, at that time, afterwards.

tabla tarang तबला तरंग - A musical instrument composed of numerous wooden *tabla* tuned to different pitches.

tabla तबला - 1) The pair of Indian hand drums. 2) The right hand drum of the pair. 3) The Arabic word for any drum.

tahe ताहे - Until, for the sake of, toward, nearby.

taj तज - Omit.

tal paddhati ताल पद्धति - A theoretical framework of rhythm.

tal ताल - 1) The Indian system of rhythm. 2) A particular rhythmic cycle (e.g., *tintal, rupak tal*, etc.) 3) The palm of the hand.

tal-lipi ताल-लिपि - Percussion notation.

tal-vadhya-kachari ताल-वाद्य-कचहरी - A percussion ensemble.

taleem तालीम - Formal training.

tali ताली - A measure which is clapped.

tamboura तंबूरा - See *tanpura*.

tan तान - A long run or trill. A fast elaboration on the *rag*.

tan तन - The body, skin.

tandava ताण्डव - An energetic, masculine dance style reminiscent of Shiva.

tanpura तानपुरा - A long necked, stringed instrument for providing the drone.

Tansen तानसेन - A famous musician of the court of Akbar (circa late 16th century)

tap तप - Devotion, worship.

tappa टप्पा - A Punjabi style of semi-classical singing.

tar saptak तार सप्तक - The higher octave.

tar shehnai तार शहनाई - An instrument similar to *esraj*.

tar तार - 1) String of musical instrument. 2) A stringed instrument of Afghanistan.

tarana तराना - A style of singing, originally of Persian origin, today characterized by meaningless syllables.

tarasay तरसाय - To long for, to strongly desire.

tasma तस्मा - The rawhide lacing of the *tabla*.

tat तत् - 1) a *tabla bol*. 2) A plucked string instrument (e.g., *sitar*, *sarod*, etc.)

te टे - A *tabla bol*.

te ते - A *tabla bol*.

teharo तेहारो - Your, yours.

tej तेज - See *tez*.

ten तें - (pronoun) They, those people.

tere तेरे - Yours.

tevra tal तेवरा ताल - See *tivra tal*.

tez तेज़ - Sharp, keen pointed, swift, intelligent.

thanh ठाँह - 1) *Vilambit*. 2) Single time.

that थाट - A musical mode.

theka ठेका - The fundamental rhythmic pattern.

thu थु or थू - A *tabla bol*.

thumri ठुमरी - A semiclassical style of singing.

thun थुं or थूं - A *tabla bol*.

ti ति or ती - Fundamental *tabla bol*.

tigun तिगुन - A *layakari* of 3:1 (i.e., triple time.)

tihai तिहाई - A cadenza composed of three identical sections.

tilak kamod तिलक कामोद् - A common *rag*.

tilang तिलंग - A common *rag*.

tilwara tal तिलवाड़ा ताल - A 16 beat *tal* similar to *tintal*.

tin तिं - Fundamental *tabla bol*.

tintal तीनताल - A very common *tal* of 16 beats.

tipalli तिपल्ली - Type of *tabla tihai* where each phrase is in a different tempo.

tisra jati तीसरी जाति - Triplets. (see *tryastra jati*)

tisra तीसरा - Third.

tisri tali तीसरी ताली - Third clap.

tit तित - At that place, there.

tivra dipta तीव्रा दीप्ता - The 20th *shruti* (microtone).

tivra tal तिव्रा or तिवरा ताल - An old *pakhawaj tal* of 7 beats.

tivra तीव्र - A note which is in the upper position. (i.e., natural for re, ga, dha, and ni and the augmented 4th in the case of ma)

tiya तीया - See *tihai*.

to तो - Then, so, in case that, thy, thine.

toda तोड़ा - A tabla *tukada*.

todi तोड़ी - 1) A *that*. 2) A common *rag*.

top तोप - (Lit. cannon.) A loud *paran* which characterizes thunder, battles, or similar moods played on the *tabla*.

tra त्र or तृ - A *tabla bol* of the right hand.

tripalli त्रिपल्ली - See *tipalli*.

triputa tal त्रिपुट ताल - An obscure *tal* of 8, 9, 11, or 13 beats.

trital त्रिताल - *Tintal*, a common 16 beat *tal*.

tryastra jati त्र्यस्त्र जाति - Any rhythm composed of 3, 6, 12, etc. beats.

tu तू - You, normally abusive except when referring to God.

tu तु or तू - A *tabla bol*.

tukada टुकड़ा - A small *tabla* composition containing a small body and a *tihai*, very similar to *paran*.

tun तुं or तूं - A *tabla bol*.

uddhare उद्धारे - Redemption, rescue, renovation.

ugra dipta ग्रा दीप्ता - The 18th *shruti* (microtone).

ustad उस्ताद - A learned man, a master.

uthan उठान - A *tabla* piece, commonly in dance and *tabla* solos, essentially a type of *mukhada*.

uttarang उत्तरङ्ग - The upper tetrachord.

vadan वादन - Instrumental music. One of the aspects of *sangeet*.

vadi वादी - 1) The key note of a *rag*. 2) A spokesman.

vajrika dipta वज्रिका दीप्ता - The seventh *shruti* (microtone).

vakra वक्र - Anything which is twisted, convoluted, or oblique.

vamadev वामदेव - The name of a *Vedic* sage.

Vashisht वशिष्ट - A saint.

Vasudev वासुदेव - An epithet of lord Krishna.

ve वे - They

veda वेद - Ancient Hindu religious text (circa 1500-900 B.C.).

vibhag विभाग - The measure or "bar".

vibhas विभास - A common *rag*.

vidh विध - Creation, arrangement.

vidhwan विद्वान - Any learned musician.

vijay विजयी - Victory.

vikari विकारी - See *chal*.

vikrat विकृत - See *chal*.

vilambit विलंबित or विलम्बित - Slow tempo.

vina वीणा - 1) Any stringed instrument. 2) The Saraswati *vina* of south India.

vishad विशद् - Elaborate.

visham (grah) विषम - The process of hiding or de-emphasizing the *sam*.

Vishnu Digambar paddhati विष्णु दिगम्बर पद्धति - A theoretical and notational system developed by
     Vishnu Digambar Paluskar.

Vishnu Digambar Paluskar विष्णु दिगम्बर पलुस्कर - A famous Indian musicologist.

Vishnu विष्णु - The preserver (i.e., God)

Vishnu Narayan Bhatkhande विष्णु नारायन भातखण्डे - A famous Indian musicologist (1860-1936).

vitat वितत - A bowed, string instrument (e.g.,. violin, *dilruba, sarangi* etc.)

yah यह - This.

yaman यमन - A common Indian *rag*.

yamuna यमुना - The river Jamuna.

zilaf झीलफ - A common *rag*.

BIBLIOGRAPHY

INDIAN MUSIC

Adesh, H.S.
1993   *Sargam*. Trinadad: Jeewan Jyoti Prakashan.
1993   *Shadaj*. Trinadad: Jeewan Jyoti Prakashan.

Agarwal, Viney K.
1975   *Traditions and Trends in Indian Music*. Meerat: Rastogi Publications.

Bhatkhande, Vishnu Narayan
1934   *A Short History of the Music of Upper India*. Bombay, India. (reprinted in 1974 by Indian Musicological
            Society, Baroda).
1985   *Hindustani Sangeet Paddhati, Kramik Pustak Malika,Vol 1*. Hathras, India: Sangeet Karyalaya.
1985   *Hindustani Sangeet Paddhati, Kramik Pustak Malika,Vol 3*. Hathras, India: Sangeet Karyalaya.
1985   *Hindustani Sangeet Paddhati, Kramik Pustak Malika,Vol 4*. Hathras, India: Sangeet Karyalaya.
1989   *Hindustani Sangeet Paddhati, Kramik Pustak Malika,Vol 2*. Hathras, India: Sangeet Karyalaya.

Bor, Joep
1987   "The Voice of Sarangi: An Illustrated History of Bowing in India". *Quarterly Journal for the National Centre
            for the Performing Arts*; Vol XV and XVI Nos. 3, 4, & 1; Sept, Dec, & March 87; Bombay, NCPA.

Chaturvedi, Balmukund
1989   *Sur Sagar*. Shri Gopal Pustakalay: Mathura

Courtney, D.R
1977   "Harmonium: Controversial Instrument", *Pallavi*. Hyderabad: India: Vol. 1, No 3, April 20, 1977: pp. 13.
1980   *Introduction to Tabla*. Hyderabad, India. Anand Power Press.
1985   "Tabla Making in the Deccan", *Percussive Notes*. Urbana Ill: Percussive Arts Society. Vol. 23, No 2,
            January 1985: pp. 33-34.
1987   "Tata and his Kamakshi Veena", *Experimental Musical Instruments*. Nicasio CA: EMI. Vol. 3, No 4
            December 1987: pp. 5-9.
1988   "Rag: Hindustani vs. Carnatic", *Svar Gnyan*. Houston: Sur Sangeet Services. April 1988: pp. 3.
1988   "Time Theory of Ragas", *Svar Gnyan*. Houston: Sur Sangeet Services. June 1988.
1988   "Rag Yaman", *Svar Gnyan*. Houston: Sur Sangeet Services. August, 1988: pp. 3
1988   "That and Mela",*Svar Gnyan*. Houston: Sur Sangeet Services. September, 1988: pp. 3-4
1988   "The Tabla Puddi", *Experimental Musical Instruments*. Nicasio, CA: EMI. Vol. 4, No 4, December 1988: pp.
            12-16.
1990   "North Indian Ragas",*Experimental Musical Instruments*. Nicasio, CA: EMI. Vol. 6, No 2, August 1990: pp.
            15-16.
1992   "New Approaches to Tabla Instruction", *Percussive Notes*. Lawton OK: Percussive Arts Society. Vol 30, No
            4, April 1992: pp. 27-29.
1993   "Mrdangam et Tabla: un Contraste", *Percussions: Cahier Bimensiel d'Études et d'Informations sur les Arts de
            la Percussion*. Chailly-en-Biere, France; Vol 28, March/April 1993; pp 11-14.
1994   "An Introduction to Tabla", *Modern Drummer*. Mt. Morris, IL: MD Publications. October 1993; Vol 17, #10:
            pp. 38-84.
1994   "The Cadenza in North Indian Tabla", *Percussive Notes*. Lawton, OK: Percussive Arts Society. August 1994;
            Vol32, No 4: pp. 54-64.
1994   *Fundamentals of Tabla. Houston:* Sur Sangeet Services. Houston TX.

Devangan, Tulsiram
1984   *Thumri-Gayaki*. Hathras: Sangeet Karyalaya

Dhavan, Devakinandan
1970   "Pad". *Bhakti Sangit Ank*. (edited by Lakshminarayan Garg). Hathras, India: Sangeet Karyalaya.

Garg, Prabhulal (Editor)
1977   *Sangit Sagar*. Hathras: Sangit Karyalya

Garg, Lakshminarayan
1973   *Bal Sangeet Shiksha, Vol. 2*. Hathras, India: Sangeet Karyalaya.
1984   *Hamare Sangeet-Ratna*. Hathras, India: Sangeet Press.

Jairazbhoy, N. A.
1971   *The Rags of North Indian Music*. Middletown CT: Wesleyan University Press.

Kripalvanand, Swami
1972   "Purush Rag, Stri Rag Aur Putra Rag", *Rag-Ragini Ank*. Hataras: Sangeet Karyalaya; pp. 7-51.

Kulshreshth, Jagdish Sahay
1983   *Sangeet Kishor*. Hathras, India: Sangeet Karyalaya.

Mital, Prabhudayal
1960   *Sangeet Samrat: Tansen: Jivani aur Rachanaen*. Mathura, India: Sahitya Samsthan.

Neuman, Daniel M.
1980   *The Life of Music in North India*. Detroit: Wayne State University Press,

Rangacharya, Adya
1966   *Introduction to Bharata's Natya-Sastra*. Bombay, India: Popular Prakashan.

Rao, B. Subba
1980   *Raganidhi: A Comparative Study of Hindustani and Karnatak Ragas, Vol. 1*. Madras, India: The Music
            Academy.
1982   *Raganidhi: A Comparative Study of Hindustani and Karnatak Ragas, Vol. 2*. Madras, India: The Music
            Academy.
1984   *Raganidhi: A Comparative Study of Hindustani and Karnatak Ragas, Vol. 3*. Madras, India: The Music
            Academy.
1985   *Raganidhi: A Comparative Study of Hindustani and Karnatak Ragas, Vol. 4*. Madras, India: The Music
            Academy.

Shankar, Ravi
1968   *Ravi Shankar: My Music, My Life*. New Delhi, India: Vikas Publishing House Pvt. Ltd.

Singh, Lal Bahadur
1977   Rag Yaman, Tintal, *Sangeet Sagar*. Hathras, India: Sangeet Karyalaya.

Stewart, Rebecca Marie
1974   *The Tabla in Perspective*. Ph.D. Disssertation, University of California (UMI: Ann Arbor)

GENERAL MUSIC

Courtney, David R.
1990   "The Value of Musical Training", *Informensa*. Houston: Gulf Coast Mensa. Vol. 23, No 9, September 1990:
            pp. 35.
1991   "Introduction to MIDI", *Syntax*. Tomball: CHUG Inc., Tomball: Dec./Jan 1991: pp. 11-13.
1991   "MIDI Protocol", *Syntax*. Tomball: CHUG Inc. Dec./Jan 1991: pp. 14-19.

Diagram Visual Information ltd.
1976   *Musical Instruments of the World*. New York: Facts on File Publications.

Randel, Don Michael
1978   *Harvard Concise Dictionary of Music*. Cambridge Mass: Belknap Press of Harvard University Press.

INDIAN DANCE

Courtney, David R.
1988   "Kathak Maestro Pt. Anju Babu", *Indo-American News*. Houston. Sat, Aug. 20 1988: pp. 13.

Shrivastava, Harish Chandra
1973   "Kathak Nritya Parichay". Allahabad: Sangeet Sadan Prakashan

LANGUAGE

Kapoor, R.K.
no date   *Kamal's Advanced Illustrated Oxford Dictionary of Hindi- English*. Delhi, India: Verma Book Depot.

Barz, R.K.
1977   *An Introduction to Hindi and Urdu*. Canberra, Australia: Australian National University Press.

Fallon, S.W.
1984   *A New Hindustani-English Dictionary: With Illustrations from Hindustani Literature and Folklore*.
              Allahabad: Bharti Bhandar

Ganathe, N.S.R.
1981   *Learn Urdu in 30 Days*. Madras: Balaji Publications.

Greaves, Edwin
1983   *Hindi Grammar*. New Delhi: Asian Educational Services.

Nathani, Sultan
1992   *Urdu for Pleasure*. Bombay: Emms Art Printers.

Srinivasachary, K.
1983   *Learn Sanskrit in 30 Days*. Madras: Balaji Publications.

Van Olphen, H.H.
1992   *Hindi Pravesikaa- Beginners Hindi: Writing and Conversation*. Austin: University of Texas.

MISC.

Allami, Abu l-Fazl
Circa 1590   *Ain-i Akbari*. (Translated by H. Blockmann). Delhi: New Taj Office.

Carterette, Edward C, K.Vaughn, and N.Jairazbhoy
1989   Perceptual, Acoustical, and Musical Aspects of the Tambura Drone. *Music Perception*. Winter 1989, Vol.7,
              No 2, 75-108. Berkeley: University of California Press.

Courtney, David R.
1989   "Timbre: Psycho-acoustic Considerations", *Svar Gnyan*. Houston: Sur Sangeet Services. September 1989,
              p. 3.
1994   "Freemasonry in India", *The North Carolina Mason*. Raleigh, NC: Grand Lodge of AF&AM of N. Carolina:
              Jan/Feb: 1994; Vol CXIX No 1: pp. 6.
1994   "Electronic Aids in Indian Music Education", *Technological Directions in Music Education*. San Antonio:
              Institute for Music Research, University of San Antonio: 1994; pp. 32-40.
1988   "Alla Rakha", *Svar Gnyan*. Houston: Sur Sangeet Services. October, 1988: pp. 2.
1991   "Tuning the Tabla: A Psychoacoustic Perspective",*Percussive Notes*. Urbana Ill: Percussive Arts Society
              Vol. 29, No 3, February 1991: pp. 59-61.
1991   "The Application of the C=64 to Indian Music: A review". Tomball:*Syntax*. June/July 1991: pp. 8-9.

1992   "Bridges: An Indian Perspective", *Experimental Musical Instruments*. Nicasio, CA:EMI. Vol 7, No 5, April 1992: pp. 8-11.

1993   "Repair and Maintenance of Tabla", *Percussive Notes*. Lawton OK: Percussive Arts Society. October 1993; Vol.31, No 7: pp. 29-36.

Mallory, J. P.

1989   *In Search of the Indo-Europeans; Language Archaeology and Myth*. London: Thames and Hudson Ltd.

Mukri, Naseem

1990   *Junoon*. Bombay: Intel Communications.

Mishra, Balaram

1979   *Konark*. Bhubaneshwar: Bibarani Prakashani.

INDEX